NEGOTIATING PEACE

NEGOTIATING PEACE

NORTH EAST INDIAN PERSPECTIVES ON PEACE, JUSTICE, AND LIFE IN COMMUNITY

SHIMREINGAM L. SHIMRAY

FORTRESS PRESS
MINNEAPOLIS

NEGOTIATING PEACE

North East Indian Perspectives on Peace, Justice, and Life in Community

Copyright © 2020 Fortress Press. All rights reserved. Except for brief quotations in critical articles or reviews, no part of this book may be reproduced in any manner without prior written permission from the publisher. Email copyright@fortresspress.com or write to Permissions, Fortress Press, PO Box 1209, Minneapolis, MN 55440-1209.

Cover image: © iStock Photo 2020; Bird's Eye View of Shillong city by Kallol Panda

Cover design: Kristin Miller

Paperback ISBN: 978-1-5064-6448-0

eBook ISBN: 978-1-5064-6449-7

CONTENTS

	Foreword	vii
	Acknowledgments	ix
	Glossary	xi
	Introduction	1
1.	Relevance of Theology and Church Leaders: Common Mission and Ministry	7
2.	Social Analysis and Theology: A Methodological Implication for Doing Tribal Theology	15
3.	Biblical Resources of Human Rights	29
4.	Promoting Peace through Human Rights: A North East Indian Tribal Theological Perspective	51
5.	Theology of Peace and the Church	61
6.	Liberation through Reconciliation	73
7.	Revisiting Patriarchy from a Human Rights Perspective	85
8.	Quest for Power Narrative on Gender Issue: Strategizing Feminist Methodology	99
9.	Methods and Values of Peacebuilding: A Contribution of Tangkhul Women	115
10.	Christian Involvement in Politics	127

11.	Holistic Child Development: Ethical and Moral Values	133
12.	Christian Theological Thinking on Children	139
13.	Against Corruption: A Social Response	151
14.	Ethical Response to the Danger of Environmental Crisis	163
15.	Understanding Conflict Situations in North East India	175
16.	Humanism and Contemporary Christianity	183
	Bibliography	191

FOREWORD

It is a privilege for me to write the foreword for the book *Negotiating Peace* by Prof. Dr. Shimreingam Shimray. Prof. Shimray is a critical and established scholar. He has been teaching at Eastern Theological College for the last thirty years and is currently serving as vice principal of the college.

All right-thinking people have been concerned with trying to develop a proper response to the crises being faced by every human being in every part of the world. It is also true that there are many people who make systematic critiques from their own theological and professional perspective toward achieving peace in their given context. More efforts should be given until we are able to fully experience the reality of peace.

Today, Prof. Shimray, who having lived through decades of difficult times and having made critical observations, has appropriately specialized in Christian ethics and tirelessly taken initiatives to inspire and evoke the minds of young people so that they take peace initiatives seriously and work with all their capacity and ability toward harmonious living among human beings and with nature.

The present book is an outcome of his deep commitment, sincere research, and his long experience of teaching under the Senate of Serampore College. It is a collection of his articles researched and written over a long period of his teaching profession.

In the history of theological education, one of the most challenging tasks has been engaging and participating in the initiatives and negotiations toward peace. It contributes toward life-changing and life-affirming status in the history of humanity.

Prof. Shimray's interest and contribution toward peace initiatives is well reflected in this book through the different articles. It is my hope that many people will consider it a privilege to go through the pages of this resourceful book.

May this book touch the hearts of the readers to commit and contribute toward the process of peace initiatives and peacemaking. May it also serve as a source of peace and understanding to many people in more aspects than one can comprehend.

Rev. Dr. Prof. Narola Imchen
Principal
Eastern Theological College
Jorhat, Assam, India

ACKNOWLEDGMENTS

I would like to first of all acknowledge God who upholds me and my family and provides me with good health to serve him. I thank the organizers of the program series that I could be part of, for the privilege to listen, discuss ideas, raise questions, and learn in many ways. My special thanks to those who invited me to write and present papers in their programs. I particularly thank the following centers for the partnership in organizing programs. I thank Rev. Prof. Dr. Razouselie Lasetso, then Dean of Institute of Leadership Enhancement Ministry Augmentation (ILEMA) of Eastern Theological College, Rajabari, Jorhat, who invited me to write an article that forms the ninth chapter in this book, "Methods and Values of Peacebuilding: A Contribution of Tangkhul Women," and I also acknowledge that this text was published in *Tribal Christian Theology—Methods and Sources for Constructing a Relevant Theology for the Indigenous People of North East India,* edited by Razouselie Lasetso and Yangkahao Vashum (Tribal Study Series no. 15, Jorhat 2007, pages 122–130). I also acknowledge Rev. Prof. Dr. Yangkahao Vashum, then Dean of Tribal Study Centre of Eastern Theological College, for publishing my article "Social Analysis and Theology: A Methodological Implication for Doing Tribal Theology" in *Journal of Tribal Studies* Vol. XV, no. 1, January–June 2010. This article forms the second chapter of this book. I am also grateful to the Tribal Study Centre for inviting me to write and present the paper entitled "Biblical Resources of Human Rights" in the Tribal Theology Institute Seminar organized by the Centre from November 3–6, 2009. This text forms the third chapter of this book. The text in chapter eleven was initially presented in the Holistic Child Development Seminar jointly organized by Compassionate International, South Asia, and Eastern Theological College, Jorhat, at ETC Conference Hall from November 22–24, 2011. I am equally thankful to the organizers of that program. I thank the program committee of Tangkhul Theological Association (TTA) who asked me to write a paper on "Liberation Through Reconciliation" for their Annual Gathering at Ramva Baptist Church in April 2012. That text forms the fifth chapter of this book. I am also thankful to Dr. Lovely Awomi

James, then Dean of the Women Study Centre of Eastern Theological College, who invited me to write the article "Quest For Power Narrative On Gender Issue: Strategizing Feminist Methodology" in its Seminar on RadFem to Pro-Women on September 21, 2018.

Another group of people that have deeply influenced me and remain a source of inspiration is the student community of Eastern Theological College, Jorhat. My experiences in the classrooms for the past thirty years have shaped and made me who I am today. Their questions in the classrooms have always inspired me to widen my scholarly readings. I am equally thankful to all my colleagues with whom I have attended programs. Their critique has sharpened my thought and their encouragement has energized me to keep going. I am thankful to many other people whom I cannot list in this section.

Shimreingam L. Shimray

GLOSSARY

Amāk	brother-in-law.
Haorā	a traditional Tangkhul shawl for men.
Hoho	council or assembly.
Jawans	Indian language referring to the soldiers.
Luira	a name of Tangkhul Naga festival of sowing of seed.
Maran kasa	feast of merit.
Mashit Sashai	feast of friendship.
Nagamese	a dialect used for communication by the Nagas.
NSCN-IM	National Socialist Council of Nagalim (Isaac-Muivah).
NSCN-K	National Socialist Council of Nagalim (Khaplang).
Pukreila	a woman who is married to a man of another village or another tribe who is generally known as *Yorla*, but in times of conflict between her brother's villagers and husband's villagers, can come in between as a kin to both villages to stop the fight, and at that point of time is known as *Pukreila*.
Sāhei	a share of good portion of meat given to a married daughter by her father or to a sister by her brother during the festivals, especially during *Luira*.
Sāhei kaphung	when a *Yorla* (see below) comes home to her father's or brother's home during a festival and when she is given *Sahei*, at which point she would call her husband's family to come and carry the meat.
Tangkhul	one of the major Naga tribes in Manipur.
Yorkhok	refers to a real daughter or sister of a father or brother married to someone from another village or tribe. She has a great responsibility in maintaining the relationship of the families and villages.

Yorla	a general term to refer to a woman married to another village or tribe.
Yorla ham	refers to a pot that is presented to a *yorla* when she comes to her father or brother with a gift during a festival or any specific occasion like marriage of her brother.
Yorla kachon	refers to a lady's shawl, commonly called *Changkhom*, that is presented to a *yorla* when she comes to her father's or brother's home with a gift during a festival or special occasion like marriage of her family member.
Yorla kakachi	a term referring to the invitation extended to all the *yorlas* for any special occasion or event in the house of her father or brother, especially during marriage or hosting of feast of merit.
Yorphāng	a term for the *yorlas* who are not the real daughters or sisters but are distant brother's sisters and daughters.

INTRODUCTION

None of us can deny the fact that our society is not in order. Every aspect of society is facing enormous problems within and outside the established structure and system. Every institution, be it political, social, economic, or religious, is in one way or the other corrupted. Human beings who are supposed to manage those systems are also corrupted. The attitude of the people does not seem to be right. That is manifested when they become custodians of the laws and make themselves capable of manipulating the law; when politics is defined as a source of financial income rather than serving the common people; when economics is understood as business, investment, and consumption only by the lawmakers who control the system; when religion becomes a source of publicity and attaining status and elitist fellowship rather than service to the spiritually dying people, etc. It is in this difficult context that the articles of this book were written at different points of time as an attempt to respond to the needs of the time.

It should also be noted that intellectuals in different fields also have deep disagreements as different people claim to own their own disciplines and fields of specialization and do not give space to understand integrated effort through which they can more meaningfully address the issues they are confronted with. For instance, politicians do not think that theologians are interested in and capable of making deep reflection that would help them understand the focus of their political thinking. On the other hand, theologians consider economists or politicians as corrupt groups and unfit to speak anything right or understand the revelation and the word of God. This reality of indifference makes it necessary for both thinkers and doers come together and give an integrated effort without which it will be more difficult for them to achieve the goal of their ministries.

I am very happy to assemble my writings of different times stretching over about a decade into a book. I am happy because these selected articles serve to affirm the standpoint of my earlier books in arguing that our services should help human beings achieve the goal of the common good rather than let individuals live excessively rich while society and social systems remain poor and weak. Each of the articles is an attempt to dwell on the issue of peace. One of the basic concerns that becomes obvious in the book is that peace cannot be derived from the outside forces, but it has to be created from within the local context by the local people through adopting their own cultural and historical system and using their own intellectual and material resources. Having said this, let me also make it clear to the readers that the context in which the articles were written is limited to the realities of the tribal people of North East India, and their own examples are used to substantiate the discussion.

The term *North East India* is used to refer to states located in the hill region bordering Bhutan, Bangladesh, Myanmar, and China. Earlier, it was known as Seven Sisters (Arunachal Pradesh, Assam, Meghalaya, Mizoram, Manipur, Nagaland, and Tripura), but later Sikkim was included, making it eight states under the umbrella term *North East India*. The people of other parts of India perceive the people of the North East region as one homogenous group with a common political problem or social system and custom. But the region is more complicated than this. There is the danger of clubbing the states together as one as far as ethnic composition and cultural differences are concerned. The region has an extraordinary diversity in ethnicity, linguistics, religion, and culture. The diversity in religious persuasion is indicated by the presence of all major world religions—Hinduism, Buddhism, Islam, and Christianity—and a small number of people still hold on to their traditional beliefs. There is a multiplicity of languages and dialects used in the region. According to L.P. Singh, they number 420 out of a total of 1,652 languages in India. All these diversities, however, do not disqualify the commonness they share in the nature of struggles and difficulties.

There are many ethnic groups in North East India who claim to be free from the Union of India and attempt to live as sovereign nations, other groups who further demand to create a new state within the Union of India, and others who demand withdrawal from the Union of India. Because of these various factors, the region has experienced decades of armed struggle against the government of India that has caused loss of lives in terms of thousands. The insurgency movement has become a part of the history of this region. However, it should be noted that today several groups have signed cease-fire agreements with the government of India and are undertaking political peace-talks. This reality of violent struggles has hampered peaceful living of the people; it has affected development processes, and it has also challenged the church (the region is dominantly evangelized by the Presbyterian, Baptist, and Roman Catholic churches) and prompted people to seriously reflect on means and prospects of restoring peace. I will not dwell too much on political struggles, but I will rather take the struggles of the people as the basis for developing the arguments in this book.

The first chapter talks about the importance of relevant and meaningful theological orientation to the context failing which theological education becomes indifferent to the realities of the people, making people do ministry for doing's sake. It calls upon the church leaders to be sensitive to the quality and value of theological education and to not make decisions based on financial involvement because theological education is a serious business of the Christian church.

The second chapter explains the importance of understanding the context for the purpose of formulating Christian theology. Unless one takes contextual reality as the basis of reading the Scripture, people will find it difficult to derive the meaning of the Bible. Theological education is a matter of interpreting the text to the context appropriately.

The third chapter is an attempt to explain that while language such as human rights is not adopted in the Judaistic literature, there are sufficient resources for us to understand the theological foundation of human rights in the Bible. It is important because unless we understand the rights endowed by Scripture and the Constitution, we will not be able to argue about the meaning of peace in the society.

The fourth chapter is a discussion on how human rights can be promoted so as to relate it to the building of a peaceful society. It calls for respect and protection of human rights in order to restore peace to the people.

The fifth chapter discusses the importance of reconciliation toward peacebuilding and argues that reconciliation should not be understood as an event but as a process because when the process ends the so-called reconciliation also ends; it is not an event to be celebrated but a process to be continuously followed.

In the sixth chapter, I present theological readings on peace and explain theories and methods of reading and understanding peace. I present an elaborative definition of peace. In regard to peace studies, Johan Galtung stands tall and thus his idea of defining peace is referred to.

The seventh chapter is a review of the long-debated issue of patriarchy from the perspective of human rights so that much of what women talk about and claim is read as human rights. In my attempt to define "rights," I have included women's rights as human rights, so that no one should violate human rights on the basis of gender.

The succeeding chapter continues the debate and calls upon women to develop a method to critique their own claims and approaches by adopting a power narrative so that they will be able to overcome passivity in feminine thought-form. The point noted here is that there is no inferiority of women, but they are being made to think inferior. This is also to mean that patriarchy is not necessarily a woman's problem but basically male attitude that colonizes the female gender and suppresses it.

The ninth chapter is a study on the specific cultural value of the Tangkhul women that can serve as a model to counter violence and conflict. The Tangkhuls of Manipur have a beautiful tradition to respect women, particularly their women who have married outside of their village or tribe. They are considered as persons with dual citizenship and are endorsed with authority even to come in between two warring groups on the condition that no one should touch or harm them. In case of any harm to them, heavy penalty would be imposed.

The tenth chapter tries to clear the confusion between "church and state" and also "religion and politics" by explaining that they should be first understood as different institutions, followed by the knowledge of the practical mode of participating in their affairs.

The eleventh chapter talks about an emerging movement relating to children and it uncovers the loopholes in the church ministries—the neglect of children's ministry. It aims to provide a perspective to the Christian church that no church has future prospects without ministering to the children of today because the future belongs to them.

The twelfth chapter further substantiates Christian theological thinking on children by highlighting the documents of the United Nations toward children's issues and advocating for a new approach of church ministry that would give sufficient focus to the children so that it lays a strong foundation for future members and leaders of the church.

The thirteenth chapter is a debate to develop an approach to address corruption in society so that every individual comes under the laws and no individuals are allowed to manipulate the law. Removing individuals' manipulation of existing laws will reduce corruption levels in society and restore peace to the people.

The fourteenth chapter discusses that even after a long debate on environmental crisis, human beings have not been able to give sufficient effort to conserve the environment. It emphasizes that environmental protection is not optional but mandatory if we want the earth to sustain itself further. Human beings need to change their attitude toward life and lifestyles. The chapter argues that no government will be successful unless it takes local people as the best partners to conserve forests.

The fifteenth chapter talks about the most needed conflict-resolution by citing North East India as a case study. This chapter argues that people should not illogically think that there are people who can come and restore peace for them, which will not happen. Peace cannot be borrowed from other people, but has to be created within the context.

The last chapter considers one of the most serious issues of religious humanism that has made many people perplexed, and resulted in a disturbance of peaceful co-existence of human beings, ideologies, systems, and worldviews. The North East region faces the problem of wrongly using religious fervor for the individual's benefit. A true religion should not lead to hatred and division, but it should rather construct a community of believers.

The primary aim of this book is to provide a sense that peace is the value that humanity has been longing for but has failed to give sufficient thought and actions toward it. Peace is a value that cannot be bought or transplanted from somewhere else, but has to be cultivated on the local soil by the local people so that they will be able to experience the reality of peace.

1

RELEVANCE OF THEOLOGY AND CHURCH LEADERS: COMMON MISSION AND MINISTRY

There is a wide vacuum between the theological community and the church ministers (Christian ministry). The former thinks that they are the most learned community who know all about the Christian doctrines and thus Christian ministers (lay and outdated) must listen to all that they have to say. On the other hand, the church ministers do not bother about the theologians who speak jargons of theology that people do not understand. They counter their allegations by saying, "They are not helpful to the life of the church as they do not understand anything that the contemporary church practically faces." There may not be any more serious issues than this if we want to continue theological education in the theological seminaries and also want to give meaningful ministry to the needs of the people.

The most important question we need to raise from the perspective of both theological educators and Christian ministers is, why are theologians being questioned on the basis of relevance to the context of the church/people? If we can find an appropriate answer to this question, we may be able to find a meeting point of the two. On the other hand, if we fail to address this seriously, it will not be a simple matter of theologians not becoming relevant but also that the Christian leaders may also become irrelevant to the people. I would like to develop a framework of hypothesis in order to draw out a line to arrest the problem. First, the core issue lies in the shaping of theological orientation. There are many people who wrongly think that Bible study and theological study are one and the same thing. There are some people who claim to be theologically trained persons, who think that the one who can preach a powerful sermon is a theologian. Others prefer to consider as theologians those who are interested in mission and evangelism, or writing, etc. It is very difficult to adopt a single criterion to define a theologian.[1] But what is important for us to determine is what is their theological orientation? What are they speaking/writing/doing? How relevant are they to the people?

Even if I am not the right person, I want to evoke the thinking of the church leaders of this region by challenging them with this question, how many of the present church leaders evaluate the standard of theological education? How far can one differentiate between theological education and theological degrees? If one thinks and has concern that the Christian church should not invest in vain, it is very necessary for them to critically evaluate theological orientation of the theologically trained people supplied by various colleges/seminaries. This is crucial, because many of us have received theological education from different places in different theological seminaries. Some of these theological seminaries are being run under accreditation of associations like Asia Theological Association (ATA) and Association of Theological Education in South East Asia (ATESEA), while others come under a university status like the Senate of Serampore College (SSC), etc., but there are others who run independent theological colleges. In certain cases, any degree is conferred to students according to their wishes or according to the wish of the teachers. Unfortunately, in those theological colleges/Bible colleges, the subjects are taught according to the availability of teachers, or teachers are given freedom to teach any subject they want to teach to the students. That is the reason why students of different theological colleges have different theological orientation and theological standards. The Christian church leaders must be made aware of this situation. Further, some of the colleges give greater emphasis on mission while others concentrate on preaching and ministry; other colleges focus on singing or the second coming or church planting, etc. As a result, when graduates come back to the ministry, their degrees do not decide what theological education is but the impact that they can make on the people. So, some graduates join the ministry to serve the people whereas some join with the aim to convert the people, then there are some who join the ministry to learn from the people's experiences whereas others join ministry to teach the people. Thus, non-uniformity of theological education/standard has caused a lot of confusion in the life of the churches in the region.

Theological education is not determined by the degree one obtains but by one's ability to meaningfully present Christian doctrinal values. It

---

[1] It is more appropriate for many of us to claim ourselves as being theologically trained, rather than theologians because most theologically trained people do not become theologians. Theologian is a term used to refer to the one who has a distinct theological idea and theological methodology, and one who has a good number of followers.

is a matter of how one can reflect upon the realities of the society with an appropriate biblical direction and give people a new meaning to understand their faith. Theological education is not about preserving and protecting the revealed truth but about relating biblical truth to the culture of the contemporary people. This is an attempt to make people involved in knowing and realizing the beauty of their selves. There are many theological interpretations of Christian principles but not all of them are considered important and accepted all over the world. Ideas are accepted based on the culture and context of the people. Therefore, as far as possible, theological studies done in the local context is encouraged because it makes people aware of their own context and enables them to learn the method of contextual interpretation of the Bible. Otherwise, students who do not study from their own context, learn the theological interpretations of other people (culture, caste, and class). In the process, when they attempt to import other people's way of doing theology, they are found irrelevant by their own people.

There is no doubt that the primary task of theological education is to produce qualified ministers who will be able to counter both religious confusion like doctrinal crises, religious fundamentalism, and fanaticism, and social issues like poverty, human rights violation, gender discrimination, etc. But this cannot be achieved only in the theological campus. Firm theological foundation cannot be established by reading many books or listening to critical lectures alone but it will be possible when a person is capable of reasoning with the realities of the society and do critical and creative reflections with scriptural insights. Theological education and Christian ministry are not separate entities but they function together toward realizing meaningful Christianity on earth. The church has a mission but many ministries. It should be clearly emphasized that the church does not produce qualified, skill-oriented ministers but they are produced by theological institutions. The church must be the partner of theological institutions in the making of ministers. If either of the two is not interested in this process, then there is no necessity for the other to exist.

In this context, we must rethink the theological education of the people of North East India. Why do most people prefer to go to the cities like Bangalore, Mumbai, Chennai, etc., and that too, mostly to independent colleges. Who recommends them? The usual unethical practice of misguiding young minds in theological studies (I am verbally told) is that the continuing students will be awarded fee concessions if they bring three students in the new academic session. In this way, some people become the agents of theological/Bible colleges to campaign for admission. Even without such a condition, many students are tempted to go to those colleges that charge relatively lower fees. The question that confronts us again is, why should we make "lower fees" as a criterion for pursuing theological education? The commitment to serve the church with better quality is what is important. While on the one hand, we think of meeting the needs of the people's aspiration and on the other hand, we continue to give our young people the freedom to choose a Bible college based on availability of friends or physical facilities or lower fee, etc. In the process, when students do not have proper theological education, the graduates undermine the people who have been Christians for generations. They come with a domineering mindset that causes conflict between theological graduates and the church leaders. So, it is high time for the churches of the region to evaluate the impact of theological education and take proper steps in order to rectify the prevalent trend.

Relevant Christian theology must bridge the gap between theological institution and the church. I want to reaffirm what Y.L. Mingthing once said, "We need to evaluate the whole content and nature of theological education, so that it will be relevant and applicable in our present situation today. At the same time, the whole question of the relationship of the theological education and the church has to be looked into afresh and the entire theological education reoriented to bridge the gap. This is a great task before us, that theological colleges in our region should take this issue seriously in our theological education process."[2] The issue we are deliberating here has been earlier expressed by Wati Longchar, "I hope Tribal Study Centre will continue to equip our pastors, missionaries, and Christian ministers to meet these new challenges and make Christian ministry effective and relevant in our times."[3] On the part of the Christian ministers, there should not be condemnation of anyone on the basis of degree/affiliation/accreditation, etc., but they should rather address the need of reorienting the new generation ministers. They should try to utilize the specialty of everyone and initiate the best way to work together in order to build a stronger Christian church. The traditional way of countering sickness, poverty and suffering, social crisis, etc., with prayer alone is no longer relevant. God has used many people to understand many things and to heal many types and kinds of disease. We must make use of these facilities.

The Christian ministers need both academic information and practical capability and will otherwise fail to respond to the varied needs of

---

[2] Y.L. Mingthing, "Keynote Address," in *Tribal Theology on the Move*, ed. Shimreingam Shimray and Limatula Longkumer (Jorhat: Tribal/ Women Study Centre, 2006), ix.

[3] Detailed discussion of what he meant by "new challenges" may be read in "The Tribal Study Centre: An Attempt for Self Theologizing," in *Advancing with Christ* (Jorhat: Souvenir of The Eastern Theological College Centenary Celebration, 2005), 75.

the people. They are not supposed to act as spiritual guide to the people by limiting their ministry to worship, prayers, and home visits. Human wholeness cannot be experienced by catering only to the spiritual needs of the congregation. The best example of Christian mission is demonstrated by Jesus Christ who began his earthly ministry by way of healing and serving the needy. That was his method of liberation, bringing wholeness and change to the life of the individuals and community.

While keeping the commitment of making life meaningful to self and to each other, both the Christian ministers and theological educators must seek together to make people realize that understanding religion is not the end. A good share of theological history has been given to that search. We must go beyond this and move to seek for the meaning of religion.

Christian ministers should continue to draw resources from theological institutions, either by pursuing higher theological degree or at least attending refreshers' course to update their knowledge. This is necessary because of their limited access to theological information such as current theological trends, current theological debate, approaches, and methodologies. For instance, while theological debate at the global level took place on different themes for a particular decade or year such as Apartheid, Gender Equality, Reconciliation, Decade of Overcoming Violence, Girl Child, Health and Wholeness, etc., Christian ministers continue to speak the same "old language" over the years. They cannot make appealing presentation to the people and therefore people are not responsive to their teaching and preaching.

To a certain extent, the Christian leaders are very critical of theological educators or institutions. They often use the term *liberal* to refer to the theologically trained people and comment that their preaching with exegetical formula is difficult to understand, whereas they approve the preaching of the so-called "pulpit guys" who speak honey-coated language without proper meaning and even distort the scriptural texts. They must realize that Christianity has to grow through a higher level and understanding of meaning.

We must all realize together that relevant theology is not a critical reading of the texts of famous European theologians like John Locke, Albreht Ritschl, Martin Luther, John Calvin, Thomas Aquinas, Karl Barth, Jürgen Moltmann, etc., and reproducing what they said about Jesus Christ in their own historical contexts. But the present need is for a more critical reading of the Bible and interpreting its message in the light of the reality of our times. This will enable us to relate the Bible to our life and culture because without doing this, we will not be able to understand the Bible meaningfully. There is no greater theological task than this.

Theological education in the North East must help the Christian ministers widen their outlook and sharpen the perspective of mission. I am once again tempted to say that the concept of Christianity in the region is still narrow in the sense that it is greatly limited to the spiritual sphere of life. At times, the participation of the church in peace making is short-lived. Her attitude toward HIV-AIDS is still negative. She is yet to make an impact on the whole context of marketization and globalization.[4] The theological educators should inspire and challenge our young generation with fresh ambitions, new dreams, and inspired visions for the community. If we say that the issue of Lesbian, Gays, Bisexual, and Transgender (LGBT) is not a theological issue, then we are contextually not relevant.

Another factor that keeps the theological education and church ministry apart is the focus of vision in mission. For instance, tribal theology attempts to articulate at the local level with local resources and culture but the local church mission aims at conversion of people in faraway lands. They simply compete over the number of missionaries they sponsor in China, Nepal, Bhutan, Myanmar, Sikkim, Jharkhand, Uttar Pradesh, etc. How much money have we spent during the last fifty years and who is evaluating the results of our church mission? Are we wasting our money, energy, and time? A time has come for the Christian church to shift the mission paradigm and focus on the local problems like people's economy, health, terrorism, child theology, etc. And when the Christians themselves are made wealthy and whole, the church's mission can flow beyond the local. "Back to the local" is the trend of contemporary Christian mission.

There is also a need to seriously attempt to deconstruct Western philosophy of mission that is centered on the numerical growth of people and local churches (though that was necessary at one point of time). It is shocking to read the remark made by Wickeri that there are today more American missionaries overseas than there have been at any time in history. The understanding of mission in relationship to Western power for many of these missionaries has not changed much since the nineteenth century, although their means and methods have been greatly enhanced.[5] Perhaps this is the reason why a missiology professor told one of the Filipino-American Pentecostal students like this, "We should no longer

---

[4] Brightstar J. Syiemlieh discussed this idea in his article, "The Future of Tribal Christian Theology in Northeast India: Possible Directions," in *Tribal Theology On The Move*, ed. Shimreingam Shimray and Limatula Longkumer (Jorhat: Tribal/ Women Study Centre, 2006), 45.

[5] Philip L. Wickeri, "Toward a Kenosis of Mission: Emptying and Empowerment for the Church and for the World," in *Scripture, Community, and Mission—Essays in Honour of D. Preman Niles*, ed. Philip L. Wickeri (Hong Kong: CCA/WCC, 2002), 333.

speak of the Christian mission, for it carries the associations of colonialism, racism, patriarchy, and hegemony."[6]

We do not need to impart theology that is not relevant to the church. Relevant theology must be shaped with the resources supplied by the people/church. Their needs, sufferings, joy, celebration, failures, etc., must become the vital source of shaping theological perspective in the institutions. In doing so, the theological products (theological graduates) will be meaningfully fitted to the ministry of the church. I want to reiterate that relevant ministry is not simply determined by thrilling sermons on the pulpit nor is it merely conversion of new converts. It has to do with realizing justice, a method to respond to different issues, making people comfortable by providing proper thinking, making them love their history, culture, and customs, and helping them understand biblical insights meaningfully. A Christian ministerial role is to identify with the people. A Christian minister must be able to create impact in the lives of both the rich and the poor. One must seriously think why many of the pastors are relevant only to the sick, poor, and weak of the society/congregation. A Christian minister must have the ability to command the entire community—a command not in terms of power but in terms of conscientizing and making them accept the truth of the Bible.

---

[6] Wickeri, "Toward a Kenosis of Mission," 332.

2

SOCIAL ANALYSIS AND THEOLOGY: A METHODOLOGICAL IMPLICATION FOR DOING TRIBAL THEOLOGY

INTRODUCTION

Social analysis and theology are two closely interlinked subjects. Theology cannot in any way be separated from social analysis. For instance, no theologian speaks of theology in a vacuum but speaks of God, of Jesus Christ, sin, salvation, etc., on the basis of human experience or context. An analysis of human realities makes people think about their own existence and the purpose of life. Theology does not come from God, but it is of the people about their relation with God and the whole of creation. Hence, theology can be developed broadly from two kinds of people, i.e., oppressors and the oppressed, which Gustavo Gutierrez calls "top-down theology and bottom-up theology." However, social analysis is the basis in both the theologies.

SOCIAL ANALYSIS

Social analysis is a subject that studies social situations by exploring historical, structural, and contextual relationships.[1] It focuses on underlying human problems like poverty, the caste system, racism, women's issues, land, ecology, human rights, etc., and addresses the structural system and policies of society. By so doing, it investigates the societal or governmental economic, political, social, cultural, and religious institutions—identifying the factors like the land-owning system, production, distribution patterns of national wealth, import-export policy, and on the whole globalization and its impacts on the people, the political parties and their

---

[1] Joe Holland and Peter Henriot, S.J., *Social Analysis Linking Faith and Justice* (Indore: Satprakashan Sanchar Kendra, 1984), 14.

ideologies, the exercise of power, the election system, the movements, etc. In the course of analysis, we are able to seriously consider the relationships of people such as that between the rich and the poor, inter-caste relationships, inter-religious relationships, etc., so that the problems are thoroughly understood and responded to at all levels. In other words, it makes it possible to discern how different kinds of people respond to the problems that confront them.

Writing from the pastoral perspective, Joe Holland and Peter Henriot in their book *Social Analysis Linking Faith and Justice* claim that there can be two approaches to social analysis. One approach is "academic," which studies a particular social situation in a detached, fairly abstract manner, dissecting its elements for the purpose of understanding, and the other approach is "pastoral," which looks at the reality from an involved, historically committed stance, discerning the situation for the purpose of action. According to them, existence is the basis; what people are feeling, what they are undergoing, and how they are responding. Then, social analysis examines the causes and consequences, identifies actors, and finds the inter-relationships. Within the context of social analysis, facts and issues are no longer regarded as isolated problems. In the third stage, theological reflection is undertaken to understand more broadly and deeply the analyzed experience in the light of living faith, Scripture, church social teaching, and the sources of tradition. These three stages will only make possible any future planning.

However, it is very clear that social analysis does not claim to solve the underlying issues/problems, but it only helps to develop perspective; creating awareness that will motivate possible actions. It helps people to find alternatives. For instance, when people are made aware of the distribution system of national wealth, it enables them to speak of their rights or see the alternative means for their livelihood. Social analysis also informs the past experiences. An analysis encourages one to rethink upon the unjust structures of the society that prohibit the poor and the backward classes from participating freely in national affairs. It creates room for deeper reflection for transformation and liberation. It leads one to envision a better society where justice reigns and equality prevails for all citizens of the society.

THEOLOGY

The term *theology* was literally translated from two Greek words *qeo* (God) and *logos* (Word), as the study of the word of God. This term has passed through a number of stages and undergone several changes in its definitions out of the new faith experiences of the people. The meaning of theology is thus no longer confined to the revealed truth of God. It concerns the whole relationship between God and humans, humans and humans, human and creation, and God and creation. According to Mithra G. Augustine, theology teaches and values human worth and quality of life and tirelessly seeks to facilitate, through individual and institutional efforts, restoration of right relations, justice, and peace among people and nations. Implications of theology encompass all life and its varied support systems.[2] It is an ongoing process of reflection on people's experience in the light of their faith in God. It advocates the wellbeing of the whole of creation. At this point of discussion, it is important to note that there has been a drastic paradigm shift in theological thinking. In its early stage, theology was developed in line with philosophy. As K.C. Abraham asserts, "classical theological paradigm has been decisively shaped by the Hellenistic philosophy and theory of knowledge."[3] Today, theology is being developed much more from the sociological aspects of human experience. For instance, James H. Cone argues that doing Christian theology is not reading the textbook of Barth, Scheiermacher, Luther, and Calvin and repeating what they said about the gospel of Jesus. Christian theology arises out of one's commitment to the struggles of the poor for justice.[4] K.C. Abraham continues to point out that the models of thought in each of these in the dominant paradigm of theology are based on the experience of the West. The paradigm is Euro-centric. Experiences of the Global South people—their culture and religions as well as their contemporary struggle for justice and liberation—have raised serious questions on the Euro-centric model of theologizing.[5] In fact, the experiences of the marginalized in every context, their suffering and their longing for a new life, demand a new paradigm of theologizing.[6] It was in that climate of shift that the Global South rejected an unpractical theology of the past and affirmed commitment as the first act of theology that is read in the Dar-es-Salaam Conference statement.

> We reject as irrelevant and academic type of theology that is divorced from action. We are prepared for a radical break in epistemology which makes commitment the first act of theology and engages in critical reflection on the praxis of reality of the Third World.[7]

---

[2] Mithra G. Augustine, "Introduction," in *Theology of Our Times*, no. 4 (January, 1997): 8.
[3] K.C. Abraham, "Paradigm Shift in Contemporary Theological Thinking," *Bangalore Theological Forum* 24 (1992): 2.
[4] Hunter P. Mabry, ed., *Doing Christian Ethics* (Bangalore: BTESSC, 1996), 119.
[5] Abraham, "Paradigm Shift," 2.
[6] Abraham, "Paradigm Shift," 4.
[7] K.C. Abraham, "EATWOT TRENDS," *Doing Christian Ethic*, ed. Hunter P. Mabry (Bangalore: BTESSC, 1996), 141.

Negotiating Peace

It will be unfair to reject the methodologies of the early classical and the modern theologians. However, when we consider methodology and contextual theology, Latin America becomes very significant where Paulo Freire developed the concept of praxis /conscientization for doing theology,[8] and Juan Luis Segundo conceptualized the "hermeneutic circle" or "method of interpretation" that sees new questions continually raised to challenge the older theories by the force of new situations.[9] In his study on ancient Israel, Norman K. Gottwald also used the sociological method that he found useful to theology. For instance, he writes, in one way sociological study is helpful to theology in order to correspond appropriately to the social setting. A sociological study of the biblical texts provides the patterns of human relations in their structure and function, both at a given moment or stage (synchronics) and in their trajectories of change over a specified time span (diachronics). This is so because, for Gottwald, the sociological method includes all the methods of inquiry proper to social sciences, i.e., anthropology, sociology, political science, and economics. This method enables us to analyze, synthesize, abstract, and interpret the Israelites' life and thought along different axes and with tools and constructs different from those familiar to us from the historical method. Such inquiry recognizes people as social actors and symbolizers who "perform" according to interconnecting regularities and within the boundaries or limits (social system).[10] In a slightly different manner, Gustavo Gutierrez also concludes that scientific application of social sciences is undeniable in its early stages and still marked by uncertainties. Nonetheless, these sciences do help us understand better the social realities of our present situation.[11]

Relationship between the two

The context and experience of the people becomes the sole criterion when it comes to constructing a theology because nothing can be said that can be meaningful to the people outside of their context. This is to say that there cannot be any relevant theology if it is not developed from the real experiences of the people themselves. For instance, in India, if the caste system, the child labor system, patriarchy, religious pluralism, communalism, ethnic conflict, etc., are not critically reflected upon, the task of Christian theology will remain unfulfilled. So, analysis of the society and its relationship to God is the beginning of theology. For example, raising a

---

[8] Paulo Freire, *Pedagogy of the Oppressed* (New York: Herder and Herder, 1970), 46.
[9] Juan Luis Segundo, *Liberation of Theology* (Maryknoll, NY: Orbis Books, 1976), 8.
[10] Norman K. Gottwald, ed., *The Bible and Liberation* (Maryknoll, NY: Orbis Books, 1983), 27.
[11] Gustavo Gutierrez, *Truth Shall Set You Free* (Maryknoll, NY: Orbis Books, 1990), 58.

question like, why are many people poor and marginalized? is a real theology because it involves the question of life and survival. The nomenclature of dalits itself is proof of the fact that they themselves no longer want to be under a suppressed condition. It is in this perspective that the role of God, his identification with the people, and his involvement in the affairs of human beings must be sought. This is theology.

It is obvious that people in a different context with different experiences while trying to make the message of Jesus Christ relevant have experienced the development of theologies such as liberation theology, black theology, and feminist theology. It also gives the impression that in doing theology, people no longer simply search for understanding but go a step beyond to find meaning. Thus, knowing who Jesus Christ is is not an end but knowing how meaningful he is to the people, particularly to the marginalized, and how he takes side with them, is important so that he will be more meaningful to them. Thus, it is undeniably true that theological trend is shaped by human experience. In the process of theologizing, history plays an important role in supplying information that lays the background for articulation. Considering the importance of time linkage, the present realities of crisis cannot be simply ignored because future society depends on what is today, as Mahatma Gandhi had correctly stated, "the future will depend on what we do in the present." His statement corresponds to what John Desrochers observes, that "the world is not threatened by catastrophe in the future. The greater part of humankind is already experiencing catastrophe today."[12] One of the underlying questions for theologians in the present situation is that, in pursuit of doing theology, one cannot neglect doing a serious reflection on the economic life of the people. Because all aspects of human life, be it politics or social, religion, or culture, evolve around the economy. In the present capitalistic structure of competitive economy, the few affluent are capturing all resources. In 1992, Manmohan Singh, then Finance Minister of India, was right when he said, in the competition, the stronger ones will survive and the weaker ones will be absorbed. The national economic growth rate is over 7 percent of the total Gross National Product (GNP). Yet, the profits do not reach the marginalized group at the outermost margin. Therefore, even if the nation claims that the percentage of people living below the poverty line is reducing, the reality remains that the number of people living below the poverty line has increased. For example, 65 percent poor people of the total population of 400 million in 1960 is 260 million. This is definitely lower than 40 percent poor people of the 100 thousand million in 2010, that is, 400 million poor people. It is in a way saying that the arithmomorphic system that simply claims that if the national production

---

[12] John Desrochers, *Toward a New India* (Bangalore: CSA, 1995), 12.

rate is higher than the population growth then the problem of poverty can be solved, is unrealistic and that poverty cannot be eradicated unless the distribution system of national wealth is drastically reformed and focus is shifted to the majority poor people. Mahatma Gandhi, while favoring the agriculture sector over industrial production, asserted that mass production will not solve the problem of poverty but production by the masses can only solve it. Referring to the system generated by globalization, Bastian Wielenga argues that because globalization, while giving much emphasis on growth (GNP), neglects the suffering of the people who have no buying power for their own productions.[13]

Today, the present trend of economic development has made it clear that the whole of humankind cannot be categorized into one level of life. For instance, the availability of economic resources becomes the criterion and so developing countries cannot be compared with those of the developed countries. At the same time, it is ecologically impossible for most Global South countries to reach the per capita levels of the rich countries. Such aspiration is thus unrealizable and undesirable for the Global South countries. Rajni Kothari opines that "there would not be sufficient non-renewable resources in the world to make it possible; there would be too much of poisonous emission."[14] A similar idea is expressed by Gamani Corea who does not approve the theory of one world, two life-styles with one life-style for the industrialized countries, and one for the Global South. Thus, he asserts, "the logic of the environmental debate points to the need for a revolution of life-style in the industrialized countries themselves so as to provide a model that can be pervasive, that can be valid, throughout the world as a whole.[15]

In his 1971 social document, "A Call to Action," Pope Paul VI challenged social activists in a manner that recalls the elements of the pastoral circle.

> It is up to Christian communities to analyze with objectivity the situation that is proper to their own country, to shed on it the light of the Gospel's unalterable words, and to draw principles or reflections, norms of judgment, directive of action from social teaching of the church.[16]

This call came into the life of one international religious community and was recovered in the 1975 documents of the 32nd General Congress of the Society of Jesus. In its Decree Four, "Our Mission Today," the Jesuits'

---

[13] Bastian Wielenga, "Market Friendly Society and Its Implications," *Theology for Our Times*, no. 4 (January 1997): 30.
[14] Quoted from Rajni Kothari in John Desrochers, *Towards A New India*, 23.
[15] See in Desrochers, *Towards a New India*, 23.
[16] Holland and Henriot, *Social Analysis*, 11.

mission underlined the importance of social analysis for evangelization as they stated: "We cannot be excused from making the most rigorous possible political and social analysis of our situation.... From analysis and discernment will come committed action; from the experience of action will come insight into how to proceed further."

It is interesting to note that the call was repeated in Cleveland in August 1978, at CONVERGENCE '78—the historical joint meeting of the Leadership Conference of Women Religious and the Conference of Major Superiors of Men. In their final statement, the religious superiors made a pledge:

> Realizing that we lack full understanding of our social, economic, and political life, we commit ourselves to structural analysis and theological reflection.[17]

While speaking of the Global South theological trends, K.C. Abraham strongly affirms the importance of social analysis in doing theology. According to him, theological and ethical reflection is rooted in the experience of a community, its experience of oppression, and its struggle for liberation. We cannot do ethical reflection without a clearer awareness of the structures of domination. Social analysis is, therefore an indispensable tool for our theological/ethical task.[18] Abraham further quotes the New Delhi Conference report that closely corresponds to his stand. It says,

> Social analysis is an indispensable mediation and basic equipment for a liberation theology. It indicates the way in which the values of the Kingdom of love, justice, and truth are being realized or denied in our situations. Without an adequate understanding of our societies, theologians cannot interpret the will of God for our societies and our times.[19]

This is exactly what Allan Delotavo claims for doing theology in Asia. He says that if a theology aims to relate Christ to the present sociopolitical condition of Asia, then a sociopolitical analysis is very important.[20] Because as K.C. Abraham once again affirms, the primary objective of theological reflection, however, is to help people in their struggle for justice and freedom.[21] Along with the above thinkers, Russell Chandran also convincingly formulated the relationship between theology and social analysis that is evident when he said, in fact, in the Christian faith based

---

[17] Holland and Henriot, *Social Analysis*, 13.
[18] K.C. Abraham, "EATWOT TRENDS," 143.
[19] K.C. Abraham, "EATWOT TRENDS," 144.
[20] Allan Delotavo, "Towards A Christ-Centered Way of Doing Theology," *Asia Journal of Theology* 3, no. 1 (April 1989): 330.
[21] Abraham, "Paradigm Shift," 2.

on the Bible, the quest for truth and the struggle for justice are integrally related. The one without the other becomes irrelevant and ineffective.[22]

RELATIONSHIP BETWEEN SOCIAL ANALYSIS AND THEOLOGY IN THE CONTEXT OF THE POOR

One of the best examples that indicate the integral relationship between theology and social analysis is an analysis of the situation of the poor. The poor are the people who experience all kinds of pain, hunger, thirst, pain of sickness, pain of heat and cold, pain of untimely death, illiteracy, long stretch of work without rest, etc. It is clear that an economically backward people will not have rich political power and socially respectable position and so on. If their situation is not critically analyzed and the causes of their poverty investigated, they will remain poor and even become poorer. A study of their situation is crucial as it is the only way for them to expect a better world, else it would mean there will be no good news for them.

Coming out of their reality of poverty is liberation that requires struggle and critical ethical/theological reflection. The human experience of domination, exploitation, and oppression in the countries of the Global South particularly in Latin America contributed to the beginning and development of the *liberation theology*. The liberation theologians defined the concept of poor. They took the side of the poor. They made the poor aware of the dehumanizing systems and forces of the oppressors and condemned the unjust social structure. In such a context, the God of the Bible who liberates the poor and the marginalized became meaningful in their theological reflections. Their faith-praxis became an important tool in developing theology based on people's experiences. As Robert McAfee Brown puts it, "for liberation theology claims that it is in the life and situation of the poor that God is to be found, that God is at work. The God of the Old Testament is the God of the poor and the oppressed, a God who takes side with them, taking their part, and identifying with them. The God of the New Testament is the same God, a God who becomes incarnate not in one who possessed wealth or influence or a good name, but in one who belongs to the "poor of the land."[23] Their faith in God became more meaningful when Christ is made to identify with the poor. This is where their theology departed from traditional to liberation. The point of departure is not simply the reality of explanation under which the oppressed suffered, but the praxis of Christians and of the poor in general, working for the transformation of the oppressive situation. The poor

---

[22] Quoted by Franklin Balasundaram in *EATWOT IN ASIA: Towards Relevant Theology* (Bangalore: ATC, 1993), 178.

[23] Robert McAfee, *Theology in a New Key* (Philadelphia: The Westminster Press, 1978), 61.

themselves give an interpretation of their misery. Critical analysis is not put aside but enriched. Thus, the poor understand themselves as children of God, created in the image and likeness of God. The resistance of the poor against oppression and their struggle for liberation became better understood, and the understanding of the poor became much clearer as read in the words of Gustavo Gutierrez. He said,

> I discovered three things. I discovered that poverty was a destructive thing, something to be fought against and destroyed, not merely something which was the object of our charity. Secondly, I discovered that poverty was not accidental. The fact that these people are poor and not rich is not just a matter of chance, but a result of a structure. Thirdly, I discovered that poor people were a social class. When I discovered that poverty was structural, that poor people were a class (and could not organize), it became crystal clear that in order to serve the poor, one had to move into political action.[24]

So, the discovery of what it means to be poor became a source of strength to many whose problems are not solved by an occasional handout or a little organized "charity." The poor, Gutierrez concluded, are poor not because they are lazy or "shiftless", but because society is so structured that the poor are destined to remain poor unless they organize to change the structure of that society.[25] Such understanding leads to two basic conclusions: One, it is "pre-theological," according to Jean Luis Segundo, a Jesuit theologian from Uruguay. Two, when we take the poor as our starting point, we arrive at another conclusion that the world should not be the way it is.[26] This can be compared to Frederick Herzog's conclusion that theology must start "where the pain is."[27]

Fitting the same methodology of liberation theology to the whole framework of the Third World Theology, K.C. Abraham writes that the starting point of theology is the life of the people, of the poor and the oppressed in particular for whom we opt and with whom we join in solidarity. He quotes Samuel Rayan who sums up this perspective: "Thus theology starts in, leads to, and calls for praxis that is liberating, and humanizing and life-giving."[28] The whole theological challenge here is that the rich must go into the life situation of the poor and become a part of them in order to bring them to life, the situation in which the poor will

---

[24] Sergio Torres and John Eagleson, eds., *Theology in America* (Maryknoll, NY: Orbis Books, 1976), 278.
[25] McAfee, *Theology in a New Key*, 62.
[26] McAfee, *Theology in a New Key*, 62.
[27] Frederick Herzog, *Liberation Theology* (New York: Seabury Press, 1972), 258.
[28] Quoted in Hunter P. Mabry, ed., *Doing Christian Ethics*, 141.

no longer feel they belong to another culture (of poor) that is against the culture of the rich.

Gustavo Gutierrez was one of the theologians who recognized the meeting point of theology and social sciences. This is clear in his discussion on poverty and theology. He explains, once the situation of poverty and marginalization comes to play a part in theological reflection, an analysis of that situation from the sociological viewpoint becomes important, and thinkers are forced to look for help from the relevant disciplines. This means that if there is a meeting point, it is between theology and social sciences, and not between theology and Marxist analysis. However, these two enable people to understand society. Theology does not end there because it does not search only to understand social realities but to have meaning to the people and for such theology to be persuasive on the basis of faith in God, God-human relationship must be incorporated. Theology must take into account the contribution of the social sciences, but in its work, it must always appeal to its own sources.[29]

POLITICAL ASPECT

Economic liberation alone is not the sole task of Christian theological reflection. There are other equally important aspects that hamper the well-being of the people that need to be analyzed and reflected upon, in order to make society grow in the right direction. For example, politics requires analysis in order to find out the flow of power. Very often, a country like India experiences the problem of law and order. A few people who hold power constantly manipulate national affairs with their vested interests to meet their own selfish ends. It is therefore the task of analysts to critically evaluate the ideologies and programs of the political parties and make people aware about whom they ought to favor. In a democratic country like India, the masses should be made to decide for themselves who they vote into power. This will be possible when the national election system is properly reformed; when every citizen is made to exercise their franchise according to their own conscience instead of casting vote for money. The root cause of Indian political corruption is seen in its election system. The whole democratic principle gets demoralized when election becomes a money-power competition. The freedom of individuals to choose their leaders is bought and their votes that decide the formation of government become a commodity to be sold and bought. Indian politics is neither stable nor decisive because power is exercised on the basis of communal interests. This is one of the reasons that has divided people. For instance, the Janata Party that was formed in 1977 has split eight times within the last thirty years. Another serious political concern in India is that Indian

---

[29] Sergio Torres and John Eagleson, eds., *Theology in America*, 66.

politicians have not learned how to run a coalition government. Very often, national interest is kept below the party's interest. Joining a coalition government may even mean a privilege to threaten the government to listen to every political party for every big and small issue. For instance, in the case of coalition government, the supporting party often threatens the leading party with the option to withdraw from the government if their interest is not considered or any decision is taken without seeking their consent.

In order to make politics more meaningful to the people, political power should not be concentrated in the center alone but should be decentralized to the lower levels of government so that the voice of the public can be heard in their own context. The Christian community can contribute the right perspectives to the political leaders through proclaiming justice values. On the other hand, people like M.M. Thomas have argued that the church can countercheck corruption in secular politics through criticism. It is the task of the theologians to critically reflect on political power so that they can make people aware of the meaning of politics in the true sense and lead to a rethink of people's rights to participate in politics in order to create a just society.

ECOLOGICAL CONCERN

In theological discussions, the issue of ecological crisis has become one of the serious concerns. It is because people have already experienced the damages done by the people themselves toward God's sustaining creation. Ecological concern developed when people started analyzing the excessive use of natural resources in order to meet the increasing demands for raising the standard of living. In a competitive world, rich people attempt to maintain the highest comfort of life. Thus, the only option to sustain their lifestyles is to increase the production of goods. As a result, there has been a rapid increase of industries and factories that produce maximum luxury goods and foods, which at the same time result in industrial wastes like uranium, plutonium, chlorofluorocarbon, etc., polluting the water, air, and damaging the ozone layer, among other things. For instance, a study paper from WCC in the Global Warming Consultation on South Asia in 1994 indicates that, the conditions of life on earth are being altered by the general depletion of the thin layer of ozone gas in the stratosphere.[30] The use of chemical fertilizers, pesticides, etc., destroys the soil quality of land, and health of other living creatures.

Unfortunately, while trying to meet their unending demands, humans have learned to use more non-renewable energy sources such as fuel, coal, and gas because they are more productive, provide more comfort, save

[30] K.C. Abraham, eds., *Global Warming* (Bangalore: SATHRI, 1994), 11.

more time, and so on. On the other hand, the unlimited felling of trees has created havoc for the earth's entire climate system bringing the existence of all living beings under serious threat. For example, Calvin B. Dewitt points out that three species are getting extinct daily. Their existence is cut off forever.[31] Human beings will also face the same end if the world's eco-system is not restored at the appropriate time.

Such an analysis draws Christians to rethink on the biblical teaching about creation or God's concern for creation itself. It is clear that God's purpose of creation is for the common good of all creatures. Thus, Michael Douglas Meeks in his famous book *God The Economist* asserts that God's creation is for sharing and for the common good of all. Moreover, people should act as stewards of God's creation.[32] It was also in the context of ecological crisis that Jürgen Moltmann in his book *God in Creation* argues that, "'rest' is the crown of creation—rest is important for all living and non-living beings in order to regenerate or come back to their original forms. Ecological crisis is therefore a challenge to the life and witness of Christians. It creates a new perspective in the process of doing theology. This is also the reason why the WCC Canberra Assembly stated, "We commit ourselves anew to living as a community which cares for creation."[33]

An analysis of ecological crisis promotes awareness of the common concern of all people around the world. It also draws attention toward alternative perspectives to sustain creation. For example, as a sign of calling people to change their attitude toward creation, the Club of Rome in 1986 declared its logo as "Limits to Growth." For E.F. Schumacher, to limit ecological crisis, human beings have to use alternative technologies that he calls "technology with human-face," that is not too destructive to nature or too traditional but an eco-friendly technology. Alternatives should be adopted because although the rich industrialists and technologists claim that they can recycle the eco-system, the energy spent for recycling resources is found to be more expensive than the results.

In relation with women's issues

The ecological problem is directly connected to women's problems. Women have gone through painful experiences in this regard. For the women in India, as in most of the Global South, ecology and the

---

[31] Calvin B. Dewitt, ed., *The Environment and the Christian* (Michigan: Baker Book House, 1991), 15.

[32] Michael Douglas Meeks, *God The Economist* (Minneapolis, MN: Fortress, 1989), 177.

[33] David G. Hallman, ed., *Eco-Theology Voices From South And North* (Maryknoll, NY: Orbis Books, 1994), 123.

Social Analysis and Theology

protection of the environment and its resources are issues of livelihood and survival.[34] As feminist ecologist Vandana Shiva puts it, poor women in many parts of India are those who "work daily in the production of survival."[35] In such a context, women suffer the most when drinking water, fuel, and healthy clean surroundings are not available. Their workload is increased and their working hours are lengthened. The present capitalistic paradigm of development, particularly the so-called scientific technologies, has done a great harm to women. This is the reason why Vandana Shiva perceives such development as patriarchal projects because women's knowledge and work that are integrally linked to nature are marginalized or displaced, and replaced by introduced patterns of thought and patterns of work that devalue the worth of women's knowledge and activities and fragment both nature and society.[36]

Much more than the above aspect of discussion, women in many societies suffer in their own homes, workplaces, and in power sharing. They are denied fair access to land and property. They are denied participation in the decision-making process. They are projected as the weaker sex. In many cases, their life experience of subjugation forces them into prostitution in order to survive. This reality empowers them to raise their voice for recognition and total emancipation. Such a demand for fuller humanity is a serious theological issue today. One cannot talk of God from a male perspective alone, leaving or ignoring the other half of humanity. The feminist theology has contributed the idea and explanation of "inclusive language" to Christian theological interpretation. It has become clear that the total liberation of women cannot be materialized through sympathy by men. The requirement for liberation is not pity but a chance or freedom to decide for themselves. The demand is not as Madhu Kiswar points out, "a ladies compartment" in the train run by men because even though they can freely sit in that compartment they do not know what men will decide and where they will be taken. Therefore, the need is their train, run by themselves. For such a task, both men and women must seriously rethink together and should decide together for the good of all humanity.

The tribals of many regions have by now realized much of their history, culture, oppressions, suffering, religion, etc. Many of them have been critically reflecting on doing theology. The pioneers of tribal theology have been successful in the sense that they have shown the younger generations why and how contextual theology is being done. We now have a

---

[34] Aruna Gnanadason, "Women, Economy and Ecology," in *Eco-Theology: Voices from South and North*, ed. David G. Hallman (Geneva: WCC, 1994), 180.

[35] Vandana Shiva, *Staying Alive* (Delhi: Kali for Women, 1989), 210.

[36] Vandana Shiva, "Let Us Survive: Women, Ecology and Development," in *Women Healing Earth: Third World Women on Ecology, Feminism and Religion*, ed. Rosemary Radford Ruether (Maryknoll, NY: Orbis Books, 1996), 65-73.

good amount of literature on tribal theology. Reading the texts of different perspectives clearly indicates that the intention is not to create a new theology besides or beyond Christ but a realistic reflection on the context. In other words, the intention is to analyze cultural values by adopting rejection and synthesis method of interpretation. One thing all tribal theologians have in common is that none of them attempts to take the tribal people back to pre-Christianity era and relive the tribal way of thinking, but they draw out liberative elements of the tribal culture for the purpose of interpreting Christ in a tribal culture. One proponent among many is K. Thanzauva who has been consistently talking of social analysis in doing tribal theology. He made his position very clear in his book, *Theology of Community*. The tribals talk of their identity, history, foreign domination, erosion of culture, modernization, etc., to set a clear context so that they can speak of Christ. This means that the reality of the people has to be first identified if at all theology has to be developed. And that is the reason why social analysis becomes *a priori* in any effort to doing relevant theology. Otherwise, any basis of interpretation of the Bible may become abstract and superficial. Christianity can fully establish its root only when people are able to realistically reflect Christ on the basis of their own cultural values and contextual realities. For the purpose of keeping religion alive, we can adopt many forms like preaching about being "born again," doing mission and evangelism, etc., but we should be very clear that that is not a way of doing theology but an expression of religious taste. Setting the context is a strong basis for making religion meaningful.

CONCLUSION

Social analysis is an indispensable step toward effective action on behalf of justice, but it must be complemented by theological reflection for a better outcome. None of these steps can be totally isolated; theology is not restricted to that moment explicitly called theological reflection. Thus, it may be possible to conclude that social analysis contains within itself, implicitly or explicitly, a theology of life and society. By doing this, it makes theology more reflective and sensitive to the current issues that people are exposed to. On the other hand, using the tool of social analysis, people who act on behalf of justice will gain clearer insight into the complexities of the situations confronting them and will design more effective action-oriented strategies in response.

3

BIBLICAL RESOURCES OF HUMAN RIGHTS

Human rights is a term used to mean a sense of equality, respect, and dignity of all human beings. It is not given by any state or religion, but it is claimed on the basis of being a human. Both Christian theology and human rights are concerned with and talk about the dignity and wellbeing of a person and community. Their concern is about protection, respect, love, sharing, equality, justice, liberation, etc. Therefore, to a certain extent they can be understood as the secular approach and religious approach to life and its fullness. It is also an affirmation that life is the most precious gift of God. My intention in this paper is not to locate the biblical references to all the thirty articles in the Universal Declaration of Human Rights and the subsequent covenants. But I will attempt to see how much biblical insights have been drawn in conceptualizing and formulating those rights that aim to protect the total humanity on earth. It would also mean investigating the biblical foundation of human rights.

The term *human rights* is not employed by classical source of the Jewish religious tradition, which means the Bible does not speak of human rights in modern terms. Hence, there are two views on the issue of biblical concept of human rights; the biblicist and fundamentalist traditions opposed to biblical basis of human rights. In fact, David Jenkin outrightly states, "I do not believe that the notion of human rights is at all biblical."[1] Eugene B. Borowitz also admits that the modern idea of human "rights" does not exist in the conceptualization in classic Jewish doctrine, for neither the Bible nor Rabbinic literature speaks of human dignity in this way.[2] Acknowledging the historical difference between biblical writ-

---

[1] David Jenkin, "Human Rights in Christian Perspective," *Study Encounter* 10, no.2 (1994): 2; cf. *The Ecumenical Review on Mission* (April 1975): 143.
[2] Eugene B. Borowitz, "The Torah, Written and Oral, and Human Rights: Foundations and Deficiencies," in *The Ethics of World Religions and Human Rights*, eds. Hans Küng and Jürgen Moltman (London: SCM Press, 1990), 5.

ing and the emergence of modern human rights, Lorenzen also admits that neither the concept nor the content of modern human rights can be derived directly from the Bible.³ But one system of values and ideas that constitutes the concept of human rights is hardly absent from the Jewish worldview. On the contrary, those values and ideas are among the beliefs that constitute the very core of Jewish sacred Scripture and the tradition of ideas and practices that flow from it. Daniel F. Polish, on the contrary, argues that the idea-set, which is represented by the phrase *human rights*, derives in the Jewish tradition from the basic theological affirmation of the Jewish faith.⁴ The Bible contains rich insights for understanding the total meaning of human beings and their relation to God and creation. Further, it is explored that the human obligations to God that require duty and responsibility to their fellow human beings are an expression of the modern idea of human rights. The system of law presented in the Torah and elaborated in Rabbinic legal literature is one that guaranteed a fair trial before an impartial court to all people, home-born and stranger alike (Lev 24:22). Judges were forbidden to accept bribes (Deut 26:19), and were prohibited from showing favoritism in any way—to the needy no less than to the powerful (Lev 19:15). The laws were aimed at safeguarding even the weaker members of the society (Lev 25).

A Christian discussion of human rights begins with a definition of "human" that requires God. This will inevitably differentiate it from any secular, humanist view of human that omits this divine dimension. For the Christians, the whole doctrine of creaturehood is the landmark to understand the dignity of human beings and their relationship with God and other living and non-living creatures. Within such a framework, the concept of human beings created in the image of God is one of the basic grounds to understand the biblical idea of human rights. The doctrine of human rights presents a challenge to the conventional understanding of a human. The present secular form of human rights does not clearly articulate the meaning of the term *human*. Rather, those articles in the Universal Declaration of Human Rights sound as assumptions regarding what being human actually entails. The Judeo-Christian understanding of humanities would begin with the concept that humans are creatures, made in the image of God, who have betrayed that dignity, sinners in need of salvation, recipients of God's loving care and mercy, a combination of both

---

[3] Thorwald Lorenzen, "Christian Perspective on Human Rights" (Unpublished paper, Canberra, 1993), 7.

[4] Daniel F. Polish, "Judaism and Human Rights," in *Human Rights and Religious Traditions*, ed. (New York: Pilgrim Press, 1982), 40. For him, the commitment to the equality of all people is embodied in the judicial system and process created by the Jewish people.

body and spirit who live in history, capable with God's help of making moral choices, and called to responsible living in community.[5]

The status of created beings and things cannot be the same as the Creator himself. Because God as Creator is the explanation for the existence of the world and for human existence,[6] the responsibility of all creation is to establish a deep and most essential relation to God. This God-creation relationship is the basis of our existence. However, there are probabilities of breaking this relation. It is because, at the time of creation, God gave to human beings freedom and intelligence that may be used either to affirm or deny the fundamental relationship of existence.

IMAGE OF GOD

God's creation of human beings in his own Image (Gen 1:26–27; 9:6)[7] is one of the key sources to place human rights within the framework of Christian thought. It signifies a unique human dignity endowed with the knowledge of right and wrong. He created them in his likeness in order that they have close relationship with himself. Therefore, humanity is defined by its relationship to God. And this dignity is shared by all human beings regardless of race, class, sex, and religion. The whole concept of creation gives "visibility" to the "invisible God." Sinclair B. Ferguson, thus, claims that the doctrine of the *image of God* can be the foundation of human dignity and for biblical ethics.[8] The creation of human beings in the image of God indicates the dignity and inviolable worth they possess and that is the given rights of every person. Charles Sherlock goes to the extent of asserting that human dignity should not be distorted because it is the object of divine concern. He says, no distinction is to be made between persons in the practice of justice, since each is made in the divine image, and is the object of divine concern.[9] The dignity of the human

---

[5] Max Stackhouse, *Creed, Society and Human Rights* (Grand Rapids, MI: William B. Eerdmans, 1984), 3.
[6] D.K. McKim, "Creation, Doctrine of," in *Evangelical Dictionary of Theology*, ed. Walter A. Elwell (Grand Rapids, MI: Baker Book House, 1984), 281.
[7] In Gen 1:26–27, God created male and female in his own image and enthroned them with the status that they may rule over all creatures. But Gen 9:6 speaks with a strong ethical condition "not to shed blood" because God made (hu)man in his own image.
[8] Sinclair B. Ferguson, "Image of God," in *New Dictionary of Theology*, ed. Sinclair B. Ferguson and David F. Wright (Leicester: Inter-varsity Press, 1994), 328–329.
[9] Charles Sherlock, *The Doctrine of Humanity: Contours of Christian Theology* (Illinois: Inter Varsity Press, 1996), 159; For him, justice is to be enacted following the divine example: "The Lord your God is God of gods and Lord of lords, the great, the mighty, and the terrible God, who is not partial and takes no bribe. He executes justice for the fatherless and the widow, and loves the sojourner, giving him food and clothing" (Deut 10:17–18).

being is not itself a human right but a source and basis for all human rights, and all human rights promote respect for the singular worth of human beings. Richard Harries is also of the opinion that God creates and at once recognizes the value of what he has created. This is the foundation for a consciously Christian approach to human rights: *God makes man in His own image and respects the worth and dignity of what he has created.*[10]

The concept of human rights has a theological foundation in the dignity and worth of the human person, created in the image of God. The basic theological understanding drawn from the sentence, "human being is created in the *image* and *likeness* of God" is that since every human being is equally created in the image of God, everyone has rights. They should be treated in ways that show care and concern, rather than disdain and disregard, for their continued existence as the beings they are. The work they have been called by God to perform, the activities by which they become the beings that God intends them to be, should be appreciated and supported rather than dismissively checked or hampered. Human rights is important not only to individuals and their relation to the state but it also remains fundamental and inviolable in our interactions with fellow human beings, for the essence of a person is found in relation with others. John Macquarrie also thus understands the content of the *imago Dei* by referring to his understanding of the personal being of human being that reads, "a person in the fullest sense can only come into being in interaction with other persons."[11] In the discussion of the image of God, Jürgen Moltmann has also made a significant contribution with his systematic concept of four propositions in order to relate to human rights.

1. The image of God is: human beings in all their relationships in life.
2. The image of God is: human beings together with others.
3. Being created in the image of God is the basis of the right of human beings to rule over the earth and of their right to community with the non-human creation.
4. Being created in the image of God is the basis of the right of human beings to their future and their responsibility for those who come after them.[12]

The Bible speaks of the one God, yet God does not belong to a particular nation or church tradition. God is the Creator of all men and women. This is the fundamental human condition, and on it is grounded the

---

[10] Richard Harries, *Questioning Belief* (London: SPCK, 1995), 137.
[11] Quoted by Douglas Pratt, "The Imago Dei in the Thought of John Macquarrie," *Asia Journal of Theology* 3, no. 1 (April 1989): 80.
[12] Jürgen Moltmann, *Theological Basis of Human Rights* (Ferney: WARC, 1976), 9–13.

ultimate dignity of human beings. Thus, "the Image of God" motif may be used as one of the useful means to elaborate the importance of a theological concept of human rights. The *imago Dei* is a relationship in which it is not we who are asking the questions or entering the claims; and in this relationship, it is the relativity not the question of our individual rights that is important.[13] For such an attempt, an example in the "theological guidelines" of the then World Alliance of Reformed Churches[14] may be cited. In identification of our humanity as created in the image of God, we affirm:

- the equal dignity and interdependence of man and woman;
- the equal validity and interdependence of personal rights (freedom and dignity) and social rights (justice and community);
- the equal dignity and interdependence of the present generation and the future generations in the stewardship of nature.

As humanity stands in a covenant relationship with God, this relationship carries with it covenant responsibilities in our stewardship of creation: the equal validity and interdependence of human rights and human duties.[15]

J.D. De puts it differently. According to him, from the biblical viewpoint, human rights are founded not in the fundamental freedom of humanity, but in the revealed truths that:

a. men and women are the fruit of the everlasting work of creation, as confirmed in the person and work of Jesus Christ (Rom 8:29; Eph 4:24; Col 1:15), and as the bearers of God's image, they have a dignity and worth guaranteed by their creator (Gen 9:6; Josh 3:9);

b. they are called and enabled by that same creative word to be the stewards of God's creation (Gen 1:28; 9:1–2), and

c. for that reason, they have a momentum in themselves and others before God.[16]

---

[13] Ramsey argues that when (hu)man ceases to reflect the image of God and begins to only reflect their own selves and their rights, they are no longer in the image of God. Thus, he is of the opinion that a Christian doctrine of rights likewise follows primarily from human's service to God, and not from human nature. Ramsey, *Basic Christian Ethics* (New York: Charles Scribner's Sons, 1954), 354.

[14] Today, they are known as World Communion of Reformed Churches.

[15] Allen O. Miller, ed., *Christian Declaration on Human Rights* (Grand Rapids: William B. Eerdmans, 1977), 145. More of personal rights, freedom, equality, and social justice have already been revealed by the eighth century prophets like Hos and Jeremiah; cf. Hosea 4 and Jer 4. At the same time, the covenantal relationship is seen in Noahic Covenant with God in Genesis 9.

[16] J.D. De, "Rights, Human," in *New Dictionary of Theology*: The Master's Reference Collection (Downers Grove, IL: InterVarsity Press, 1988): 594–595.

All these discussions of human beings created in the image of God uncover the ultimate purpose of God toward creating them in such a condition. God's image is seen neither in disassociated individuals nor in collectives that require a loss of individual identities, but in person-in-community. God is not partial but loves the whole of creation. God will therefore not tolerate injustice done to any fellow being, for the worth of a person is irreplaceable. In this connection, Karol Gabris writes that the image of God brings us to the basic human rights according to which people are equal in principle and have, in principle, equal rights to life and its values. Gabris affirms his stand by observing three standpoints concerning human beings made in God's image:

a. the value of human beings, their equality with others, and at the same time, full respect for the situation in which they are living.

b. Man's communion—a unique understanding derived from the Bible is that considerably more place must be given in our lives to collective stances that have been given until now—and, basically, human rights introduce a person to a communion and presuppose its continued existence.

c. Service for the well-being of one's fellow human—such is the sense of the realization of a person's mission with regard to another person; this is to say that the method of implementing human rights helps to reveal very clearly that right corresponds to duty.[17]

Such theological conceptualization of all humankind as the children of God is a way of radicalization in the sphere of human rights, cautioning against violations and the preservation of God's creation. Human beings are unique but they are not apart from the rest of God's creation for they cannot survive without relating to other creatures. Human beings have a capacity for responsible relationship with God.[18] And it is with such capacity or reasoning ability that they can differently respond to God, acknowledging the partnership in creation and greater responsibility toward maintaining and sustaining God's creation. While referring to the relationship between God and human beings, Kuitert Harry states that human beings being created in the image of God is not something we can do simply by being rational creatures but it has to do with the purpose

---

[17] Karol Gabris, "The Issues of Human Rights," in *Human Rights is More than Human Rights*, eds. Eric and Marilyn (Rome: IDOC International, 1977), 9. Pope John XXIII also supports this when he said, "since men are social by nature, they are meant to live with others and to work for one another's welfare" (*Pacem in Terris/Peace on Earth*), 31.

[18] Clifton J. Allen, ed., *The Broadman Bible Commentary*, vol. I (Nashville, TN: Broadman Press, 1969): 84.

God has for humans—to live as covenant partners with God and with our fellow humans on earth.[19]

It may also be asserted that human beings are not only created in the image of God but also endowed with freedom. This endowment of freedom provides a theological bridge to human rights, as the modern concept of human rights appropriately begins by declaring every person's right to freedom. Human beings were created not for slavery but for freedom, and it is this original freedom that distinguishes humans as being in the image of God and exalts them above all other creation (Ps 8:5–6). Because of one's capacity of owning and exercising freedom, one is inviolable. However, this human capacity for freedom cannot be described as a person's capacity to do what one pleases. It is to be defined rather as one's capacity to become what one ought to be.[20] In other words, a person's freedom has to be exercised within the limit of divine will and control.

COVENANTAL IMPLICATION

The Hebrew concept of covenant is again an important area in the attempt to understand the relationship between God and humanity. In the context of the Hebrew Bible, it is the covenant and law that obligated human duties and responsibilities to God, to humans, and to the creation. The meaning of the word *berit* itself is probably "fetter" or "obligation," coming from a root word *bara*, "to bind."[21] The term *covenant* means an agreement of coming together between two or more groups.[22] Such a practice has been found in every society. It was also widely practiced in the Ancient Near East. The covenant played a vital role, particularly in the Old Testament settings. The covenantal relationship between God and Israel is in fact a central feature in the Hebrew Bible. Eichrodt therefore asserts that the covenant between God and Israel provided the key both to the unity and the uniqueness of Israel's faith.[23] In other words, God's

---

[19] Kuitert Harry, *Signals from the Bible* (Grand Rapids, MI: William Eerdmans, 1972), 32.

[20] Helmut Thielicke, *Theological Ethics: Foundation Vol. 2* (Philadelphia: Fortress Press, 1969), 281; "Covenant," in *The Encyclopedia of Judaism*, ed. Geoffrey Wigoder (New York: Macmillan, 1989), 181.

[21] G.L. Archer, Jr. "Covenant," in *Baker's Dictionary of Theology*, ed. Everett F. Harrison (Michigan: Baker Book House, 1979), 299–301.

[22] Nowel Irene, "Covenant," in *The New Dictionary of Theology*, ed. Joseph A. Komonchak, Mary Collins, and Dermot A. Lane (Dublin: Gill and Macmillan, 1987), 243–246; Covenant is made frequently between two individuals like Abimelech and Abraham in Gen 21:27. It was made between ruler and state, like David and Israel in 2 Sam 3:21; and between state and state like Israel and Tyre in 1 Kgs 5:12, Israel and Assyria in Hos 12:1.

[23] D.G. Spriggs, *Two Old Testament Theologies* (London: SCM Press, 1974), 12–14.

covenant with Israel serves as the basis for the Jewish faith. The Torah is traditionally said to contain 613 commandments.[24]

A covenant is a binding agreement or bond between two parties. It is a solemn promise bound by an oath, which may be either a verbal formula or a symbolic action.[25] The covenant history in the Old Testament begins with Noah and Yahweh in Gen 9:1–17,[26] followed by God with Abraham in Gen 12:1–9; 15:1–21; 17:1–27.[27] The first account of a covenant in Genesis is the story of God establishing the covenant with Noah but one intended for all of humanity.[28] It is a covenant of God's own initiative, unconditional, and everlasting.[29] The Noahic covenant, then, is universal in the widest sense imaginable. It is fundamentally an ecological covenant that includes not only human beings everywhere but all animals (Gen 9:16). The relatedness of the members of the human family to each other and to God is underscored and formalized in the announcement of an eternal covenant with Noah in Gen 9:1–17. Underlying this covenant is a theology that places all peoples in a relationship of grace and accountability with God. Because the Noah story is essentially a tradition about one eternal covenant established with humanity, it contains an aspect of universality, humanity after creation, and of totality, God's concern for the world.[30] This Noahic covenant differs from the Mosaic covenant as interpreted by Deuteronomic theologians. Deuteronomic covenant is one in which a party is bound to the covenant maker, who imposes conditions and sanctions (blessings for obedience and curses for disobedience).

Later, the Sinai covenant was made between Yahweh and the people of Israel at Mount Sinai in Horeb. It was binding on both God and Israel. It is a condition that can be broken. And if it is broken, it might result in the loss of covenant privilege, the loss of land and descendants, and

---

[24] Dan Cohn-Sherbok, "Covenant and Law," in *Creating Old Testament*, ed. Stephen Bigger (Oxford: Basil Blackwell, 1989), 135.

[25] G.E. Mendengall, "Covenant," in *Interpreter's Bible Dictionary*, ed. George A. Buttrick et al. (New York: Abingdon Press, 1962), 714.

[26] This is the most universal covenant found in the Bible. This covenant covers every living creature and the descendants of the sons of Noah.

[27] Another individual covenant with David in 2 Sam 7:1–17 is modelled on the covenant with Abraham. The basic difference between these two and the Sinai Covenant is that the individual covenants are unconditional; they are bound only by God. They cannot be broken.

[28] Ellen J. Christiansen, *The Covenant in Judaism and PaulA Study of Ritual Boundaries as Identity Markers* (New York: E. J. Brill, 1995), 30–31.

[29] J. Arthur Thompson, "Covenant," in *The International Standard Bible Encyclopaedia, Vol. I*, ed. Geoffrey W. Bromiley (Grand Rapids, MI: William B. Eerdmans, 1979), 790–792.

[30] Christiansen, *The Covenant in Judaism and Paul*, 32.

return to slavery in a foreign land.[31] The fall of the northern kingdom of Israel (722 B.C.E.) and the fall of the southern kingdom of Judah (587 B.C.E.) were directly attributed to covenant breaking. However, they were not left unheeded forever. They were required to show repentance and in response, God was always graciously ready to forgive their sins.

According to the Old Testament, most Israelite laws are associated with YHWH, Moses, and Sinai. This association says something important about the theological place of law. Law has to do not only with human norms but also with the recognition and carrying out of divine will. "The proclamation of the divine will for justice is like a net thrown over Israel: it is the completion of her conveyance to Jahweh."[32] Thus, Israel understood and celebrated the revelation of the commandments as a salvific event of the first order. "The covenant is made, and with it, Israel receives the revelation of the commandments."[33] In the case of God and Israel, this set of laws with their sanctions was purely religious,[34] a moral guide. With regard to this, Henry McKeating thinks that Old Testament ethics at that point of time did not distinguish between right moral conduct and right religious conduct. The law indiscriminately mixed commands on moral matters with commands on religious matters.[35]

Human rights is an instrument to protect individuals and groups against the institutional abuse of power. It is a noble function of law to curb selfishness, ruthlessness, and injustice, and to protect the interest of the vulnerable, the weak, and the marginalized groups in society. Such conviction is closely in line with the Judeo-Christian belief that God is concerned with liberating, sustaining, guiding, and accompanying people who are being pushed to the margins of life.[36] The story of the Israelites in Exodus testifies to the struggle for their basic human rights. Or the story of Israel shows that it is not the history of any person. Rather, it is a collective response of a particular community toward God. Reading it from another angle indicates that the context of liberation of Israel from Egyptian bondage already revealed God's concern for human rights. For instance, the Israelites under the power of Egypt did not even know how to pray to

---

[31] Irene, "Covenant," 244–245.
[32] G. von Rad, *Old Testament Theology*, vol. I (Edinburgh: Oliver and Boyd, 1962), 192.
[33] G. von Rad, *Old Testament Theology*, 194.
[34] George Mendenhall, *Law and Covenant in Israel and the Ancient Near East* (Pittburgh: Biblical Colloquium, 1955), 23; cf. D.J. McCarthy, *Old Testament Covenant: A Survey of Current Opinions* (Oxford: Basil Blackwell, 1973), 10.
[35] Henry McKeating, "Old Testament Ethics," in *A New Dictionary of Christian Ethics*, ed. John Macquarrie and James Childress (London: SCM Press 1986), 434.
[36] God's concern for Israel applies to all people who are left half dead on the sides of the roads of life. Cf. Exod 3:7.

Negotiating Peace

God for their liberation. They only cried. And it was God who heard their cry and initiated the whole process of liberation.[37] And this action helped them to become a nation in history. Their bitter experience in Egypt was a driving force for them to look for alternatives based on freedom, equality, and justice. Therefore, they took maximum care to not repeat the experiences in Egypt. Meanwhile, liberating them from Egypt was not simply to free them. Its purpose was to make Israel holy as Yahweh is holy (Lev 19).

In the whole of Israelite history, there had been changes and development in their laws. This process of development is important because it was done in order to safeguard the human rights; to incorporate the rejected ones into the society. For instance, the ancient traditional laws were exploitative against women and servants. For them, the slavery system was a denial of human rights. Hence, they gave the right of freedom to the slaves; to gain freedom after six years of service. That was the essence of the Sabbatical year. Another example that may be cited is in regard to stealing, the Israelites maintained a different approach from their neighbors. Though they did consider the act of stealing and robbery as immoral, unlike the neighboring states, the Israelites demanded only the lost things. One can discern from the Israelites' law recorded in Exodus 22:21–24 that the laws are for the protection of the poor, weak, and lowly whose rights could easily be snatched by the powerful people. At the same time, their law protected them from becoming landless people. Assets like land and other properties sold at the time of an economic crisis could be purchased back for the same amount. It means that each family must have some land, the basic means of production (Lev 25:25). Even if a person had to sell themselves for sustenance, according to the rule of the Sabbatical year, he or she would be released at the end of the sixth year (Lev 25:54; Deut 15:12). Further, the whole intention of the Jubilee Year read in Leviticus 25:8–55 is a basic humanitarian concern.[38] Many of the Old Testament scholars try to trace the date of this institution to the postexilic period. According to R. H. Charles, the period could be between 153 and 105 B.C.E.[39] It speaks mainly about *hashed* (restore) and *teror* (liberty) when

---

[37] Bastian Wielenga, *It's a Long Road to Freedom Perspective of Biblical Theology*, rev. ed. (Madurai: TTS,1988), 72.

[38] Cf. Neh 5:1–13; Num 36:4; Deut 15:12–23.

[39] R.H. Charles, *The Apocrypha and Pseudepigrapha of the Old Testament with Introduction and Critical Explanation Note of the Several Books*, vol. II (Oxford: Clarendon Press, 1913), 6–7; Gnana Robinson, "A New Economic Order: The Challenge of the Biblical Jubilee," in *A Vision for Man*, ed. Samuel Amirtham (Madras: CLS, 1978), 365; Sharon H. Ringe, *Jesus, Liberation and the Biblical Jubilee* (Philadelphia: Fortress Press, 1985), 26.

Jubilee is declared, the slaves are to be freed and their properties are to be restored.[40]

The various Law Codes enshrined in the Hebrew Scriptures were formulated at different periods of Israel's history, but all of them recognized the fundamental concept of justice and liberativeness of God. Acknowledging the long historical setting of the Israelites, scholars like McKeating and Jon D. Levenson admit that we do not, therefore, expect Old Testament ethics to be totally homogeneous and consistent, especially when we consider that the Old Testament contains materials from a period covering at least a thousand years.[41] Further, R.K. Harrison affirms the long stretch of the formulation of the covenant codes. He says, "some of the legislative elements of the covenant code had been formulated during the period when the Hebrews were living in the land of Goshen... at Kadesh and even in trans-Jordan to represent the nucleus of materials relating to social behaviour."[42]

It is clear that it was inevitable for the Israelites to re-interpret their legal heritage in the context of their socioeconomic, political changes in order to protect the weaker sections of the society from further exploitation and the worst excesses of the elites. These two passages may be used for comparison: Exodus 21:2–6 and Deuteronomy 15:12–18. In both the accounts, a male slave is to be released after six years of service. The Exodus account then treats the case where a master gives a wife to a male slave and children are born of the union. Here, only the male slave is to be released at the end of the six-year period; the wife and children remain with the master. We see an unequal treatment of women here on the basis of the status of sex. But in the Deuteronomy passage, the law is expanded in order to include equal treatment of all people. Hence, in Deuteronomic law, a female slave is to be released in the same manner as a male slave.[43] Deuteronomy still accepts the Exodus account and in both the cases, the obligation to release slaves after six years is binding. In another example,[44]

---

[40] Robert North, *Sociology of Biblical Jubilee* (Rome: Pontifical Biblical Institute, 1954), 1; R.S. Foster, *Restoration of Israel* (London: Darton Longman & Todd, 1970), 194.

[41] Henry McKeating, *Old Testament Ethics*, 434; Jon D. Levenson, "The Universal Horizon of Biblical Particularism," in *Ethnicity and the Bible*, ed. Brett, M. G. (Leiden: Brill, 1996), 145.

[42] R.K. Harrison, *Introduction to the Old Testament* (Michigan: William B. Eerdmans, 1969), 584; cf. Gerald A Larue, "Biblical Ethics and Continuing Interpretation," in *Biblical Vs Secular Ethics—The Conflict*, ed. R. Joseph Hoffman and Gerald A. Larue (New York: Prometheus Books, 1988), 19.

[43] Calum M. Carmichael, *The Laws of Deuteronomy* (London: Cornell University Press, 1974), 54–55.

[44] See Deut 25:1–3 whose original text is found in Exod 21:18–21, 26–27; here we see the shift of emphasis while dealing with the disputing parties.

the Deuteronomic law represents a stage in legal development in which the disputing parties are encouraged to bring their cases to the court.[45]

Walter Harrelson, one of the scholars who has greatly contributed toward the discussion on the biblical laws and modern human rights also at the first instance, admits that the Bible knows little about human rights in the sense of the modern terms.[46] He was aware that the ambiguity of the biblical material that has inspired the quest for social justice has been appealed to and used as an instrument for rejecting that quest. He points out the example of slavery: That the Bible, though it did not strive to abolish slavery, at least did something to regulate it. But, this argument cannot be universalized because the degree of regulation was in fact limited to a certain class of slaves (free Israelites who had become temporary slaves through debt. Exod 21:2–6), that is coupled with a provision through which a temporary slave may become a permanent slave and thus envisages an extension of his slavery.[47] However, for Harrelson, the "relevance" of the Hebrew Bible is not something that has to be painfully searched for or ingeniously derived, but something that is present and immediate, waiting only to be stated.[48] He, on the other hand, found a rich knowledge and immediate relevance of human rights in the Hebrew Bible. For him, the reality is in fact that one has obligations to others and in which case, the others have the rights to expect.[49] God is just, loving, and merciful to humankind. And in return, he requires certain obligations from human beings. In this case, these divine rights became the standards for human rights and thus, they became for us divine obligations. This is what the Baptist World Congress declaration in Toronto in 1980 aimed at, by stating, "Human rights are derived from God—from his nature, his creation, and his commands. Concern for human rights is at the heart of Christian faith. Every main doctrine is related to human rights, beginning with the biblical revelation of God."[50]

---

[45] G. von Rad, *Deuteronomy* (London: SCM Press, 1966), 154; S.R. Driver, *Deuteronomy* (Edinburgh: T&T Clark, 1902), 135–136.

[46] He discusses the relevance of the biblical laws to human rights in his book, *Ten Commandments and Human Rights* (Philadelphia: Fortress Press, 1980), xv, hereafter referred to as Walter Harrelson, *The Ten Commandments*; cf. D. M. Walker, ed., *The Oxford Companion to Law* (Oxford: Oxford University Press, 1980), 591.

[47] "Human Rights," in D.M. Walker, ed., *The Oxford Companion to Law* (Oxford: Oxford University Press, 1980), 591.

[48] He discusses this point at length in his book, *Ten Commandments*.

[49] Harrelson, *Ten Commandments*, xv,

[50] Baptist World Alliance, *Celebrating Christ's Presence Through the Spirit: Official Report of the Fourteenth Congress, Toronto, Canada, July 8–13, 1980* (Nashville: Broadman Press, 1981), 77.

Biblical Resources of Human Rights

The above discussion on biblical laws underlines the basis to affirm that human duties and responsibilities logically imply human rights. One cannot speak of human rights without the direct implication that society has a duty to uphold rights. It is in the sense of duty that human rights are implied. "To one man's natural right there corresponds a duty in other persons: the duty, namely, of acknowledging and respecting the right in question."[51] Accordingly, as Gerhard Luf understands, standing up for the rights of one's fellow man is an essential consequence of the very commandment to love one's neighbor.[52] Thus, an important task of Christian commitment to human rights is to counter a one-dimensional individualistic idea of entitlement, and to oppose it by emphasizing the dimension of social obligation in the human freedom of action. For, if this social dimension of freedom remains unattended to, there is a great danger that human rights will be used as mere instruments, thus degrading them to mere means of egocentric self-advancement, leading as has been pointed out above, to new inequality. Christian work for human rights now means "work at the most basic level toward a society without unjust structures."[53]

The biblical perspective of human rights is subsequently derived from its association with justice. Rights are particular statements of the demands of justice. Justice is a most basic ethical demand of Scripture. The Hebrew word *mispat* is widely used to refer to the *right* without differentiating what right and to whom it belongs. The term generally reflects the notion of legal proceedings, and since the maintenance of justice was the responsibility of the kings, the word is often also used in connection with royal functions.[54] It was, on several occasions, used by the rulers to claim their rights against their subjects. However, there is a second definition of *righteous* in the Old Testament. Not only is he righteous who fulfills the demands of a relationship, but also, he who has had his right taken away from him within such a relationship. God intervenes to restore the right to him who has been deprived of it. He decides in favor of the deprived one, of him who is needy.[55] "They do not defend the *mispat* (rights) of the needy" (Jer 5:28), "A righteous man knows the *din* (rights) of the poor"

---

[51] John Paul XXIII, *Pacem in Terris*, 30.

[52] Gerhard Luf, "Peace and Human Rights as seen by the Churches," in *Peace for Humanity*, ed. Andreas Bstch (New Delhi: Vikas Publishing House, 1996), 147.

[53] *Religious Freedom—Main Statement by the WCC*, Report of Section V of the Fifth Assembly, Nairobi, 1975 on "Structure of Injustice and Struggles for Liberation—Human Rights," 73.

[54] Helmer Ringgren, "Miswa," in *Theological Dictionary of the Old Testament*, eds. G. Johannes Botterweck, Helmer Ringgren, and Heinz-Josef Fabry (Grand Rapids: William B. Eerdmans, 1997), 506.

[55] E.R. Achtemeier, "Righteousness in the Old Testament," in *The Interpreter's Dictionary of the Bible, vol. 4*, ed. George Arthur Buttrick (Nashville, NY: Abingdon Press, 1962), 83.

(Prov 29:7). The character of rights as claims that one possesses, that are due to one, is most clearly perceived when Hebrew words for justice are combined with the possessive case for person(s) to whom justice is due. The *"mispat* of the afflicted" (Job 36:6) are rights or claims for justice that belong to the afflicted. An underlying contribution of the Bible to the proper understanding of human rights is that it does not advocate individualism. Rights are not attached, however, to individuals as creatures isolated from the community. Biblical justice pertains to what is essential for membership in community, and the articulations of that provision we recognize as rights. Individuals have their own dignity through creation and God's historical act of redemption, yet the concept of justice is in accord with the communal view of human nature. Individuals are creatures who belong in community.[56]

With all these, it should be noted that God appears constantly in Scripture as the protector of the rights of human beings over against those who trample on these rights. God has an unceasing program to restore the dignity of the violated people. Here, Jacques Ellul pointedly asserts that "the ultimate manifestation of God's justice reveals God's will to restore… when God judges, he does so in order to restore what has been distorted, the relationship between God and humans and among human being themselves."[57] God is just and it is his personal will that renders justice (Deut 1:17). Therefore, the unfailing obligation of the covenantal relationship is justice. In Deuteronomic code, we find that the right to live is also affirmed in the form of gleaning rights—the poor are protected with the provision to share with the rich; feeding the underprivileged people, such as aliens, orphans, widows through gleaning rights (Deut 14:19–22);[58] the economic rights to just wages (Deut 24:14–15); rights of refugees/asylum (Deut 19:1–13); protection of life (Deut 22:8); and ecological rights (Deut 20:19–20). With all these, it becomes clear that the key motive of Deuteronomic concern for the human rights of the poor and defenceless is justice. It is only through the maintenance of justice that the community will be able to guarantee right relations between humans and God as well as humans with other fellow-humans.[59]

Further, though there is no direct reference to the phrase *human rights* in the Bible, it is erroneous to think that the idea of human rights is absent

---

[56] Stackhouse has closely dealt with this when he identified rights as dealing with the membership of individuals in community rather than with the question of individualism versus collectivism. See, Stackhouse, *Creed*, 104.

[57] Jacques Ellul, *The Theological Foundation of Law* (London: SCM Press, 1961), 47.

[58] Blenkinsopp, "The Book of Deuteronomy," in *The New Biblical Jerome Commentary* (Bangalore: Theological Publication of India, 1991), 105.

[59] Lalfakzuala, *Human Rights in Deuteronomy—A Sociological Approach* (Delhi: ISPCK, 2004), 124.

in the Bible. Human rights is God's will and concern. The Deuteronomic theology clarifies the will of God. "You shall not violate any of these rights; you shall not show partiality; and you shall not take bribe, for a bribe blinds the eyes of the wise and subverts the cause of the righteous. Justice, the only justice, you shall follow, that you may live and inherit the land which the Lord your God gives you" (Deut 16:19–20).[60] Thus, violation of human rights is against the will of God, rather it is his will that humans should live on the basis of the covenantal condition made with God to preserve human life.

The argument here is not to simply universalize Israel but to see that God's concern is not limited to Israel alone but expands to the whole of humankind in the cosmos. At one point, the national character of covenant is clear-cut in both biblical and rabbinical literature. The covenant is specifically between God and the Jewish people.

> Now therefore, if you obey my voice and keep my covenant, you shall be my treasured possession out of all the peoples. Indeed, the whole earth is mine, but you shall be for me a priestly kingdom and a holy nation (Exod 19:5-6).
>
> I the Lord am your God; I have separated you from the peoples... You shall be holy to me, for the Lord am holy, and I have separated you from the other peoples to be mine (Lev 20:24, 26; cf. Exod 34:10; Lev 25:39–46; Deut 7:1–11; 10:12–22; 33:4; Jer 11:1–13).

Another indication of this is what is said about the Sabbath, which is the symbol of the ongoing covenant between God and Israel and thus, according to the rabbis, the equivalent of all the other commandments. Exodus 31:16–17 reads, "The Israelites shall keep the Sabbath, observing the Sabbath throughout their generations as a perpetual covenant. It is a sign forever between me and the people of Israel . . . ." But on the other hand, it is understood that Jews are required to obey the law because they are part of God's covenant with Israel at Sinai; non-Jews were never part of the Sinai covenant and therefore they are not obligated under it.[61] But, this does not mean that they are excluded from God's concern or prevented from enjoying God's favor; on the contrary, as mentioned earlier the Noahic covenant is a distinct basis to understand God's universal concern.

It may also be necessary to see how universalism can be understood in the light of Israel. According to Jon D. Levenson, the term *universalism* can carry a number of divergent meanings. It may simply refer to the

---

[60] Jacques Ellul, *The Theological Foundation of Law,* 80; J.G. McConville, *Law and Theology in Deuteronomy* (Sheffield: JSOT Press, 1984), 11.

[61] Elliot N. Dorff, "A Jewish Theology of Jewish Relations to Other Peoples," in *People of God, Peoples of God,* ed. Hans Ucko (Geneva: WCC Publications, 1996), 53.

universality of the deity: No other god exists, and the whole world without exception, is his.[62] The placement of the story of cosmic creation by God ('elohim) at the beginning of the Bible (Gen 1:1–2:3) establishes a universal horizon for the particular story of Israel that occupies most of the rest of that sacred book.[63] It is also highly significant that in both creation accounts at the beginning of Genesis, it is humanity in general and not any people in particular that is created.

Israel emerges in history, twenty generations after the creation of the human species in the image of God. "Israel," in the words of a contemporary scholar like Stuhlmueller, "has no particular supernatural status by birth and early history."[64] Therefore, biblical concern for human rights is universal in the sense that it is applicable to all people, to all nations, to all religions, and cultures of all times.

JESUS'S TEACHING

Christian theology grounds human dignity in its doctrine of God. Human beings have dignity because God created them in his own image, and then restored the lost image (by sin) by living, dying, and rising in Christ.[65] The concern for human rights is deeply rooted in biblical faith and is an essential part of the gospel. Jesus particularly identified himself with the powerless, with those who were denied rights and social status.

One thing that Jesus made very clear during his ministry on earth was that no one should be deprived of basic humanhood. And therefore, it is to those whose rights were violated that the kingdom of God is announced (Mark 1:15). His message of the coming of the kingdom must be seen in the context of human search for peace, freedom, justice, and life. In order to understand this connection between human's fundamental hopes and the promise of the coming of the kingdom of God, we must start from the fact that, in the common view of the Bible, humans are seen as incapable of possessing peace, justice, freedom, and life through their own unaided resources. Life is constantly threatened, freedom suppressed and sold, and justice trampled underfoot. In such a context, Jesus establishes the kingdom of God by restoring the living condition of those who were physically, economically, socially, and politically denied the right of humanhood.

---

[62] Jon D. Levenson, "The Universal Horizon of Biblical Particularism," in *Ethnicity and the Bible*, ed. Mark G. Brett (New York: Brill, 1996), 144.

[63] Levenson, "The Universal Horizon," 146.

[64] Carroll Stuhlmueller, "The Foundation for Mission in the Old Testament," in *Biblical Foundations for Mission*, eds. Donald Senior and Carroll Stuhlmueller (New York: Orbis Books, 1983), 11.

[65] This is concerning the fall of human beings due to sin before God. Humans thus became sinners who need God to save them.

Biblical Resources of Human Rights

Jesus's Nazareth Manifesto informed what his public ministry would be and for whom. He opened his ministry by reading the text from the book of the prophet Isaiah that says, "The Spirit of the Lord is upon me, because he has anointed me to preach the gospel to the poor. He has sent me to proclaim release to the captives and recovering of sight to the blind, to set at liberty those who are oppressed, to proclaim the acceptable year of the Lord" (Luke 4:18-19 RSV). Jesus's attitude is a significant demonstration to show that the very people who are ignored, despised, and defamed by society, have a right to recognition, that there is an inalienable dignity of humans, a right to which also the "sinner," the outcast, or the criminal, is entitled. God himself makes his "good government" present among us in Jesus Christ, the rights of the poor mark the trust of his ministry. He said so because their place is confirmed by the beatitudes in Matthew 5:3-11. What then, does the poor mean? In the words of Gustavo Gutierrez, "The 'poor' person today is the oppressed one, the one marginalized from society, the member of the proletariat struggling for his/her most basic rights; he/she is the exploited and plundered social class, the country struggling for its liberation."[66]

Though it is not the dominant theme, violence provides a backdrop for much of the New Testament narratives. The drama of salvation starts and ends with violence. On the first page of the New Testament, when Jesus Christ enters the stage of history, king Herod, fearing for his throne, slaughters the innocents to eliminate a potential rival (Matt 2); and in the central act of the New Testament drama, the rulers of this age plan and execute the brutal murder of Jesus Christ using a mock trial to give it political legitimacy.[67] Jesus was aware of the differences and conflicts that confronted the people of his time. These include the conflict between the Jews and Gentiles, Sadducees and Pharisees on the ground of racial status, and occupational professionalism such as priesthood. Therefore, his concern focused on reestablishment of a just and equal society. This is visible in his symbolic recruitment of twelve disciples representing the twelve tribes of Israel.[68] The twelve are the remnants of Israel[69] and "the

---

[66] Gustavo Gutierrez, *Theology of Liberation* (Maryknoll, NY: Orbis Books, 1973), 301. (The female pronoun is added by the writer to express inclusiveness).

[67] Miroslav Volf, *Exclusion and Embrace: A Theological Exploration of Identity, Otherness, and Reconciliation* (Nashville, TN: Abingdon Press, 1996), 290-291.

[68] Mark 3:13-19; Matt 19:25; Luke 22:30; D.E. Nineham, *Saint Mark—The Pelican New Testament Commentaries* (Middlesex: Penguin Books, 1975), 114-115; Joachim Jeremias points out that the number twelve does not signify exclusion of salvation for non-Jewish people, rather to every individual in the world. Joachim Jeremias, *New Testament Theology*, vol. I (London: SCM Press, 1971), 235.

[69] A. Feuillet, "The Reign of God and the Person of Jesus According to the Synoptic Gospels," in *Interpreters Bible* (New York: Abingdon, 1951), 785-786.

symbolic nucleus of the New People of God."⁷⁰ Jesus, in order to manifest the universal humanhood, included *amharez* "the people of the land" into his "little flock" (Luke 12:32). It is clear that he intended to create an authentic human relationship against bitter oppositions and deep misunderstandings. He thus categorically refused to admit any group or class distinction in his kingdom.⁷¹

Jesus's approach to total liberation⁷² of humankind is not an event once and for all but an ongoing process guiding people to establish their society in which no conflict should exist. His concern centered around the meaning of life. It was also for the cause of human well-being that he proclaimed sociopolitical and religious restructures.⁷³ Jesus's revolutionary tool was much different from the expectation of all around him during his lifetime on earth. He consciously rejected violence.⁷⁴ He was not ready to identify with and strengthen any single political party or nation. Jesus's liberation motive and the Zealot rebel movement are therefore not identical.⁷⁵

Jesus, in his liberating ministry, did not bluntly go against the laws of the land. In fact, in many cases, Jesus's understanding was similar to that represented by the Pharisees. Like them, he offered a way of life in which religion would seem relevant to every activity; he based his teaching on the "will of God" as revealed in the law. But at the same time, there are striking differences too. He adopted a radical stance to be more humane and less ritualistic. For instance, he says, "If you are offering your gift at

---

[70] C.H. Dodd, *The Founder of Christianity* (Fontana, London: Collins, 1973), 136–137; G.B. Caird, *Saint Luke—The Pelican NT Commentaries* (Middlesex: Penguin Books, 1974), 100.

[71] Desrochers, *Christ the Liberator*, 119.

[72] Jesus has been seen as close to the Zealot national liberation movement. S.G.F. Brandon, *Jesus and the Zealot* (New York: Scribes, 1968), 3; Martin Hengel, *Was Jesus a Revolutionist?* (Philadelphia: Fortress Press, 1971), 9; Alan Richardson, *The Political Christ* (London: SCM Press, 1973), 142–144; André Trocmé, *Jesus and the Nonviolent Revolution* (New York: The Plough Publishing House, 2011), 100, 130; Dennis Eric Nineham, *Saint Mark—The Pelican NT Commentaries* (London: Penguin Books, 1972), 413; Far from being a violent liberator and militant, Jesus constantly chose to heal the sick and bind up wounds. His attitude excludes militant action for Christians. Hengel, *Was Jesus a Revolutionist?* 20. He did not call for an armed revolt.

[73] Cleansing of the Jerusalem Temple in John 2:14–17 and refusing to pay tax to the Roman government are examples of his revolutionary mission. His refusal was because it was a Roman policy to strengthen Emperor worship by granting religious freedom. The Jews were allowed to practice their particular cult so long as they agreed to venerate Caesar. André Trocmé, *Jesus and the Nonviolent Revolution*, 95.

[74] Hengel, *Was Jesus a Revolutionist?*, 26.

[75] Joachim Jeremias, *Jerusalem in the Time of Jesus* (Philadelphia: Fortress Press, 1969), 119–120.

the altar, and there remember that your brother has something against you, leave your gift there before the altar and go; first be reconciled with your brother, and then come and offer your gift." In such teaching of humanization, Jesus does not abolish the sacrifice, but enlarges its scope. A similar meaning may be found in his statement, "Man is not made for Sabbath but Sabbath is made for man" (Mark 2:27), and also his question, "Is it lawful on the Sabbath to do good or to do harm, to save life or to kill?" (Mark 3:4) that indicate the problem of institution's role (cf. Matt 12:12). This is to show that as E.F. Scott puts it, "His ethics was not only different from that which had gone before but was in a real sense its antithesis."[76]

All that Jesus did was contrary to violence and to enable Israel to fulfill its role as the chosen people. The plain truth is, the option left to Jesus was difficult. It was a situation in which people talked of national threat or religious threat and overlooked human beings. There was a section of people, the Zealots who chose violence, shedding the blood of thousands of victims in the name of a better future. Thus, if Jesus opted to violate human rights and wage war, it would greatly please the Zealots. Again, if he completely withdrew from the world it could be interpreted as favoring the Essenes.[77] Thus, Jesus chose the middle way to give himself unto death and be raised again (Matt 16:21). That choice culminated in his non-violent entry into Jerusalem to undergo many forms of suffering from the authorities. Hence, despite the grim predictions Jesus was making about himself and the outcome of his trip to Jerusalem, he had no doubts about the final success of the campaign he had inaugurated a year and a half earlier in Nazareth's synagogue.

The God of the Bible is a loving God who first loved the world and made himself known to the world (John 1:14; 3:16). As Clement of Alexander says, God himself is love, and for the sake of love he made himself known.[78] Therefore, the teachings of Jesus constantly insist that love should be our response to God without question. Following this, that very love to God should take the form of loving our fellow beings by showing care and concern, protection and support, recognition of others' dignity, etc. This love alone can fulfill the Divine requirement.[79] Such teaching

---

[76] E.F. Scott, *The Ethical Teaching of Jesus* (New York: The Macmillan Company, 1957), xii.

[77] Jesus's ethic differs from that of the Essenes for it does not grow out of a pessimistic view of the world. It does not propose asceticism, nor does it demand escapism from the world.

[78] Alister E. McGrath, ed., *The Christian Theology Reader* (Cambridge: Blackwell, 1995), 177.

[79] Emmanuel E. James, *Ethics: A Biblical Perspective* (Bangalore: Sevadasan Training Institute, 1992), 97.

may be possibly collected from his parable of the Good Samaritan recorded in Luke 10:29–42. This was spoken in the context of the question raised to him by an unidentified lawyer of how to inherit eternal life. Jesus interestingly picked up the issue of the Jews and the Samaritans. It has also to be noted that in that world of Jesus, the Jews despised Samaritans and generally excluded them from the category of neighbor. His answer, "Go and do likewise" in verse 37b proves the acceptance of every human's dignity; the universalization of love and service. A narrow categorization of people on the basis of a rigid racial concept was a humiliation to the forcibly-made lower section of the people. This parable defends that there is no rational explanation of higher and lower race. In the Lukan context, this means that people who belong to God's covenant community show love (i) that is not limited by the clean-unclean laws (Acts 10:15); (ii) that does not limit itself to friends but has a universal scope (cf. Luke 2:32; 3:6; 4:25–27; 10:1–12); and (iii) that does not look for recompense (cf. Luke 6:32–36).[80] While speaking of love, Susan Gillingham also supports that in the biblical sense, "doing the right thing" is not only culturally conditioned; it is also an expression of the heart and mind of God. We cannot have the one without the other.[81]

Another very important reference of love made in the teaching of Jesus Christ is found in his summarization of the Ten Commandments of the Old Testament into the New "Commandment of Love" (Matt 22:37-39; cf. John 13:34; 15:12-13). Here, love covers all the conditions of human relationships. This is a direct challenge to all forms of separatism, division, and deprivation. This commandment promises that human rights will be observed because in love, there will be no room for injustice and violation of human dignity. This also implies that standing for the rights of others is one practical way of expressing love for the neighbor. Jesus's idea of love is not a vague love for the world, which can so easily become sentimental illusion. But it is a realistic command of concrete involvement (cf. Matt 15:31-39). It cannot be reduced to material assistance. For instance, his reference to pray for the persecutors in Matthew 5:44 underlines the requirements of love.[82] Love is the central ground of Jesus's teaching. According to Joseph Fletcher, all the rules, principles, ideals, and norms are only contingents but love is the key principle.[83] Because of teaching

---

[80] Charles H, Talbert, *Reading Luke* (New York: Crossroad, 1986), 122.
[81] Susan Gillingham, "The Ethics of Love Doing the Right Thing in the Christian Tradition," *The Expository Times*, 106, no. 8 (May 1995): 234.
[82] Cf. Wolfgang Schrage, *The Ethics of New Testament* (Philadelphia: Fortress Press, 1988), 79.
[83] Joseph Fletcher, *Situation Ethics: The New Morality* (London: Westminster John Knox Press, 1966), 17–39.

and practice of love, John Robinson calls Jesus as a "man for others."[84] When Jesus taught about love, it covered all the aspects of human life. According to him, love cannot be expressed with an individual alone but it has a relational aspect. Valson Thampu also points out that the love that Jesus teaches is relational and, at the same time, subjective and objective. It is subjective because it involves the subject's concern, but this concern is related to the objective well-being of the other person.[85]

Hence, human rights remind the church of its struggle for the rights of the people. In human rights, therefore, the church sees a pointed reminder to its own task, and the secular promises contained in human rights recall the church itself back to the message entrusted to it: that the world is not yet finished and salvation in its totality is still in the future, the new heaven, and the new earth (Rev 22; Acts 3).[86]

The inclusiveness of God's love is for all humankind—male and female and all races and nations—all of whom are created equally in the divine image and are equally inviolable as persons. The Bible is permeated with the themes that one's love of one's neighbor is second only to one's love of God; the denial of one's love for one's fellow human being is a denial of love for God. The cluster of "love your enemies" *logia*, also known as the "hard sayings" of Jesus preserved in the Matthean Sermon on the Mount (Matt 5:38–48) and the Lukan Sermon on the Plain (Luke 6:27–36) have been used as the textual basis for Christian pacifism. For instance, Hengel sees in the Sermon on the Mount the "conscious rejection of violence" by Jesus.[87] Social ethicists have also combined ethics and biblical exegesis to claim that the kingdom proclaimed by Jesus was non-violent.[88] On the other hand, Horsley categorically denies that the set of "love your enemies" sayings has anything to do with the issue of Jesus and violence. He argues that the themes of non-violence, non-resistance, and non-retaliation are not part of the message of these sayings.[89]

---

[84] John Robinson, "Honest to God," in *The Honest to God Debate*, ed. David L. Edwards (London: SCM Press, 1955), 76.

[85] Valson Thampu, "The Church and the Nation," *Evangelical Review of Theology* 22, no. 2 (April 1998): 119.

[86] Günter Krusche, "Human Rights in a Theological Perspective: A Contribution from the German Democratic Republic," *Lutheran Word* 1 (1977): 64. He consistently maintains that Human Rights remind the Church of the promise still outstanding.

[87] Hengel, *Was Jesus a Revolutionist?*, 26–27.

[88] J. H. Yoder, *The Politics of Jesus* (Grand Rapids. MI: William B. Eerdmans, 1972); S. Hauerwas, *The Peaceable Kingdom* (Notre Dame: Notre Dame Press, 1983).

[89] Richard A. Horsley, *Jesus and the Spiral of Violence* (Minneapolis, MN: Fortress Press, 1993) 261.

Concluding remark

This perspective of human rights does not rest upon an occasional prooftext from an obscure book of the Bible. It has its roots in one of the most fundamental aspects of theology, namely the nature of God and of God's relationship with humanity. The Christian concern for human rights has been awakened by the frightening injustice done to the lives of the people, but it is important for us to realize that this concern for human rights is ultimately grounded in the nature of God the Creator and Redeemer. This is also the reason that it can never be reduced to the level of an optional extra or even be considered simply as a necessary implication of the gospel.[90] It may also be considered that the biblical concept of human rights is more inclusive than that of the modern definition of human rights. For instance, the latter does not speak about ecological rights but the former has a clear reference to it. It claims that rights to life and existence enjoyed by human beings are valid only as long as they respect the rights of the earth and other living creatures.

By insisting on the importance of human rights, we in no way question God's sovereignty,[91] nor do we identify human rights directly with God's will.[92] This could be summed up in S. C. Mott's assertion: "It is God who provides human dignity and consequently human rights . . . when oppressed, they are valid claims, not against the sovereignty of God but rather they are valid because of God's sovereignty."[93]

This brief discussion has enabled us to understand that the resources of the Bible are richly enshrined in the conceptualization and formulation of modern human rights. It is a different form of expressing how the God of humanity wants people to keep intact the dignity of his creation. This is so that human beings can understand him better and his kingdom may be realized through all means of human efforts. However, it is not to claim that human rights that is understood in the modern world is based on biblical teachings. Human rights is not limited to a single religious group. But, it is important to note that the idea of promoting well-being of total humanity is richly reflected in the Bible.

---

[90] William H. Brackney and Ruby J. Burke, eds., *Faith, Life, and Witness: The Papers of the Study and Research Division of the Baptist World Alliance, 1986–1990* (Birmingham: Samford University Press, 1990), 244.

[91] Stephen Charles Mott, *Biblical Ethics and Social Change* (Oxford: Oxford University Press, 1982), 52–54.

[92] Thorwald Lorenzen, "Christian Perspective," 5.

[93] S. Charles Mott, "The Contribution of the Bible to Human Rights," in *Human Rights and the Global Mission of the Church*, ed. Arthur J. Dyck (Massachusetts: Boston Theological Institute, 1985), 6.

4

PROMOTING PEACE THROUGH HUMAN RIGHTS: A NORTH EAST INDIAN TRIBAL THEOLOGICAL PERSPECTIVE

"Give Peace a Chance" has been a cry in the world where conflict and violence have created countless victims. There are many young adults who were born in violent situations and have never experienced the taste of peace; they only know the history of conflict, hatred, violence, and killing. It is also true that the value of peace has not been permanently restored in the world. This is not because it is not possible for the people to think and restore it for themselves, but because there has been a lack of realization amongst the people. For a long time, every individual and group has been speaking about peace but very few people work for it and thus, we have not been able to create peace in our world according to our expectations. This correlates with the argument often being made that peace is a value that no other people will bring and deliver in a package from outside to a region, but one that local people have to create for themselves in their own land. Peace and human rights are like the two sides of the same coin. However, the process of the two cannot be reversed in the sense that we cannot have peace for the purpose of protecting human rights but human rights has to be respected for the creation and restoration of peace. Therefore, I take human rights as the framework for this section to discuss the search for lasting peace in the world; however, I would also use North East India as the context of reference.

A human right is a right claimed not because one is a citizen of a nation or endowed by the law but it is one claimed on the basis of "being human." A human is a historical being, and therefore subject to change. Similarly, human rights are historical realities, and are therefore subject to change. This indicates that the rights that are claimed on the basis of one's humanity are not statically fixed but their meaning, change according to the context.

For instance, from the eleventh century onwards, wars for freedom played an increasing part in Europe's development. Although these were people's movements, the freedom sought was religious freedom rather than freedom for people[1] and they did not challenge the feudal structure of society.[2] But with the signing of the Magna Carta[3] at Runnymede, England in 1215, new possibilities emerged. It became an encouragement to people's movements throughout Europe. Subsequently, following the First World War, a series of treaties were signed by the European nations demanding the protection of racial, religious, and national minorities. Thus, the provision of the League of Nations Charter came into being. Of all the predecessors of the United Nations, the League of Nations was the most significant one. The League was the brainchild of then-President Woodrow Wilson of the United States who proposed,

> A general association of nations must be formed under specific covenants for the purpose of affording mutual guarantees of political independence and territorial integrity to great and small states alike.[4]

The history of the United Nations starts with the declaration made by then-President Roosevelt on January 6, 1941, to the Congress of the United States.[5] The four freedoms declared in his speech as being of universal importance were: (1) Freedom of speech and expression; (2) Freedom of every person to worship God in their own way; (3) Freedom from want; and (4) Freedom from fear. These ideas formed the basis for the establishment of the United Nations.

The Second World War marked a turning point in the development of international concern for human rights. Supporting this view, Burns H. Weston argues that the term *human rights* came into use only after the Second World War.[6] The experience of the war resulted in the widespread conviction that effective international protection of human rights was an essential condition of international peace and progress, and this

---

[1] Egon Schwelb, "Human Rights," in *Encyclopaedia Britannica*, 15e. (1975), 1183.
[2] R. O'Grady, *Bread and Freedom: Understanding and Acting Human Rights* (Geneva: WCC, 1979), 4.
[3] Among many rights provided to the minorities, the most important is that "no punishment could be imposed without due process of law." Cf. Loulla-Mae Eleftheriou-Smith, "Magna Carta: What is It—And Why is It Still Important Today?" in *INDEPENDENT,* Monday, February 2, 2015, 1.
[4] Rumki Basu, *The United Nations: Structure of Functions of an International Organisation* (New Delhi: Sterling Publishers, 1993), 11.
[5] Basu, *United Nations*, 17.
[6] Burns H. Weston, "Human Rights," in *Human Rights Quarterly* 257 (1984): 27.

conviction found expression in a number of statements, declarations, and proposals made while the war was still being fought.

The idea of human rights as we understand it today is something that has developed in Western civilization.[7] The emphasis of the First or capitalist world or Liberal Approach[8] is on the right of the individual. Civil and political rights become the standards of liberty. In the liberal thought, the main inspiration for nurturing of the concept of human rights (natural rights of man) is the resistance to political absolutism that had derogated the basic rights of man to freedom and equality. The liberal democratic state promises to guarantee such rights as freedom of religion, speech, and assembly; the right to be secure in one's person and property; and the right to due process of law.[9] It is these rights that David Hollenbach terms as "the freedom of individual person."[10]

Justifying the arguments of O'Grady and S.C. Kashyap, John Desrochers summarizes their views by stating that the liberal concept of human rights was progressively developed in Europe.[11] It contributed to the emancipation of society from feudalism and the growth of capitalism.[12]

The Global South has yet another understanding of human rights that is a product of these countries' own human, social, and political situation; interest in specific rights related to the individual is put in the background to make room for the rights to existence itself. This is another context where one sees the problem of interrelationship between the state and the individuals. And often the state is blamed for not safeguarding their individual rights. The Global South perspective focuses neither on individual political rights nor on collective rights to social participation. Rather, the focus is on the right to human survival and liberation. According to Robert Evans and Alice Evans, as the people of the Global South attempt to distinguish rights of necessity from rights of preference, "survival" and

---

[7] Hans Kung and Jürgen Moltmann, eds., *The Ethics of World Religions and Human Rights* (London: SCM Press, 1990), 12.
[8] This term is used by John Desrochers.
[9] Robert A. Evans and Alice Frazer Evans, *Human Rights: A Dialogue Between the First and Third Worlds* (Maryknoll, NY: Orbis Books, 1983), 8; cf. K.M. Panikkar, *In Defence of Liberalism* (Bombay: Asia Publishing House, 1962), 32.
[10] David Hollenbach, *Claims in Conflict: Retrieving and Renewing the Catholic Human Rights Tradition* (New York: Paulist, 1979), 13.
[11] The liberal ideas were greatly influenced by three English documents: The Magna Carta (1215), the Petition of Rights (1627), and the Bill of Rights (1791).
[12] George Joseph and John Desrochers, *Development, Human Rights and Action Groups* (Bangalore: Centre for Social Action, 1985), 78; cf. O'Grady, *Bread and Freedom: Understanding and Acting Human Rights* (Geneva: WCC, 1979), 6–10; S.C. Kashyap, *Human Rights and Parliament* (Delhi: Metropolitan, 1978), 1–4.

"liberation" became the two basic human rights in the Global South.[13] Affirming this new context, George Lobo asserts that, in poor countries like India, basic human rights are denied to the majority of people.[14] The Global South understanding of human rights is categorically affirmed by Jürgen Moltmann when he stated,

> The demand for the most fundamental human rights can be heard in the people of the "third world" (sic) today, who have to fight against the death of hunger for their survival: it is the right to exist, the right to survive.[15]

Let me mention that the Christian church, for that matter, the World Council of Churches (WCC) from its inception in 1948 has been very active in the promotion of human rights. In August 1946, the Commission of the Churches on International Affairs (CCIA) was established at a meeting in Cambridge, England, as the joint agency of the WCC and the International Missionary Council. The CCIA was granted early consultative status with the Economic and Social Council under arrangements worked out in accordance with Article 71 of the United Nations Charter. The CCIA, in its formative years, considered human rights as intrinsically worthwhile and thus gave great emphasis on the inclusion of religious liberty in the Universal Declaration of Human Rights. The CCIA took active part in the drafting of the United Nations Charter, and was primarily responsible for the wording and inclusion of the Article on Religious Liberty in the United Nations Universal Declaration of Human Rights. The memoranda of the CCIA submitted to the working group on the Declaration at the December, 1947 meeting of the Human Rights Commission in Geneva appear in the final text of Article 18 of the Universal Declaration of Human Rights,[16] which has continued to provide valuable benefits.[17] The CCIA was equally concerned that the preamble should reflect a basic approach to the observance of human rights that was acceptable from the Christian standpoint, even though it did not contend that a Christian

---

[13] Robert Evans and Alice Frazer Evans, *Human Rights A Dialogue between the First and Third Worlds* (Maryknoll, NY: Orbis Books, 1983), 10.

[14] George Lobo, *Human Rights in Indian Situation* (New Delhi: The Commission for Justice and Development Catholic Bishops' Conference of India, 1991), 2.

[15] Jürgen Moltmann, "Christian Faith and Human Rights," in *Adventurous Faith & Transforming Vision*, ed. Arvind P. Nirmal (Madras: GLTC & Research Institute, 1989), 63.

[16] Everyone has the right to freedom of thought, conscience, and religion. This right includes freedom to change one's religion or belief, and freedom, either alone or in community with others and in public or private, to manifest one's religion or belief on teaching, practice, worship, and observance (Art. 18).

[17] *Evanston to New Delhi 1954–1961, The Report of the Central Committee to the Third Assembly of the World Council of Churches* (Geneva: WCC, 1961), 135.

position had to be enunciated therein. At this point, it is worthy to note the inclusiveness of the Christian contribution toward the development of human rights. It is noteworthy that there was no effort to secure rights or freedoms for Christians that would not be available to all persons, no matter what faith they professed, or even if they professed no faith. Hence, at its inaugural Assembly in Amsterdam in 1948, the WCC affirmed its conviction of the churches' role in the struggle for human rights.

> We are profoundly concerned by evidence from many parts of the world of flagrant violence of human rights. Both individuals and groups are subjected to persecution and discrimination on grounds of race, color, sex, religion, culture, or political conviction... They must work for an ever wider and deeper understanding of what are the essential human rights if men are to be free to do the will of God.[18]

Laying the foundation for further participation, the First Assembly issued a "Declaration on Religious Liberty." The four cornerstones of religious liberty were listed as the following:

1. Every person has the right to determine his (or her) own faith and creed.
2. Every person has the right to express his (or her) religious belief in worship, teaching, and practice, and to proclaim the implications of his belief for relationship in a social or political community.
3. Every person has the right to associate with others and to organize with them for religious purposes.
4. Every religious organization, formed or maintained by action in accordance with the rights of individual persons, has the right to determine its policies and practices for the accomplishment of its chosen purposes.[19]

Under the initiation of the CCIA, an international consultation on "Human Rights and Christian Responsibility" was held in October, 1974 at St. Pölten, Austria. For the first time, representatives of churches from all parts of the world were brought together to discuss and make recommendations to the Fifth Assembly of the WCC, 1975 in Nairobi. The Consultation proposed sweeping adjustments in the approach of the

---

[18] Kathleen Bliss et al., "The Church and the Disorder of Society" (Amsterdam: WCC, First Assembly, 1948).

[19] Quoted from *A Declaration on Religious Liberty* (Amsterdam: WCC First Assembly, 1948); cf. Erich Weingartner, *Human Rights on the Ecumenical Agenda* (Geneva: WCC, 1983), 9. This was again reaffirmed by the WCC Third Assembly at New Delhi; cf. *The New Delhi Report—The Third Assembly of the World Council of Churches, 1961* (London: SCM Press, 1962), 160.

WCC on the responsibility of the churches in this field. It listed a number of issues for the churches' attention.

1. *The right to a full human life*—No rights are possible without the basic guarantees for life, including the right to work, to adequate food, to guaranteed health care, to decent housing, and to education for the full development of the human potential.
2. *The right to enjoy and maintain a political and cultural identity*—Issues involved here are national sovereignty and self-determination; recognition and respect for cultural, linguistic, religion, ideological, and ethnic pluralities; rights of minorities; inter-cultural exchange, based on mutual respect, across and within national boundaries. All people have the right to determine their own political system; free from undue foreign influence or international oppression and discrimination, and to pursue their own economic, social, and cultural development. This includes the right to dispose freely of their natural wealth and resources.
3. *The right to participate in decision-making within the community*—This includes the right of people to decide how it shall be governed, who shall exercise authority, and what legal system shall be adopted, and continually and responsibly to participate in the governing process at all levels.
4. *The right to dissent*—Preserves a community or system from authoritarian rigidity.
5. *The right to personal dignity*—Certain phenomena have become common: disappearances, assassinations, bombings, torture, deportation, death sentences, etc.
6. *The right to choose freely a religion or belief*—Human solidarity demands that we should be aware of the inter-relatedness of all rights including the rights of people of other faiths and of no faith.[20]

The recommendations of the St. Pölten consultation were considered and adopted in Section V of the Nairobi Assembly on Structures of Injustice and Struggle of Liberation.[21] Later, in June 1993, The World Conference on Human Rights at Vienna reaffirms the solemn commitment of all states to fulfill their obligations to promote universal respect for, and observance and protection of, all human rights and fundamental freedoms for all in accordance with the Charter of the United Nations,

---

[20] *Work Books for the Fifth Assembly of the WCC, Nairobi, Kenya, 23 November–10 December 1975* (Geneva: WCC, 1975), 55–56.

[21] David M. Paton, ed., *Breaking Barriers, Nairobi 1975: The Official Report of the Fifth Assembly of the WCC, 23 November to 10 December 1975* (London: SPCK, 1976), ix.

other instruments relating to human rights, and international law. The universal nature of these rights and freedoms is beyond question.²² In 2019, we have celebrated the seventy-first anniversary of the Universal Declaration of Human Rights focusing on caring for and nurturing young people. And, we need to develop a new perspective in order to make human rights a meaningful source of creating and promoting peace.

At the global level, the seventieth year of the Universal Declaration of Human Rights was considered as a time for serious re-introspection on why peace is distorted in almost every part of the world. It is also very appropriate for the people of this region to rethink our approach to human rights. I have called for a paradigm shift in thinking about human rights; that we should no longer think of human rights and its violations from the grievance narrative but rather learn to adopt the power narrative.²³ One of the best examples to understand the need of paradigm shift may be cited from the reality of the people of North East India. They have submitted thousands of memorandums to the government of India and to the state governments against human rights violations but almost no one has read these and thus, there has been a minimal response to people's demands. We live in a world where there is little response to the cries of the people. Therefore, voices of "I am weak, help me; My right is violated, protect me; I am poor, save me," are not relevant voices. But, what are relevant are the voices of "show and prove that this is my inviolable identity; this much is what I have achieved; this is what I can do and this is my dream to realize. Each of you who has resources, it is your turn to positively participate toward materializing my dream of humanizing people." We must not give options to the people in power to either decide to decline or respond, but they must be made to respond.

If we take the stories of the same context for the last five decades, on the pretext of national security, too many violations of human rights against the innocent civilians have been meted out while at the same time too much of harm is being done against the Indian armed forces by the so-called freedom fighters. The reports of the effects of the Armed Forces Special Powers Act, 1958, that was amended in 1978 are shocking and terrifying. No one will like to expect such atrocities to happen in a civilized world. We often ask whether the difficult situation in North East India is created by the backwardness of the people, economic poverty, political instability, failure of law and order, trust deficit, and political unwillingness. Today, we must be very clear that many of the violations of human rights are taking place because of the lack of political will.

---

[22] *Vienna Declaration and Programme of Action.*
[23] Shimreingam Shimray, "Towards Paradigm Shift of Human Rights," *Asia Journal of Theology* 27, no.1 (April 2013): 70.

We are only experiencing reduced incidents of violence, a temporary situation after the government of India and state governments signed the Suspension of Operation Agreement or Cease-Fire Agreement with some "insurgent" groups in the region. But the way these groups are being treated and handled seems to be unsatisfactory, and there is constant argument that they would prefer to take arms if no political negotiation is initiated (from the examples of Manipur and Assam). This is a dangerous trend. On the other hand, the people of this region have been trapped by a harmful ideology of protest that results in repeated calling of bandh (general strike) in different parts of the region. The question we are confronted with is, have we at any point of time assessed the difference between gain and loss of 24-hours bandh? When a state or a region stops business transaction for a day, how much is the economic loss? It is very much understandable that when the government or authority does not take up welfare programs or does not meet the needs of the people, then they protest against the authority. But the question is, why should we resort only to bandh? This is a practice that violates the rights of the people. It is also necessary to raise a question to the concerned authority of each department and government why they should always wait for the call of bandh to respond to the needs of the people.

On the part of civil societies, there is a grave weakness of mediating (communication gap) between the people and the state. Because of this, unconsciously, the state is often unaware of people's needs and dreams because they are not made known to the policy makers. We need strong social movements that would creatively mediate between the people and the authority so that all available resources are utilized for meeting the needs of the people. If the civil societies are able to achieve such mediation, the so-called human rights violations will be drastically reduced and peace would be restored.

Toward this end, I would like to reiterate that the people of the region need to realize two things: (1) If the available resources are utilized properly, the entire population will be able to live satisfactorily. This means that the so-called corruption has to be checked by adopting a system that prohibits anyone from doing unfair practices to fulfill their selfish motives. (2) The composition of people in the region is a beautiful thing. We have varied races and tribes. If we are able to understand each other's beauty and respect each other, the diverse cultures of the people can be assembled into a beautiful chain of cultures. They are like scattered gems, and the only thing is to put them together in order to make a beautiful necklace. This calls for a pluriform society where each and every ethnic identity is respected, and co-existence of different communities in a well knitted single community is promoted.

Peace in the region will not come until people of the region realize the importance of human rights of every individual and community. There is always a possibility of differences among the people, but there is also a way to sort them out through proper negotiation without conflict. There is no issue that is beyond solution. What we need is a trust and respect for each other. There are sufficient laws and traditions that will help us to find the best way of coexistence. For this, we need to understand the force of human emotions that may lead to unreasonable actions that will be marked with regret throughout history. Reading human rights from a Christian point of view, we understand that it is a means to maintain a human relationship that is beautifully enshrined in the kingdom values. Jesus talks about love, equality, peace, righteousness, etc., to mean that human beings only need to know how to relate with each other because none of these values is possible without realizing the importance of a human relationship. And, a human relationship is not possible without respecting human rights of every individual and community.

5

THEOLOGY OF PEACE AND THE CHURCH

WHY PEACE?

By way of shaping perspective, I would like to make these introductory lines that today, every group, region, nation, institution, etc., is talking about peace. It is so because peace has become an abstract rather than a reality. Peace is the most envied value of the world, but not many people are committed to its pursuit. Victor Cancino, while referring to the Middle East, states that peace is merely an abstraction for millions living in this region. Peace will continue to be, moreover, an abstraction for the near future until enough people are willing to acknowledge the source of the conflict.[1] It is as if we are waiting for someone to come and restore peace to our land; that is likely to never happen. Peace can be created only by the local people for themselves. It is more realistic to think in terms of overflowing peace to the outside world than borrowing peace from the external environment.

MEANING

According to Baker's Dictionary, the English word *peace* conjures up a passive picture, one showing an absence of civil disturbance or hostilities, or a personality free from internal and external strife. The biblical concept of peace is larger than this and rests heavily on the Hebrew root *slm*, which means "to be complete" or "to be sound." The verb conveys both a dynamic and a static meaning, "to be complete or whole" or "to live well." The whole idea can be grouped into four categories: (1) shalom as wholeness of life or body (i.e., health); (2) shalom as right relationship or harmony between two parties or people, often established by a covenant (see

---

[1] Victor Cancino, "Efforts Towards Reconciliation in the Middle East," in *Prospects and Challenges for the Ecumenical Movement in the 21st Century*, eds. David Field and Jutta Koslowski (Geneva: Globethics.net Global, 2016), 161.

"covenant of peace" in Numbers 25:12–13; Isaiah 54:10; Ezekiel 34:25–26) (3) shalom as prosperity, success, or fulfillment (see Lev 26:3–9); and (4) shalom as victory over one's enemies or absence of war. Shalom was used in both greetings and farewells, to mean, "your life be filled with health, prosperity, and victory." In the New Testament, the Greek word *eirene* is the word most often translated by the word *peace*.

The paradigm of history has been changed again and again and it will continue to change. Sometimes, one finds illogical conclusions that shaped differences of attitude. Before I try to define the term *peace*, let me quote Guro Bert Domingo: "Rationality requires a logical mind with enough knowledge to base judgment and make appropriate choices. Knowledge with a sensible mind, leads to a reasonable attitude. Courage is achieved with knowledge and reason, thus, banishing fear. Without fear, we can be free to seek for the truth. For me, *ecumenism* in all faiths is necessary for people to converge to achieve world peace. There are many good ideas in every religion where people can agree. In philosophy, I am *eclectic* selecting the best, but respecting others' point of view. Politically, I would consider myself *centrist*, conservative in morality but progressive in economic and other social concepts. Every society should seek the greatest good for the greatest number. I live in *moderation,* to have comfort without upsetting homeostasis and symbiosis with myself and with other humans. I also follow the *"golden rule and mean,"* as a responsible free individual. Socially, I believe in co-existence and *interdependence* among equal and free people. Furthermore, I firmly believe against competition, since everyone is unique and different. There should never be comparison, since each has a special contribution to make in the total scheme of things . . . . Every free, responsible individual needs to sharpen all sensory abilities to detect truth from falsehood. One should also use all available information, tools, and instruments to verify what one doubts. Finally, using intuition, logic, and reasoning determine the nature of things as it affects life and existence."[2]

One of the first and most common reactions to the question, "What is peace?" is, it is "the opposite of war." Peace in classical Judaism was seen as a necessary precondition for the preservation of the existence of humanity and also a requirement for its development. This means that peace was defined with an explicit reference to the internal working structures of a society. For instance, the term *shalom* is used to define the conformity between God and human, and the condition of peace is the total defeat of the enemies of Israel. Of course, the whole exercise of peace on earth was understood within the framework of divine rule, the system of justice.

---

[2] Guro Bert Domingo, *God: Rational Theology, Prescription for World Peace*, 2nd ed. (np, 2008), 37–38.

Peace and striving for peace are at the heart of all major religions, even if groups of followers abuse their religion for violence and war. The Muslim greeting "As-Salaamu-alaykum" translates to "peace be upon you"—an indication of the fundamental desire for peace in Islam. The word Islam itself means "peace." The Qur'an commands Muslims to be kind to each other and to not act violently. The following order to establish peace might explain what this entails: Whosoever killed a person—unless it be for killing a person or for creating disorder in the land—it shall be as if he had killed all (hu)mankind" (Al Mahida, 5:33). This means that unlawful shedding of the blood of a single life is to be seen like killing the whole human race. Thus, according to the Qur'an, acting violently is a sin; an act that violates peace.[3]

Johan Galtung is one of the most renowned researchers in the field of peace studies. One of his main contributions is the definition of Structural Violence as the systematic way in which a regime prevents individuals from achieving their full potential. Institutionalized racism and sexism are examples of this. He then introduced the concept of peace in two ways, which are:

Negative peace

It refers to the absence of war, fear, direct violence, and conflict at the individual, national, regional, and international levels. It requires institutional reforms to prevent acts of direct physical violence committed by individuals or groups. Negative perception of a former enemy or conflicting party is neutralized or shifted after a violent conflict is settled. "During the period of negative peace, there is no emphasis on dealing with the causes of violence or conflict. Rather, it is limited to addressing the manifestation of factors that led and lead to violence."[4]

Positive peace

It refers to the absence of indirect and structural violence, the absence of unjust structures and unequal relationship; it refers to peace at different levels like behavior, attitudes, or structures. Positive peace is filled with positive contents such as the restoration of relationships, the constructive resolution of conflict, and the creation of social systems that serve the needs of the whole population. Positive peace encompasses all aspects of a good society that one might envisage for oneself: universal rights, economic well-being, ecological balance, and other core values.[5]

---

[3] Katharina Schilling, *Peacebuilding & Conflict Transformation: A Resource Book* (Berlin: Brot für die Welt, 2012),18–19.
[4] Schilling, *Peacebuilding*, 22.
[5] Galtung Johan, *Cultural Violence*, 1990, 291. Cf. Schilling, *Peacebuilding*, 22–23.

Peacebuilding

It refers to the process of work that has peace-enhancing outcomes. It is the set of initiatives by diverse actors in government and civil society to address the root causes of violence and protect civilians before, during, and after violent conflict. It consists of a wide range of activities associated with capacity building, reconciliation, and societal transformation. Peacebuilding is a long-term process that occurs after the violent conflict has slowed down or come to a halt.

Peacebuilding includes building legal and human rights institutions as well as fair and effective governance and dispute resolution processes and system.

It is not primarily concerned with conflict behavior but looks at the underlying context and attitude that give rise to violence, such as unequal access to employment, discrimination, unacknowledged and unforgiven responsibility for past crimes, prejudice, mistrust, fear, or hostility, between groups.

Peacebuilding dimensions

Peacebuilding has three dimensions—namely, the structural dimension, the relational dimension, and the personal dimension.

Peacebuilding agents

The role and possibilities of intervention are different for those in the elite leadership positions, religious leaders, or the masses and their local leaders at the grassroots level. Peacebuilding measures should therefore integrate civil society in all efforts and include all levels of society so that they play their specific roles in building a lasting peace.

Peace education

It is an important aspect of peacebuilding. Creating a realistic and inclusive goal that everyone strives for is a serious business in this education pattern. Peace education finds its motivation in peace utopias and in the vision of people who have shown that hopes and dreams are not necessarily individualistic, but can be combined with political commitment. An example is the vision of Martin Luther King Jr. that he spelled out in his "I have a Dream" speech.[6]

---

[6] He gave this speech on August 28, 1963, the steps of Lincoln Memorial, Washington D.C., accessed April 15, 2020, https://kinginstitute.stanford.edu/king-papers/documents/i-have-dream-address-delivered-march-washington-jobs-and-freedom.

Theology of Peace and the Church

The concern of peace education is to provide a positive mindset to the children and a free space to grow and live a whole life. It is in this kind of environment that we can expect children to be successful.

Conflict: What is conflict?

Conflict happens when two or more groups have, or think they have, incompatible goals. It is a difference of interest or attitude. It is a matter of not agreeing with another group with reason or without reason. It is logic that leads to violence and destruction. So, conflict is not simply "not agreeing" but a source of violence; a threat to harmonious living. Several pertinent factors are identifiable, as given below.

Conflict is a fact of life. God made each one in his own image, but he also made each one with unique identity. Therefore, some of our views and opinions will differ from those of others. Conflict often occurs because of a lack of respect for one another's needs and views.

Factor 1: Power

Power is the ability or capacity to do something or to control and influence what others do. It determines who makes decisions and what decisions are made. Power is often shown when two or more people interact. People often think that power lies in the hands of public leaders like politicians and directors of commercial companies. It is so because they hold power to decide for and against the people they represent or the people who work for them and buy their products. Market is a power center in today's context. For instance, today most people find it difficult to understand the force behind their definition of "basic needs." It is no longer we who define the meaning but the market compels us to define basic needs much different from what we actually need. It becomes a need only because our neighbor has it or we have explored and seen it in the showroom.

Similarly, a closer look shows that there are many other forms of power that operate to dominate certain sections or groups. For example, patriarchy is all about power crisis between the genders. Cultural norms are used by males as tools to justify oppression while female groups protest that these are biased and unjust norms.

At another level, we see that every individual has power of a certain degree. Even the masses have strong power if they are made to realize that they can also shape the direction. For example, when the trade unions call for bandh in India, business comes to a standstill causing the nation to lose thousands of crores. As for the tribal people, they find it very difficult to claim public power even as they face discrimination in the name of religion and ethnicity and fail to protest even for their rights. Their understanding of patience and meekness is turning out to be more of ignorance.

But, what is most important for us to understand is that there are two types of power. And it is useful to distinguish between the two: (a) Hard power, which is the ability to command and enforce. Hard power usually represents physical or military power. It is dominant in violent conflicts as opposing groups struggle for victory; (2) Soft power, which is the ability to bring about co-operation. This type of power is vital for peace-building.[7] This power enables one to be capable of forming a strong voice that will determine the function of the government or pull together resources to sponsor ten theological students; this becomes power but a soft power.

Factor 2: Money

Money and wealth hold a strong ability to perform many activities. Money is a powerful source for success. Without it, people will find it very difficult to sustain life. It is also a source of creating crisis if people do not properly understand their attitude toward money and wealth. Any form of manipulation is an unfair stewardship and it brings crisis to the community life. People without proper discipline often find it difficult to manage wealth. They often become either greedy or selfish. This is the attitude that Jesus Christ was very critical of. We must also distinguish two kinds of money, private money and public money. Private money refers to the money that an individual owns. An individual can make independent decisions on private money. The other, public money, is owned by the public over which no individual should exercise power so as to meet vested interests. But, what is more important for us is that anyone who is involved in financial management must possess qualities of transparency, accountability, and honesty. Financial crisis is one of the main causes of conflict. The Christian churches must now be able to take strong position to combat corruption without leaving it to the NGOs. That is, we need to understand combating corruption as Christian participation in nation building.

Factor 3: Politics

Politics in the modern period has become an institution of money and muscle that produces power. It controls the system of the society and has strong influence on many aspects of every society. One of the identified aspects that calls for our attention when we think and talk about peace is its influence on religion. It has become an issue because of the nature of Hinduism that is not only a religion but at the same time a culture (Hindu

---

[7] Rachel Blackman, *Peace-building Within Our Communities* (Teddington: Tear Fund, 2003), 9–11.

culture) and so politics also finds its place in Hinduism. The philosophy that "what is politically right is religiously right as well" is the most serious threat to other religions in India. It is so because that is not acceptable to Christianity and more seriously to the Baptists who hold its distinctiveness as a "complete separation between the Church and the state." This is so because we do not understand whose culture they refer to.

Another aspect that needs to be explained is politics that is narrowed down to party politics. Indians in general have not been able to develop the right attitude to politics, as the system of governance to look after the welfare of the people is defined along party-line and those who belong to different political parties are considered as enemies. The Indian democratic system of election is also not doing well as people's rights are being sold and bought or controlled through caste, tribe, clan, etc. Moreover, the deciding majority is in many cases wrong (to illustrate, when the vote share out of 100 votes is 40, 35, and 25, and the one who received 40 votes is declared as the winner in an election). When leaders who do not have the people's mandate come into power, they do not command people's support. Thus, it encourages them to get involved in political corruption.

All these factors harm the majority of citizens who very often are left without any option to respond and participate in peacebuilding processes. Most people do not strive toward common goals. Many people consider that pacifism is a better option although they do not want to survive in misery and poverty. At the same time, many Christians remain indifferent to the crises generated by politics. We need to think of a concrete Christian position to politics.

Factor 4: Religion

The more important aspect of this area is not so much to do with religion itself but it becomes a serious matter when the followers are not able to sincerely follow religious teaching and make biased (exclusive) religious claims. This may be understood through religious fundamentalism. Religious imposition on others is one serious factor in our country. For instance, an attempt to make Hinduism as the national religion is a serious threat to the peaceful co-existence of many religious groups. Also, waging war in the name of religion is equally dangerous. A terrorist attack allegedly by Brenton Harrison Tarrant, a twenty-eight-year-old Australian man at Christchurch, New Zealand on March 15, 2019 that killed 50 Islamic worshipers at mosques is said to have led to negative retaliation of suicide bombing in three Christian churches and three luxury hotels at Colombo, Sri Lanka, when Christians were worshipping on Easter Sunday morning on April 21, 2019, killing over 300 innocent people.[8]

---

[8] *Assam Tribune* (April 22 and 23, 2019).

Negotiating Peace

A related issue in religious manifestation is when two or more denominations are not able to understand their own differences and appreciate one another. The other aspect is when religion is used with vested interest—leadership crisis under the cover of religion that is equally destructive. People in the present day are wrongly interpreting the definition and meaning of religion because no religion teaches violence and intolerance. But, people in the name of religion are becoming very intolerant creating fear and insecurity in the minds of the public.

Journey through the world of the Bible

The Bible is the source book for Christian moral principles. It provides perspective rather than the ready-made answer to every modern crisis. However, we also find that the Bible contains contradictions (if one considers verse against verse). But, this is not a problem when it comes to methodology and proper reading of the Bible. The historical and contextual interpretation of the Bible provides meaning and perspective to all situations.

There are several incidences of war and violence in the Old Testament. This is the reason why there are many people who purchase the Bible do not read it for their devotion but read it as a comic book or to find fault in it. We find God being portrayed as the mastermind of war and a leader in the battlefields. How do we then relate to the discussion of peace? We cannot question the total truth of the Bible but we also need to make positive deconstruction in order to understand the core purpose of the book. The context where much violence was executed needs to be understood—that it was in the context of Israelites' extreme fundamentalism of faith in Yahweh. In their monotheistic understanding, it was only Yahweh who was the true God and besides him, no other gods should exist. Their exclusive religious faith prompted them to think that other faiths must be abolished. Further, in order to fulfill such a claim, they must have put their words into the mouth of Yahweh to command and participate in the war as the hero. The idea of "our God" and "their gods" had become the basis of all those undertakings. But, we should be able to read the entire Bible with the strong undercurrent of the message of salvation and liberation of the total cosmos.

The Bible is a strong advocate for peace and its pursuit. Even the statement in Exodus 21:24, "An eye for an eye, a tooth for a tooth," is also a call for peace. In Palestine in the past, for any harm done to a woman among the Jews (particularly the Bedouins) the punishment was fourfold. For the life of one woman, the lives of four men had to be taken. Such was the inclination for revenge in those days. Even though that was the law, practically, the action of revenge was very different. For instance, in Genesis 34, for the harm done to Dinah, the sons of Joseph destroyed the entire Shechemite community. According to their practice, if a person harmed the eye of another person, that person and his people did not stop with harming the other person's eye, but they went on to destroy that person's community as a whole. In such a context, Moses had to intervene to reduce their feeling of vengeance and said, "Stop, you cannot do that. If the other person has taken your eye, be content with taking his eye. But don't go beyond that." That means, do not think of taking revenge, as it is always more harmful than the first act. In other words, no human being can maintain and count the destruction during the heated moments of taking revenge. So, the original message of the text is a proclamation/declaration of life; a great teaching to sustain life.

Reconciliation

It will be wrong on the part of human beings (Christians or other faiths) to expect to live without any form of conflict and problem. But what is important is how they handle the conflict at different levels. Conflict should not be left to increase and do greater harm. Reconciliation is the first step toward peacebuilding. We often refer to different levels of reconciliation like God-human, men-women, rich-poor, inter and intra tribal conflict, factional conflict, border conflict, etc. We have also experienced a series of events for reconciliation. However, much of them have been associated with celebration or event. This is the reason why we have not been able to create lasting peace. After all these experiences, we should now call for a paradigm shift in Christian thinking for peace. The coming together of two enemy parties to shake hands in front of the public is not the answer if the attitude of coming together is not understood. After the event, if forgiveness is withdrawn and feeling of enmity exists, then that is not reconciliation.

It is so because people have wrongly understood reconciliation as an event. Therefore, the concept of reconciliation has to be an unending process. The moment the process ends, the reconciliation ceases. Thus, people who agree to reconcile should be prepared to maintain it as a process, failing which one is responsible to harm and violence. Everyone should respect the principle of reconciliation and sincerely oblige to sustain the process.

Quest for Meaning

What is the meaning of an individual and community life? What history are we writing? Is our record clean? Do people admire us and try to learn how we live or find many reasons to criticize us? Are people waiting for me to relinquish the office or give me their support to the fullest? A theology of peace should examine all these.

In a Christian language, we all seek for wholeness and happiness. But what motif we adopt matters the most. Are we looking for wealth, position, or power, for the purpose of achieving happiness? These can give us temporary happiness. The theological vision needs to be made very clear, otherwise our endeavor may be distracted. Take for example, current science and technology, which offer a vista of the future without any limit. The discoveries in genetics and DNA research point to the eradication of diseases. But, we must also understand that the misery caused by diseases and calamities does not contribute much to human suffering. They contribute roughly about 25 percent; the remaining 75 percent of human misery is caused by injustices (corruption of all forms). Guro Bert Domingo thus states, "we all must seek for lasting and anxiety free happiness."[9]

Keeping in mind the idea of positive peace, I would like the Christian leaders to critically reflect on the execution of political power in the so-called democratic system as indicated above and formulate a concrete position of the Christian church. Common citizens have suffered for long without hope for a better future. Their rightful share is not available; the welfare service does not reach the villagers. The condition of the people inspires us to question the concept of politics. The following points may be considered.

1. The established political system and politicians seem to have defined politics within a narrow frame of individual kingdom in which "others" do not find a space to claim right to life.
2. The public has become too weak that their votes can be bought and their rights sold. The clean election campaign is not making enough impact in this chronic election system.
3. The Christian churches have become dependent on the generous donations of the rich politicians.
4. A time may come when a politician may openly dictate the pastor on what to speak and what not to speak from the pulpit and defile the sanctity of the pulpit if we are not vigilant.
5. The fates of many politicians belong to the voters who belong to the Christian church. Can the voters dictate or provide moral principle to them? They can and they should be able to execute such privilege and power and not allow a few individuals to ruin the church.

---

[9] Domingo, *GOD: Rational Theology*, 38.

Today, the Christian church leaders need to take appropriate steps on two contemporary realities. First, they need to develop a clear concept/position on how to deal with politics. A mature approach to electoral politics does not allow money to play a decisive factor because it steals the development of the society. Second, they need to develop a positive approach toward neighbors. Then, it will be easier for them to look into other local issues.

6

LIBERATION THROUGH RECONCILIATION

While writing about the vision of reconciliation, Robert Kennedy put it this way: "Some [people] see things as they are, and say why; I dream of things that never were, and say why not?"[1] We should not only think and talk about conflict and division, but look toward the beauty of reconciliation that had not happened in the past.

Liberation has a wide range of concepts. It is concerned with all forms of domination, disorderliness, chaos, division, conflict, etc., relating to economic, political, social, ideological, cultural, and religious aspects. The contemporary Christian world uses the term *liberation theology*[2] when it

---

[1] These are the words of Robert Kennedy, who paraphrased the words of George Bernard Shaw. See in Jules Witcover, *85 Days: The Last Campaign of Robert Kennedy* (New York: William Marrow, 1988), 8.

[2] Simply put, liberation theology is an attempt to interpret Scripture through the plight of the poor. It is largely a humanistic doctrine. It started in South America in the turbulent 1950s when Marxism was making great gains among the poor because of its emphasis on the redistribution of wealth, allowing poor peasants to share in the wealth of the colonial elite and thus upgrade their economic status in life. As a theology, it has very strong Roman Catholic roots.

Liberation theology was bolstered in 1968 at the Second Latin American Bishops Conference that met in Medellin, Colombia. The idea was to study the Bible and to fight for social justice in Christian (Catholic) communities. Since the only governmental model for redistribution of the wealth in a South American country was a Marxist model, the redistribution of wealth to raise the economic standards of the poor in South America took on a definite Marxist flavor. Since those who had money were very reluctant to part with it in any wealth redistribution model, the use of a populist (read poor) revolt was encouraged by those who worked most closely with the poor. As a result, the liberation theology model was mired in Marxist dogma and revolutionary causes.

As a result of its Marxist leanings, liberation theology as practiced by the bishops and priests of South America was criticized in the 1980s by the Catholic hierarchy, from Pope John Paul on down. The top hierarchy of the Catholic Church accused liberation theologians of supporting violent revolutions and

interprets the Bible from any of these perspectives. However, I do not attempt to define the term here, but will keep its meaning as referring to the discovery of "the new world"; a new experience among the Christians. For this, I use the religious experiences of the Tangkhul Baptist Christians of Manipur.

CONCEPTUALIZATION OF RECONCILIATION

The term *reconciliation* simply means agreeing to be united; to be partners in all undertakings. It is a matter of acceptance. However, reconciliation may not be used to refer to any act of coming together to celebrate an event alone. Two conflicting people called to come together to the stage in a big gathering to shake hands in front of many people is an event. If the meaning of shaking hands ends when they leave the hall and revert to the same attitude of conflict, such an event cannot be considered as reconciliation. It has to be understood in terms of an "ongoing process" and that agreement of the two should not end in any circumstances. Further, such unending reconciliation cannot be established if one of the parties hesitates. Therefore, we need *dual-positive* attitude. This requires that both the parties must be positive toward coming together for positive negotiation. It cannot be for the benefit of one party alone. Charles Villa-Vicencio understands the term as follows: "Reconciliation must by definition reach beyond the restrictive ghetto of any creed, culture, or ideology. It must necessarily be both conceptually and substantially available to everyone."[3] Reconciliation can be processed through a pure and open heart. Anyone

---

outright Marxist class struggle. This perversion is usually the result of a humanist view of man being codified into church doctrine by zealous priests and bishops and explains why the Catholic top hierarchy now wants to separate itself from Marxist doctrine and revolution.

However, liberation theology has moved from the poor peasants in South America to the poor blacks in North America. We now have *black liberation theology* being preached in the black community. It is the same Marxist, revolutionary, humanistic philosophy found in South American liberation theology and has no more claim for a scriptural basis than the South American model has. False doctrine is still false, no matter how it is dressed up or what fancy name is attached to it. In the same way that revolutionary fervor was stirred up in South America, liberation theology is now trying to stir up revolutionary fervor among blacks in America. If the church in America recognizes the falseness of black liberation theology as the Catholic Church did in the South American model, black liberation theology will suffer the same fate that the South America liberation theology did; namely, it will be seen as a false, humanist doctrine dressed up in theological terms. Cf. *The Moody Handbook of Theology* by Paul Enns.

3   Charles Villa-Vicencio, *The Art of Reconciliation* (Östervåla: Life & Peace Institute, 2002), 23.

Liberation through Reconciliation

who wishes to enter into the process must be willing to avoid all forms of exaggeration and fanaticism.

The purpose

Where there is tension and conflict, the churches are called to be bearers of Christ's presence, to be agents of reconciliation and justice. Sometimes, however, churches are so closely identified with particular groups, institutions, nations, and their interests that they cannot play this reconciling role, and indeed may make conflicts worse by legitimizing and promoting the interests of one party over others. When divisions among the churches reflect and reinforce divisions in society, the results are often destructive, even deadly. Reconciliation is for the benefit of both parties; for the well-being of all people together. It aims to cast off biasness or self-interest that creates distance between the two conflicting parties. It is a step to explore all possible means to live together and strengthen the structure and system of any given society/church.[4]

The need is for what has been called "a relationship-centric approach to reconciliation."[5] It is a process of learning. It is the beginning of a new way of living. It involves different attitudes toward and relationships with those from whom one often continues to be estranged. It is a relationship that places dialogue and reciprocity at the center of the struggle to be fully human, suggesting that people are incomplete to the extent that they are alienated from one another. This quest for humanity is never in isolation

---

[4] A genuine unity is based on a just relationship among its component parts. Whatever reconciliation is necessary among these parts must be achieved in order for the unity to be genuine, and lasting. A paradigm of reconciliation between individuals, ethnic groups, or nations can be found in the reconciliation between Jacob (Israel) and Esau (Edom) in Gen 32–33. The conflict between the twin brothers configures also ethnic tension and rivalry over territory. In order to return home, Jacob must face the problem of his broken relationship with Esau. He shows repentance and good faith as he appeases his brother through gifts that are more than generous. Reconciliation is achieved because there has been a re-establishment of justice, through Jacob's return of the blessing that he had stolen from Esau. To be sure, Jacob could not fully compensate Esau for what he had lost, but was ready in his heart to make an honest "return" so as to restore justice. The witness of this biblical story—whether it reflects a peace historically made between Judah and Edom, or a hope that twin brothers like Esau and Jacob can reach reconciliation after a story of strife—suggests that reconciliation is possible if there is a conversion of heart and a genuine attempt to engage the issue of justice. Reconciliation requires that the contending parties take the initiative to face what is required in order that restitution can be made.

[5] John Paul Lederach, "Five Qualities of Practice in Support of Reconciliation Processers," in *Forgiveness and Reconciliation: Religion, Public Policy and Conflict Transformation,* eds. Raymond G. Helmick and Rodney Petersen (Philadelphia: Templeton Foundation Press, 2001), 185.

from others. It is inherently in communion with others, where the mutual shaping of one another is possible. As such, it is necessarily opposed to a sense of fatalistic surrender to estrangement. It involves the creation of the kind of future that pursues the creation of a society that transcends exclusion and alienation, and attains inclusivity and reconciliation.

Reconciliation is not needed when there is no conflict. So, it is necessary to all conflicting people and to all those people who are divided on all grounds; be it political, economic, social, or religious.

THE ISSUE

What happens if conflicting people are left without reconciliation? There will be power struggle among and between people and nations. There will be an interest to exercise power against one another that can be very expensive in terms of life and property. Take the example of the conflict between the Nagas and India. The cost has been very heavy. The loss has been incalculable.[6] Generations have remained stagnant. And more may be expected if reconciliation is denied. Socially, people cannot live together. There are many reasons that people may claim to differentiate among themselves. One may think of ethnic superiority; others may think of geographical and cultural inaccessibility. And slowly, the gap of difference would widen. The same has happened to the Naga tribes. There are several factors for their unwillingness to compromise. Differences are upheld and distance created even to the extent of not allowing certain tribes to live in other tribal dominant areas. The Tangkhuls have experienced that during the 1990s in Nagaland. This issue can be debated from many different perspectives. There is an issue of jealousy, as well as the issue of the Tangkhuls being too active in violence, etc. Another example may be cited from the relationship between the Kukis and the Nagas that has been very different from the past. The ethnic conflict between the two during 1992–93 has created insecurity in both the ethnic groups. The relationship of living together as good neighbors was broken and it has been very difficult to restore normalcy even after almost twenty years. If the same attitude continues and the seed of ill feeling allowed to grow, then the younger generations would face total disconnect because there is deep "trust deficit" between the two ethnic groups. Again, in Manipur, the Meiteis in the valleys and the hill people, particularly the Nagas, have not been able to find ways to live together. The Nagas' insistent claim of ownership of land has led to the Meiteis developing a contradictory political ideology under which the entire state government is being run. As a result, the Nagas have been deeply victimized. The resources of the

---

[6] Shimreingam L. Shimray, *Theology of Human Rights: A Critique on Politics*, Chapter 3 (Jorhat: Ruth Shimray, 2002), 84–127.

state have been strictly controlled; the employment opportunity has been captured, and more seriously, a very systematic policy to control development is applied by withdrawing power facility. One can easily understand that when there is no electricity, there cannot be any production. No industry, factory, or good agriculture, is possible. Above all, it has turned out to be a cutting off of any means of competition because the education of the hill people is restricted. A student who studies with electricity light cannot be compared with the one who studies under candle light. And when certain groups of people are made to lose a few years of education, definitely, they will never ever be able to compete with other privileged groups in all aspects of life. This is a method of stealing away generations. And this situation is being faced by all the hill people. Liberation cannot be referred to as related to physical control, but it should be related to ideological manipulation.

The Tangkhuls are the people who first received Christianity in Manipur in the late nineteenth century. They were the leading people for two generations, but today they are losing their glorious Christian identity because of unreasonable differences created by themselves. In terms of religion and denomination, they follow the same religious denomination and yet, many of them are not in a position to worship together. This living reality is a sign of the need of liberation from internal religious crisis to make us understand that religion has to construct community and not destroy the values of the Christian community.

All these different forms of conflict have created tension and insecurity for the people to live and worship freely. They need to be liberated from all these crises. Otherwise, the coming generations will face a much greater consequence. One must also ask whether people are not able to understand the need of reconciliation or what factor keeps them away from reconciliation. At this juncture, they must also consider that reconciliation is one of the greatest challenges to every group who has restricted freedom. People need to seriously work on the factors that prevent them from open reconciliation, especially those who feel insecure of losing their individual position and status. This is to mean that any insecure person cannot think of wider relationships; as such, a person will not be able to freely relate with others.

As indicated above, reconciliation has to be initiated with an open mind. I am critical of the historical reality of initiating reconciliation because it can cause greater loss to certain kinds of people. As far as the North East Indian experience is concerned, they have not been successful in political negotiation. The outcome of negotiation has mostly been submission to a greater nation that has sufficient money to disintegrate people through different methods.

In this connection, one may also consider a question, who should initiate reconciliation? There are three actors involved in this, namely: (i) oppressor does it to suppress any group who claim to share power, to avoid violence, and to keep the weak under control/constitution; (ii) oppressed/victims—this is normally more liberative and moves toward a total change of power system. Sometimes this happens when certain people are under too much pain and suffering. For example, the initiative of peace process between the government of India and the Naga nationalists during the 1960s was because of the extreme suffering meted out at the Naga civilians. It was not based on the ideology of liberation but initiated on the basis of a desperate desire to end human suffering; (iii) middle path—in this process, it is not who initiates that is important, but the issue to be negotiated becomes more important. This is possible when there are no conditions set for reconciliation; when the table is open for logical debate.

The present Indo-Naga Peace Talk began on a good note and high hope. That was so because it was initially started at the highest political level, but later it missed the status of talk as it was conducted at the emissary level. Over one hundred rounds of talks have not brought any tangible solution. Such a delay has confused people and made them to ask about the direction of the twenty-two years of peace talks, as the government of India seems to have taken the driver's seat to drive the Nagas to its choice. A Framework Agreement was signed in August 2015 to serve as the basis and guideline of final solution, but after that there has been a long period of silence. The issue for us is clear that if the talks fail, then the conflict will continue to haunt many people and the situation would become worse. The whole national life would be endangered. Moreover, war may break out that would cause unimaginable loss to both the parties. This is the reason why we need reconciliation to sort out things amicably.

The ideological framework of the middle path theory has been strongly voiced by the Forum for Naga Reconciliation. Its main concern is that there cannot be fragmented freedom of any distinct Naga tribe but there can only be the Nagas as a single nation. If they are not able to move together as a nation to liberate themselves from all forms of domination and influence, they will not be able to do it individually. The Forum has given sufficient attention toward bringing together all factions of the Naga national movement and it has been successful to a great extent though the work is yet to be completed.

While talking about reconciliation, one must also keep in mind that in today's highly intellectual world with highly sophisticated weapons, there is no space for anyone to claim victory because violent confrontation can only result in loss of life and property and ecological imbalance. Most people in the present world have come to agree that violent power is incapable of bringing liberation and freedom. Therefore, this method of war is becoming irrelevant to this world.

RECONCILIATION AS PROCESS

The theological demands for confession, repentance, resistance, and forgiveness are important. They are enduring and need to be addressed. Any suggestion that they are a necessary precondition for the possibility of getting reconciliation underway is, however, likely to be counter-productive in deeply divided societies. An alternative approach, which identifies reconciliation as a process rather than a goal is more helpful. This pastoral approach is not an alternative to, but an inherent part of, a viable prophetic ethic of reconciliation and forgiveness. It may well be the more viable way of attaining the elusive goal of justice.

Theology is at its creative best when and where it embraces the realm of the artistic—in liturgy, symbol, and ritual, where imagination and new possibilities dwell, rather than the realm of dogma and legal codes. The former offers the possibility of forging new options through the celebration of human creativity and compassion, the latter lends itself to the kind of rigidity that defends past practices and entrenched rules concerning what is possible in the future. Religion that is reduced to legalism and moralism, stripped of its flexibility, humanism, aesthetics, intellectual quests, and spiritual devotion, is essentially a thing of power, not of the soul. It is a limited and time bound agenda that turns away from what Horkheimer calls the "theological moment" that takes us beyond "mere business."

Take an example from the African experience where many church leaders in South Africa find themselves trapped in a different approach to reconciliation and forgiveness. A reading of a series of interviews conducted by Bernard Spong with church and other religious leaders suggests that repentance needs to necessarily precede reconciliation—as a necessary price to be paid.[7] There is a concern throughout the interviews about "cheap grace," which is attributed to a failure of individuals and the church as a whole to "publicly confess their involvement in the evil of apartheid." It is argued that a failure "to provide adequate restitution and compensation" to victims and "to compensate for the legacy of the past" undermines any possibility of reconciliation. These, suggests one of the interviewees, are "the requirements for reconciliation." "In the end," says another, "reconciliation ... is really only going to happen when people experience economic transformation and economic justice." The concerns of the leadership and their understanding of the goals that need to be

---

[7] This is quoted from the interviews conducted on behalf of the American Association for the Advancement of Science, 2001.

pursued are both noble and necessary. But, we cannot rely on material benefit or an important event. It must continue in the hearts of the people and needs to be continually lived out to others.

In addressing the importance of the Truth and Reconciliation Commission (TRC), as it was beginning to be conceptualized, Dirkie Smit reminded us of the roots of the gospel:

> According to the Christian gospel, it only becomes possible for this truth—about who we really are, about our pasts, about the suffering we have inflicted upon others and the guilt we have brought upon ourselves—not to become unbearable, not in fact to become something that we must push aside, repress, avoid, and deny, when we acknowledge the more comprehensive truth of the love, mercy, forgiveness, and acceptance of God.[8]

Reconciliation is often as painful as it is costly. It is not for the faint-hearted or easily defeated. And clearly, some have no obvious desire to go in search of it at all. Reconciliation is a first step beyond enmity. It makes "time for speech," sometimes in the midst of violence, without any guarantee as to whether such talk can have any long-term benefit.[9] Seen on a continuum extending from temporary suspension of the logic of established patterns of cause and effect to a rupture of such patterns that contain the possibility of new life, the interruption offers no guarantee of enduring success. It happens in different ways, at different levels of intensity. An important exercise in capturing the scarcity of reconciliation initiatives and the lure of such moments in time is to collect and reflect on stories of reconciliation, exploring their relevance to other situations in life. Theologies of reconciliation are more about stories than about theory. We should be able to constructively respond to the reality of crisis.

Conflict or division refers to the existence of two faces of truth. You listen to the first group and hear about the problems created by those who fail to follow law and order, and therefore methods to control are found necessary for the sake of justice. You then turn to the other group and hear their claim about protection of their own people's identity, protest for equal treatment, justice to the poor and the weak, etc., and realize that both are fighting for justice. Thus, there is a clash in the perceptions of justice. When justice clashes with justice, the peacemaker is helpless. However, a peacemaker, for the purpose of liberation, should be prepared to fail but at the same time determined never to give up.

---

[8] Dirkie Smit, "The Truth and Reconciliation Commission—Tentative Religious and Theological Perspectives," *Journal of Theology for Southern Africa* 90 (March 1995), 6.

[9] Doxtader, "Middle Voices in Transition: The Form of Public Speech in Post-TRC South Africa," *The Public* 8 (2001), 3, 23–34.

Reconciliation involves understanding

Understanding does not necessarily lead to reconciliation. When, on the other hand, the story of a perpetrator is thoughtfully told, heard, and deeply understood, it can soften the perception that the victim, survivor, or observer, has of the perpetrator. It opens space for the possibility of a new kind of interaction between adversaries. Many perpetrators are themselves victims of one kind or another—of propaganda, religious indoctrination, fear, disillusionment, and a culture of submission.

What then is reconciliation in relation to liberation?

Consideration of reconciliation techniques is imperative, talk about reconciliation is important, and the identification of lessons learned from reconciling initiatives is essential. The spirit nevertheless blows where it wills and reconciliation happens in different places in different ways. Vigilance is required in order to discern the possibilities of reconciliation when and where they occur. And tragic is the initiative, whether theologically grounded or not, that seeks to curtail these possibilities in the name of one or another prescribed code or doctrine. Liberation of any form (new order of life) is not possible without successful reconciliation. At the same time, reconciliation can never be successful unless the motive is clear and the method is genuine. Again, I would refer to the same example and say that the present peace-talk on Naga political issue would fail if the Nagas and the government of India cannot understand the concept of freedom and sovereignty.[10]

Therefore, I would like to assert liberation from two perspectives. First, politically, a nation can be defined as people with ethnic affinity who claim to be governed by a single government. It means the end of factional ideology. Such can be the first outcome of reconciliation that can generate a strong mandate to further the process of negotiation. It would mean that people would not be subjugated to outside force. In such a case, people are not concerned with what kind of government system would fit the people, but the manifestation of self-national government is what is important.

Second, religiously they will be able to realize true religious faith and genuine human values if people are liberated through reconciliation. In this context, I understand that liberation means realizing that the Tangkhuls are one people predominantly following Baptist Christianity. They do not need three church governments but one. And even if they

---

[10] The world no longer thinks of individual national freedom anymore. There is no nation that would prosper without connection with the others. There is no isolated sovereignty anymore; this is not what the world understands today. Sovereignty is understood within the context of partnership.

want more than one, it should not be based on reaction or confusion. The rationale must be made clear. Therefore, we are concerned with freeing ourselves from all enmity, ego, selfishness, etc. Liberation would therefore mean creating an environment to live together as people without conflict; it means overcoming rejection by any system. In many parts of the world, different people have been talking about the evil of political and theological colonialization and acted against it. Thus, we have the story of liberation in Latin America, Africa, and Asia. It means that this is not the time for them to colonize themselves by unacceptable systems, but freeing themselves from all that exist among them.

Brief Reflection

Let me cite one of my observations about the Tangkhul Christians. For them, liberation would first of all mean integrating the identity of one people and drawing communities to a committed lifestyle. Melanie A. May calls this "The Unity of the Church and the Renewal of Human Community."[11] They seriously need to overcome their fragmented identity through which other people take advantage and undermine them. I know the problem of division among the Tangkhul Baptist Christians in Manipur and thus prefer to use their condition as an example to explain the rationale. Among them, no one denies being a Tangkhul Baptist Christian but because they attest to different Baptist associational structures, they invite other people to question their identity. For example, if one says one is a Tangkhul, then the insulting question would be to which Tangkhul church one belongs. It is a matter of shame and loss. But again, if it is all about shame and loss for them, the issue does not end there because it would mean that they are weakening themselves and inviting defeat from others. The Christian community should not allow this to continue.

Liberation would further mean restoring the lost value of friendship. In reconciliation, not only is the debt forgiven, the obstacle removed, but the relationship is renewed and restored. For such long years, many of them had worked together, shared success and failure, but today they are not on talking terms because of the difference within the Christian church. This is very questionable—Is this the way they should strengthen their Christian ministry? "I do not want to work with them," 'I will not work under their leadership," are some remarks that we have heard. From where do they draw and develop this attitude? A true Christian has to move against this attitude because it is not biblical, neither theologically

---

[11] Melanie A. May, "The Unity We Share, the Unity We Seek," in *A History of the Ecumenical Movement: Volume 3, 1968–2000*, eds. John Briggs, Mercy Amba Oduyoye, and Georges Tsetsis (Geneva, WCC Publications, 2004), 89.

sound nor ethically justifiable. Tangkhul Christians need a theological perspective and reconciliation spirit that would bring liberation toward political, social, and ideological realms. They should note that as long as they maintain a divided voice, they will not be able to speak about economic equality and political justice. My argument is simple. It is wrong to try to adopt a system that would in the process colonize people to a more difficult situation. People need to understand reconciliation and liberation for the common good.

All that I am trying to initiate is that people need to think together to generate a strong force that can question the wrong system.[12] The church can easily determine people who should serve in politics. It can control the political election because church members' votes decide the success and failure of political candidates standing for election. The church forum can evaluate the credibility of those who claim to serve the people and support or reject them based on the findings. The Christian politicians should belong to the people rather than the people belonging to them.

In the end, I want to make it clear that the frame of thought I maintain is to critically evaluate the whole ideological basis of sociopolitical and religious reality. If we are able to reconcile among ourselves as Christians, we have the future to critique our faith-system like, Is God only for worshiping while our practical life is based on bureaucratic advice, friend-circles, and soothsayers? Is our local church administration system good enough? Are we able to protect the sanctity of the office of the pastor? Have we become sensitive enough to the suffering of the women and children in the church? Liberation must include all these aspects.

---

[12] The lustration process in European countries may be borrowed here. In the period of post-communism after the fall of the various European communist states in 1989–1991, the term came to refer to governments' policies of "mass disqualification of those associated with the abuses under the prior regime." They excluded participation of former communists, and especially informants of the communist secret police, in successor political positions, or even in civil service positions. This exclusion was part of the wider decommunization campaigns. In some countries, however, lustration laws did not lead to exclusion and disqualification. Lustration law in Hungary (1994–2003) was based on the exposure of compromised state officials, while lustration law in Poland (1999–2005) was based on confession. Lustration law "is a special public employment law that regulates the process of examining whether a person holding certain higher public positions worked or collaborated with the repressive apparatus of the communist regime." The "special" nature of lustration law refers to its transitional character. The "public employment" nature of lustration law distinguishes it from other methods of criminal justice, such as criminal trials, amnesties, or qualified amnesties. "The process of examining" refers to the very process of "lustration," which means examining or screening against secret police archives.

7

REVISITING PATRIARCHY FROM A HUMAN RIGHTS PERSPECTIVE

Introduction

Today, at the global level, people across the world have developed a different mindset from that of traditional patriarchy that was prevalent in different parts of the world. The attitude of most men toward women is changing. The support for gender equality is becoming greater, and that is shaping a new definition of humanity. In 2015, United Nations (UN) Women organized two major public events under the umbrella campaign "Planet 50-50 by 2030: Step It Up for Gender Equality": a street march and a celebratory evening event. Both events celebrated the gains and achievements made by the global women's movement over two decades and urged for global action to achieve gender equality no later than 2030. The slogan they used was "Empowering Women—Empowering Humanity: Picture It!" Giving stronger emphasis on achieving the goals of women's struggle for human rights, Phumzile Mlambo-Ngcuka, then UN Women executive director, states that "2015 must mark the beginning of the end of gender inequality, with 2030 as the expiry date."[1] "Today, we are calling on governments, everywhere in the world, to Step It Up," says Ms. Mlambo-Ngcuka. She continues, "By 2030 at the latest, we want to live in a world where at least half of all parliamentarians, university students, CEOs, civil society leaders, and any other category, are women. Real progress requires 50-50."[2] We are journeying to achieve a great goal;

---

[1] Phumzile Mlambo-Ngcuka, "Gender Gap Figures Must Give Us a Sharper Hunger for Change," accessed September 29, 2016, *UN Women*, https://www.unwomen.org/en/news/stories/2014/11/ed-speech-spring-forward-for-women-conference.

[2] "Planet 50-50 by 2030. Step It Up for Gender Equality," accessed October 5, 2016, www.unwomen.org/stepitup.

a difficult road to journey that requires active and energetic activities because 2030 is not too far from us.

Keeping this goal of 2030, we do not find it much necessary to talk about gender inequality because "male" and "female" are included in the definition of human rights. However, it is necessary to investigate the issue for the purpose of establishing our own position.

There is not much necessity to design "rights" for women because enough rights are already enshrined in both international and national laws. I would therefore, briefly refer to the discussions and debates initiated at different levels basically within the umbrella of the United Nations, and present the frame of women's rights as human rights so that constructive steps may be made on the basis of the definition of this topic.

Key concepts

In the past, human rights had been conceptualized in a way that did not take account of women's lives and the fact that women routinely faced violence, discrimination, and oppression.[3] Until the middle of the twentieth century, women's rights in public and political life were restricted and few parliamentary democracies recognized women's right to vote. In 1945, when the United Nations was established, more than half of the 51 nations that ratified the Charter still did not allow women to vote or gave them only restricted voting rights.[4] Consequently, women's experiences were, until relatively recently, not adequately addressed by the human rights framework.[5] Therefore, human activists all over the world had been demanding for the recognition of women's rights and better protection of

---

[3] Discrimination is defined as Direct and Indirect discrimination. Direct discrimination occurs when a difference in treatment relies directly and explicitly on distinctions based exclusively on sex and characteristics of men or of women that cannot be justified objectively. Indirect discrimination occurs when a law, policy, or program, does not appear to be discriminatory, but has a discriminatory effect when implemented. This can occur, for example, when women are disadvantaged compared to men with respect to the enjoyment of a particular opportunity or benefit due to pre-existing inequalities. … a gender-neutral law may leave the existing inequality in place, or exacerbate it.

[4] Francoise Gaspard, "Unfinished Battles: Political and Public Life," in *The Circle of Empowerment: Twenty-five Years of the UN Committee on the Elimination of Discrimination Against Women*, ed. Hanna Beate Schöpp-Schilling and Cees Flinterman (New York: Feminist Press, 2007), 145; The percentage of women parliamentarians as of July 2013 is Sub-Saharan Africa (21.3), Americas (24.8), Asia (18.8), Europe (24.4), Middle East and North Africa (15.7), the Pacific (12.8). Cf. Inter-Parliamentary Union's website www.ipu.org.

[5] United Nations, *Women's Rights are Human Rights* (Geneva: United Nations Publications, 2014), 25.

women. The key concept of gender equality covers a wide range of human aspects. Some of them are shown below:

a. *The Public-Private Divide*: Human rights require state agents to respect, protect, and fulfill human rights standards and rules established at the international, regional, and national levels. Historically, this set of rules and the concomitant scrutiny have focused on actions directly attributed to state agents, based on their commission or acquiescence, such as killings, torture, and arbitrary detention. The obligation of the state to respect human rights, including women's rights, referred to the obligation to refrain from doing anything that could violate those rights. Any wrong committed within the private sphere, without any direct intervention by state agents, was not considered a human rights violation. However, since the 1980s and 1990s, the women's rights movement has increasingly criticized this interpretation of human rights as perpetuating violations of women's human rights and stemming from male bias.[6]

b. *Universality of Human Rights:* Since the adoption of the Universal Declaration of Human Rights, states have repeatedly emphasized the universality and individuality of human rights. At the World Conference in Vienna, they specifically recognized that women's human rights are part of universal human rights and they have subsequently reaffirmed this, including at the Fourth World Conference on Women. The universality of human rights and their validity in a given local context have often been contested through relativist discourses that brand them as foreign ideas incompatible with local culture. This calls us to understand that culture is not static but changing and therefore, any oppressive and discriminatory aspect of culture must be challenged while retaining its positive aspects.

c. *Non-Discrimination and Equality between Women and Men:* Non-discrimination and equality between women and men are central principles of human rights law. Both the International Covenant on Civil and Political Rights and the International Covenant on Economic, Social, and Cultural Rights prohibit discrimination on the basis of sex and guarantee women and men equality in the enjoyment of the rights covered by the Covenants.

d. *Equality and Equity:* The Convention on the Elimination of All Forms of Discrimination Against Women (we will discuss this

---

[6] Sheila Dauer, "Indivisible or Invisible: Women's Human Rights in Public and Private Sphere," in *Women, Gender, and Human Rights: A Global Perspective,* ed. Marjorie Agosin (New Brunswick, NJ: Rutgers University Press, 2001), 12.

later) requires that women be accorded rights equal to those of men and that women should be able to enjoy all their rights in practice. While international human rights treaties refer to "equality," in other sectors the term *equity* is often used. The term *gender equity* has been used in a way that perpetuates stereotypes about women's role in society, suggesting that women should be treated "fairly" in accordance with the roles that they carry out.[7] It also refers to the concept that all human beings, regardless of sex, are free to develop their personal abilities, pursue their professional careers, and make choices without the limitations set by stereotypes, rigid gender roles, and prejudices. This understanding risks perpetuating unequal gender relations and solidifying gender stereotypes that are detrimental to women.

e. *Gender:* Gender refers to socially constructed identities, attributes, and roles for women and men. The term *gender* is not interchangeable with women. Society's social and cultural meaning for these biological differences results in hierarchical relationships between women and men, and in the distribution of power and rights favors men and disadvantages women. This social positioning of women and men is affected by political, economic, cultural, social, religious, ideological, and environmental factors, and can be changed by culture, society, and community. This argument is made because gender constructions are dynamic and fluid; they change over time and can be different in different cultures.

GLOBAL COMMITMENTS

Women's rights have been at the heart of a series of international conferences that have produced significant political commitments to women's human rights and equality. The International Women's Year was celebrated at Mexico City in 1975, which resulted in the World Plan of Action and the designation of 1975–1985 as the United Nations Decade for Women. This decade stands significant in our attempt to understand women's rights as human rights. The Convention on the Elimination of All Forms of Discrimination against Women (CEDAW), adopted in 1979 by the UN General Assembly, is often described as an international bill of rights for women. Consisting of a preamble and 30 articles, it defines what constitutes discrimination against women and sets up an agenda for national action to end such discrimination.

---

[7] In development parlance, *equity* is a term commonly used to speak about inequalities on a variety of grounds, not only on gender grounds.

Revisiting Patriarchy from a Human Rights Perspective

The CEDAW defines the right of women to be free from discrimination and sets the core principles to protect this right. It establishes an agenda for national action to end discrimination, and provides the basis for achieving equality between men and women through ensuring women's equal access to, and equal opportunities in, political and public life as well as education, health, and employment. CEDAW is the only human rights treaty that affirms the reproductive rights of women.[8]

Further, the Convention defines discrimination against women as "any distinction, exclusion, or restriction made on the basis of sex which has the effect or purpose of impairing or nullifying the recognition, enjoyment or exercise by women, irrespective of their marital status, on a basis of equality of men and women, of human rights and fundamental freedoms in the political, economic, social, cultural, civil, or any other field."

By accepting the Convention, states commit themselves to undertake a series of measures to end discrimination against women in all forms, including:

- to incorporate the principle of equality of men and women in their legal system, abolish all discriminatory laws, and adopt appropriate ones prohibiting discrimination against women;
- to establish tribunals and other public institutions to ensure the effective protection of women against discrimination; and
- to ensure elimination of all acts of discrimination against women by persons, organizations, or enterprises.

The Convention has been ratified by 180 states, making it one of the most ratified international treaties. State parties to the Convention must submit periodic reports on women's status in their respective countries. CEDAW's Optional Protocol establishes procedures for individual complaints on alleged violations of the Convention by state parties, as well as an inquiry procedure that allows the Committee to conduct inquiries into serious and systematic abuses of women's human rights in countries. So far, the Protocol has been ratified by seventy-one states.[9]

Meanwhile, another international conference on women was held in Copenhagen in 1980 and the CEDAW was opened for signature and most of the member states of the United Nations signed this Convention in 1981. The third World Conference on Women was held in Nairobi, with the Committee on the CEDAW having begun its work in 1982. These three world conferences witnessed extraordinary activism on the part of

---

[8] Nafis Sadik, *The State of World Population 2000* (Geneva: UN Population Fund, 2000), 47–50.
[9] "The Human Rights of Women," *UNFPA*, accessed September 27, 2016, http://www.unfpa.org/resources/human-rights-women#sthash.2HrW9XK1.dpuf//.

women from around the world and laid the groundwork for the world conferences in the 1990s to address women's rights, including the Fourth World Conference on Women held in Beijing in 1995.

The impact of activism of women during the 1980s became significant for the World Conference on Human Rights held in Vienna in 1993. It sought to review the status of the human rights machinery in place at the time. Women's rights activists mobilized to ensure that women's human rights were fully on the agenda of the international community under the rallying cry "Women's Rights are Human Rights."[10] Particularly around the issue of violence against women, civil society activists organized tribunals to put the spotlight on violations of women's rights, previously unaddressed because they were considered part of the private sphere. The struggles of many women at that point of time were successful as they could make the Vienna Declaration and Programme of Action state that "the human rights of women and of the girl-child are an inalienable, integral, and indivisible part of universal human rights,"[11] and strongly endorsed elimination of all forms of gender-based violence.

Beijing Declaration and Platform for Action

The Beijing Conference in 1995 became significant in the struggles of the women for their rights. Its mission statement was very strong as it reads:

1. The Platform for Action is an agenda for women's empowerment. It aims at accelerating the implementation of the Nairobi Forward-looking Strategies for the Advancement of Women and at removing all the obstacles to women's active participation in all spheres of public and private life through a full and equal share in economic, social, cultural, and political decision-making. This means that the principle of shared power and responsibility should be established between women and men at home, in the workplace, and in the wider national and international communities. Equality between women and men is a matter of human rights and a condition for social justice, and is also a necessary and fundamental prerequisite for equality, development, and peace. A transformed partnership based on equality between women and men is a condition for people-centered sustainable development. A sustained and long-term

---

[10] "Women's Rights are Human Rights," is a phrase used in the feminist movement and is the title of a speech given by Hillary Clinton, the First Lady of the United States, on September 5, 1995, at the United Nations Fourth World Conference on Women in Beijing.

[11] Read para 18 of the Vienna Declaration 1993; Also, see "the eradication of any conflicts which may arise between the rights of women and the harmful effect of certain traditional or customary practices, cultural prejudices, and religious extremism" (para 38).

commitment is essential, so that women and men can work together for themselves, for their children, and for society to meet the challenges of the twenty-first century.

2. The Platform for Action reaffirms the fundamental principle set forth in the Vienna Declaration and Programme of Action, adopted by the World Conference on Human Rights, that the human rights of women and of the girl child are an inalienable, integral, and indivisible part of universal human rights. As an agenda for action, the Platform seeks to promote and protect the full enjoyment of all human rights and the fundamental freedoms of all women throughout their life cycle.

3. The Platform for Action emphasizes that women share common concerns that can be addressed only by working together and in partnership with men toward the common goal of gender equality around the world. It respects and values the full diversity of women's situations and conditions and recognizes that some women face particular barriers to their empowerment.

4. The Platform for Action requires immediate and concerted action by all to create a peaceful, just, and humane world based on human rights and fundamental freedoms, including the principle of equality for all people of all ages and from all walks of life, and to this end, recognizes that broad-based and sustained economic growth in the context of sustainable development is necessary to sustain social development and social justice.

5. The success of the Platform for Action will require a strong commitment on the part of governments, international organizations, and institutions at all levels. It will also require adequate mobilization of resources at the national and international levels as well as new and additional resources to the developing countries from all available funding mechanisms, including multilateral, bilateral, and private sources for the advancement of women; financial resources to strengthen the capacity of national, sub-regional, regional, and international institutions; a commitment to equal rights, equal responsibilities, and equal opportunities, and to the equal participation of women and men in all national, regional, and international bodies and policy-making processes; and the establishment or strengthening of mechanisms at all levels for accountability to the world's women.[12]

---

[12] "World Conference on Women, 1995," accessed April 15, 2020, https://en.wikipedia.org/wiki/World_Conference_on_Women,_1995.

Adopted during the Fourth World Conference on Women in September 1995, the Beijing Declaration and Platform focused on 12 areas[13] concerning the implementation of women's human rights and set out an agenda for women's empowerment. It builds on the results of the previous three world conferences on women, but is considered a significant achievement in explicitly articulating women's rights as human rights. The Platform for Action includes a series of strategic objectives to eliminate discrimination against women and achieve equality between women and men. It involves political and legal strategies on a global scale based on a human rights framework. The Platform for Action is the most comprehensive expression of states' commitments to the human rights of women. The Beijing Declaration states, "In a world of continuing instability and violence, the implementation of cooperative approaches to peace and security is urgently needed. The equal access and full participation of women in power structures and their full involvement in all efforts for the prevention and resolution of conflicts are essential for the maintenance and promotion of peace and security. Although women have begun to play an important role in conflict resolution, peace-keeping, and defence and foreign affairs mechanisms, they are still underrepresented in decision-making positions. If women are to play an equal part in securing and maintaining peace, they must be empowered politically and economically and represented adequately at all levels of decision-making."[14] Hillary Clinton in her speech on September 5, 1995, at the World Conference on Women in Beijing stated,

---

[13] The 12 areas are as follows:
- Women and poverty
- Education and training of women
- Women and health
- Violence against women
- Women and armed conflict
- Women and the economy
- Women in power and decision-making
- Institutional mechanism for the advancement of women
- Human rights of women
- Women and the media
- Women and the environment
- The girl-child

See more at: http://www.unwomen.org/en/how-we-work/intergovernmental-support/world-conferences-on-women#sthash.xGrNjkao.dpuf, accessed October 5, 2016.

[14] UN Women, *Beijing Declaration and Platform for Action: Beijing+5 Political Declaration and Outcome* (Geneva: United Nations Publications, 1995, reprinted in 2014), point no. 134; cf. UN Women, *Summary Report: The Beijing Declaration and Platform for Action Turns 20* (New York, March 2015), 36.

- I believe that, on the eve of a new millennium, it is time to break our silence. It is time for us to say here in Beijing, and the world to hear, that it is no longer acceptable to discuss women's rights as separate from human rights . . . . It is a violation of human rights when babies are denied food, or drowned, or suffocated, or their spines broken, simply because they are girls.
- It is a violation of human rights when women and girls are sold into the slavery of prostitution.
- It is a violation of human rights when women are doused with gasoline, set on fire, and burned to death because their marriage dowries are deemed too small.
- It is a violation of human rights when individual women are raped in their own communities and when thousands of women are subjected to rape as a tactic or prize of war.
- It is a violation of human rights when a leading cause of death worldwide among women ages 14 to 44 is the violence they are subjected to in their own homes.
- It is a violation of human rights when young girls are brutalized by the painful and degrading practice of genital mutilation.
- It is a violation of human rights when women are denied the right to plan their own families, and that includes being forced to have abortions or being sterilized against their will.

She concluded with the statement, "If there is one message that echoes forth from this conference, let it be that human rights are women's rights and women's rights are human rights once and for all."[15] With the same tone, Lemmon, while writing the Clinton Doctrine said, "As long as discrimination and inequities remain so commonplace everywhere in the world, as long as girls and women are valued less, fed less, fed last, overworked, underpaid, not schooled, subjected to violence in and outside their homes—the potential of the human family to create a peaceful, prosperous world will not be realized."[16]

Subsequent reviews of the implementation of the Beijing Declaration and Platform for Action have revealed that although significant progress has been made in some areas of women's human rights, "discriminatory legislation as well as harmful traditional and customary practices and negative stereotyping of women and men still persist" particularly in family, civil, penal, labor, and commercial laws or codes, or administrative rules

---

[15] H.R. Clinton, *Statement at the United Nations Fourth World Conference on Women, Beijing, China* (September 5, 1995). See gopher.undp.org/00/unconfs/women/conf/gov/950905175653 (emphasis added), accessed September 30, 2016.

[16] Gayle Tzemach Lemmon, "The Hillary Doctrine," *Newsweek*, June 3, 2011.

and regulations.[17] Both the 2005 and the 2010 reviews of the Platform concluded that total equality had not been achieved in any country in the world and the 2010 review recognized that even where legal reforms had taken place, they were often ineffectively enforced.[18]

We may refer to India's status according to its report on the implementation of the Beijing Declaration and Platform for Action 20 years after the historic World Women's conference in 1995, in which it has admitted that deep rooted gender inequalities continue to undermine the country's potential to translate economic growth into inclusive development.

In the report of the goals set at Beijing under a review process recently, India said the gender-based inequalities, for instance in education, income, and employment, limit the ability to protect women's health. This lack of power of women in most cultural settings also impacts nutritional intake and health status of women and girls. Along with the policy initiatives, a lot needs to be done to realize the policy measures on the ground.[19] However, all these failures are not due to the lack of sufficient laws to ensure equal treatment of women and men in India; we have enough laws to protect women.[20]

---

[17] General Assembly Resolution S-23/3, Annex, Para. 27.
[18] United Nations, *Women's Rights are Human Rights*, 14.
[19] Meena Menon, "Empowering the Perpetrator," *The Hindu*, November 14, 2014.
[20] The laws that are supposed to protect women in India are:
   a. Protection of Women from Domestic Violence Act (2005) is a comprehensive legislation to protect women in India from all forms of domestic violence. It also covers women who have been/are in a relationship with the abuser and are subjected to violence of any kind—physical, sexual, mental, verbal, or emotional.
   b. Immoral Traffic (Prevention) Act (1956) is the premier legislation for prevention of trafficking for commercial sexual exploitation. In other words, it prevents trafficking in women and girls for the purpose of prostitution as an organized means of living.
   c. Indecent Representation of Women (Prohibition) Act (1986) prohibits indecent representation of women through advertisements or in publications, writings, paintings, figures, or in any other manner.
   d. Commission of Sati (Prevention) Act (1987) provides for the more effective prevention of the commission of sati and its glorification on women.
   e. Dowry Prohibition Act (1961) prohibits the giving or taking of dowry at or before or any time after the marriage from women.
   f. Maternity Benefit Act (1961) regulates the employment of women in certain establishments for certain period before and after child-birth and provides for maternity benefit and certain other benefits.
   g. Medical Termination of Pregnancy Act (1971) provides for the termination of certain pregnancies by registered medical practitioners on humanitarian and medical grounds.
   h. Pre-Conception and Pre-Natal Diagnostic Techniques (Prohibition of Sex Selection) Act (1994) prohibits sex selection before or after conception and prevents the misuse of pre-natal diagnostic techniques for sex determination leading to female feticide.
   i. Equal Remuneration Act (1976) provides for payment of equal remuneration to both men and women workers for the same work or work of a similar nature. It also prevents discrimination on the ground of sex, against women in recruitment, and service conditions.
   j. Dissolution of Muslim Marriages Act (1939) grants a Muslim wife the right to seek

MILLENNIUM DEVELOPMENT GOALS

In 2000, the international community agreed to eight time-bound development goals to be achieved by 2015, including a goal on gender equality and the empowerment of women. But, there has not been satisfactory progress because at the most, the visible change is in the elimination of gender disparities in education by 2015. Although it is recognized that girls' access to education is imperative for achieving gender equality, this narrow target is insufficient for measuring progress on achieving gender equality and empowering women.[21]

---

    the dissolution of her marriage.
- k. Muslim Women (Protection of Rights on Divorce) Act (1986) protects the rights of Muslim women who have been divorced by or have obtained divorce from their husbands.
- l. Family Courts Act (1984) provides for the establishment of Family Courts for speedy settlement of family disputes.
- m. Indian Penal Code (1860) contains provisions to protect Indian women from dowry death, rape, kidnapping, cruelty, and other offences.
- n. Code of Criminal Procedure (1973) has certain safeguards for women like obligation of a person to maintain his wife, arrest of woman by female police, and so on.
- o. Indian Christian Marriage Act (1872) contain provisions relating to marriage and divorce among the Christian community.
- p. Legal Services Authorities Act (1987) provides for free legal services to Indian women.
- q. Hindu Marriage Act (1955) introduced monogamy and allowed divorce on certain specified grounds. It provided equal rights to Indian man and woman in respect of marriage and divorce.
- r. Hindu Succession Act (1956) recognizes the right of women to inherit parental property equally with men.
- s. Minimum Wages Act (1948) does not allow discrimination between male and female workers or different minimum wages for them.
- t. Mines Act (1952) and Factories Act (1948) prohibits the employment of women between 7 p.m. to 6 a.m. in mines and factories and provides for their safety and welfare.
- u. The following other legislations also contain certain rights and safeguards for women:
  - i. Employees' State Insurance Act (1948)
  - ii. Plantation Labour Act (1951)
  - iii. Bonded Labour System (Abolition) Act (1976)
  - iv. Legal Practitioners (Women) Act (1923)
  - v. Indian Succession Act (1925)
  - vi. Indian Divorce Act (1869)
  - vii. Parsi Marriage and Divorce Act (1936)
  - viii. Special Marriage Act (1954)
  - ix. Foreign Marriage Act (1969)
  - x. Indian Evidence Act (1872)
  - xi. Hindu Adoptions and Maintenance Act (1956).
- v. National Commission for Women Act (1990) provided for the establishment of a National Commission for Women to study and monitor all matters relating to the constitutional and legal rights and safeguards of women.
- w. Sexual Harassment of Women at Workplace (Prevention, Prohibition and Redressal). Act (2013) provides protection to women from sexual harassment at all workplaces both in public and private sector, whether organized or unorganized.

    See *Women Rights in India*, accessed September 28, 2016, http://edugeneral.org/blog/polity/women-rights-in-india/; see more at http://ncw.nic.in.

[21] United Nations, *Women's Rights are Human Rights*, 15.

Based on the recommendations that emerged from the review process, UN Women is leading multiple initiatives to galvanize urgent action toward the implementation of the Beijing Platform for Action (BPfA). In September 2015, in collaboration with the People's Republic of China, UN Women co-organized a Global Leaders' Meeting on Gender Equality and Women's Empowerment: A Commitment to Action with the participation of heads of states and governments. In the lead-up to the event, UN Women launched a "Planet 50-50 by 2030: Step it Up for Gender Equality" campaign, calling upon governments to make concrete commitments to advance gender equality and women's empowerment in the post-2015 development framework.[22]

The September high-level meeting provided member states with an opportunity to announce their commitments and initiatives. On the margins of this event, UN Women also organized a Global Civil Society Dialogue. Throughout the Beijing+20 commemoration, UN Women has organized and co-hosted a series of global thematic events focusing on the twelve critical areas of concern of the Beijing Platform for Action. The events have been instrumental in bringing together experts, decision-makers, activists, and global leaders to share cutting-edge experience and knowledge on each critical area of concern. UN Women Country and Regional Offices around the world have also actively engaged in this process and organized national and regional events on the critical areas of concern.

Global Fund for Women is another international organization that works for a world where every woman and girl can realize and enjoy her human rights. It supports women's movements to create shifts in power and lift voices for change. It maintains the principle that only when women and girls have full access to their rights—from equal pay and land ownership rights to sexual rights, freedom from violence, access to education, and maternal health rights—will true equality exist. Only when women have taken leadership and peacemaking roles and have an equal political voice will economies and countries be transformed. And only then will all women and girls have the self-determination that they are entitled to.[23]

Concluding remarks

The efforts being made by the women leaders at the global level have been greatly recognized, and the results of their struggles so far have also been

---

[22] That was the same time that United Nations held the World Conference on Sustainable Development.

[23] *Women's Human Rights*, accessed October 4, 2016, https://www.globalfundforwomen.org/womens-human-rights.

encouraging. They have a great and realistic dream and every person is called to participate to help realize their dream; a genuine call! We are made to realize many things and respond to the call with much sincere effort at any time, in any place. With all these, we need to keep in mind a few important things.

1. The present dynamic global leaders will be in office for a limited term, however, the platform created by them must continuously encourage us all until every human being realizes that dream.
2. There are people (women and men) who refuse to give in to the initiatives taken at the global level. For, they prefer to run their own society according to their own set of rules. It must be noted that there are sharp critiques and also criticisms on women human rights movements.[24]
3. The issue is not an issue of half of humanity but of the whole humanity. However, while male members are called to develop a political will, the female members are called to double up their efforts and convince their counterparts not by words, but by actions.
4. The issue is not simply to be decided by an individual but an issue that requires a fight against the social construct. We need to avoid traditional ways of doing things become much more innovative, creative, and see that development that cares for all of humanity is designed by us; academic excellence is produced by us, and creative social transformation is initiated by us. Otherwise, when we are not capable of showing people our achievements, we will not be able to convince them to accept our viewpoints.
5. We must work very hard to critique the existing tribal culture that refuses to share responsibility with women, especially in social and political undertakings. I say this because the core issue of refusal to share equal responsibility does not lie in the Christian church but more on the socio-cultural system. This will be changed when the rights of women are properly respected and endorsed by the social and political organizations.
6. Another important matter we need to seriously take up is to actively follow the global debate or international events and statements/declarations and systematically and consistently localize them to the local context so that we will be able to make impact of global concern to the local people and help them reshape their worldview. We may decide to intensify our commitment and work toward 2030 to see great change among the tribal communities.

---

[24] Read Annelise Riles, "Rights Inside Out: The Case of the Women's Human Rights Campaign," *Cornell Law Faculty Publications,* Paper 1035, http://scholarship.law.cornell.edu/facpub/1035.

8

QUEST FOR POWER NARRATIVE ON GENDER ISSUE: STRATEGIZING FEMINIST METHODOLOGY

INTRODUCTION

> In 2018, men of all ages and all across the country, married or single, educated or not, are far more feminist than ever before. This needs to be acknowledged. The struggle to transform our institutions, our politics, and our culture will succeed much faster if more men join the fight. But if you want an ally, you have to at least acknowledge they're on your team, not your rival.[1]

During the last 50 plus years, feminist theology has been one of the most interesting theological debates initiated by comprehensive ideology, rooted in women's experience of sexual oppression, that engages in a critique of patriarchy, embraces an alternative vision for humanity and the earth, and actively seeks to bring this vision to realization.[2] In each wave of feminism, movements have been shaped to best reflect the grievances and struggles of the present time. The first wave took hold in the nineteenth and early twentieth centuries, focusing on the fight for equal voting rights: focused on vote, then property and education. In 1919, women gained the right to vote, and the suffrage movement[3] largely got diffused. During the 1960s, the class distinction in capitalism was modelled into a "sex" issue and the second wave of feminism took hold, advocating equality between

---

[1] Scott Gilmore, "Want Men to Support Feminism? Stop Treating Them as the Problem," i *Maclean's Newsletter* (February 2018): 2.
[2] Sandra Schneiders, *Beyond Patching: Faith and Feminism in the Catholic Church* (New York: Paulist, 1991), 15.
[3] The suffragist movement fought for these rights, and the people who were part of that movement were suffragists. The word suffrage means the right to vote in elections.

men and women, and the end of damaging patriarchal systems that dominated nearly all corners of society. This wave gained momentum in the idea of "women's liberation," which took on a conservative form of feminism and focused on defining gender roles and empowering the female voice in a male-led society.[4] But what followed was, after that stage of feeling liberated, "We're told Betty Friedan and Gloria Steinem liberated us, but American women still spend $7 billion a year on cosmetics. Women had more than 10 million surgical and nonsurgical cosmetic procedures in 2013;[5] the definition of beauty and dress code could not be changed." The second-wave feminism was able to motivate many young women to dedicate work toward empowering women but after achieving a lot of progress, most of them refused to identify themselves as "feminist." I am referring to Katy Perry, Billboard's Woman of the year (2012) and Salma Hayek[6] as examples. Radical feminism was challenged in the 1990s by a third wave of feminists, who championed a more diverse and inclusive approach to what it means to be a woman. Today, mainstream feminism seeks to break away from the limitations of the second wave, as well as stereotypes that are sometimes encouraged and perpetuated by smaller "RadFem" organizations and movements that are still in existence.

Today, a lot of women and some men, will say, "I'm not a feminist, but...," and then go on to add that they hold certain beliefs about women's equality and traditional gender roles that actually fall into a feminist framework. The reluctance to self-identify as feminists underscores the negative image that feminists and feminism have, or that the actual meaning of feminism may be unclear.

---

[4] See "Women's Liberation Movement—A History of the Name," accessed September 14, 2018, http://womenshistory.about.com/od/feminism-second-wave/a/Womens-Liberation.htm.

[5] Brianna McGurran, "The Bitter Pill: How Second-Wave Feminism Failed, and Why It Doesn't Matter," 2014, accessed August 28, 2018, https://academicworks.cuny.edu/cgi/viewcontent.cgi? article=1009&context=gj_etds.

[6] In 2013, Salma Hayek Pinault co-founded *Chime for Change* with singer Beyonce and international fashion powerhouse Gucci. The campaign supports nongovernmental agencies with the mission of empowering women and girls around the world through initiatives focused on education, health, and justice.

Chime for Change has so far raised $7.3 million with 153 non-profit partners to fund projects in 88 countries, benefiting 400,000 women and girls. "All the issues with poverty affect women double," Hayek says. "When it comes to access to education, it's always going to be the boys who have the few chances." "This is her heart" and "she is truly passionate about the rights of women and young girls," says Caryl Stern, president of the US Fund for UNICEF, and an advisory board member for *Chime for Change*. Accessed October 6, 2015, http//variety.com/2015/film/news/salma-hayek-pinault-nonprofit-chime-for-change-beyonce-1201610707/.

Feminism and sexism are generally two sides of the same coin. Feminism refers to the belief that women and men should have equal opportunities in economic, political, and social life, while sexism refers to a belief in traditional gender role stereotypes and in the inherent inequality between men and women. With this, what is important for us to further note is that while we acknowledge and endorse strong feminist principles, we still need to identify certain weaknesses in feminism, especially radical feminism, and strategize our approach to make it real and meaningful.

Let us first differentiate between feminist theology and Christian theology before any further discussion. Christian theology is exclusively for the Christians but feminist theology is for all women without religious and racial borders. Although the patriarchal system is found in the Bible and in Christianity, and although it is several Christian women who had initially taken initiatives toward gender equality, Christianity cannot claim credit for launching the gender equality movement for it has a wider perspective and greater vision to emancipate women across faiths. Therefore, it is not quite appropriate to place feminist concern within the frame of Christian theology. Christian feminist thinking can only serve as one of the perspectives of feminist thinking.

A FEW GENERAL OBSERVATIONS

In the initial undertaking of feminism, there has been a linguistic misconception that God could be fully expressed and explained by human language with gender reference. With this assumption, many have believed that "He" or "She" matters much to believe in the God who is divine, and this was applied as the theological framework to redefine humanity without realizing that God is beyond human language and all these "pronouns" have little importance to define and express the divine. Gender biased language has not helped us to perceive God in a better way.

While trying to critique patriarchy, Radical Feminism (RadFem) intends to create matriarchy that has an equal amount of wrong like that of patriarchy. The radical feminists' interest in terminological debate has led to a rewriting of the Bible called *The Woman's Bible*[7] and established

---

[7] *The Woman's Bible* is a two-part non-fiction book, written by Elizabeth Cady Stanton and a committee of 26 women, published in 1895 and 1898 to challenge the traditional position of religious orthodoxy that woman should be subservient to man. By producing the book, Stanton wished to promote a radical liberating theology, one that stressed self-development. The book attracted a great deal of controversy and antagonism at the time of its introduction. Many women's rights activists who worked with Stanton were opposed to the publication of *The Woman's Bible*; they felt it would harm the drive for women's suffrage. The biblical scholars did not even accept it as a major work.

the Women-Church movement.[8] However, the enthusiasm is almost lost today because God cannot be understood from a gender-biased approach. Not many people prefer to read and follow the *Woman's Bible* nor do many people participate in the Women-Church movement and their worship. Initially, they envisioned establishing a beautiful world where women would find full leadership and enjoy full freedom; and in that world, male members are not required. The basic problem was that the Radfems took extreme positions even to the extent of exaggerative blame on men. Perhaps the most damaging position of the RadFems is the view that all problems are literally *man*-made, and that men should not enter the world of feminism as they are bound to always be the problem. The emphasis on the "sisterhood" being the only legitimate voice in the fight for equality actually eliminates any hope for equality, as it does not allow for ally-ship and collaboration with males for positive change. The Radfems Conference 2013 has this to say:

> Man's damage to the environment is irreparably destroying our chance and our children and our children's children of a patriarchal-free future. It is male violence and greed, which is causing this long-term irreversible damage. Increasing numbers of women are being badly affected by climate change. They are trapped, unable to flee from floods/droughts, and are climate migrants trapped in poverty and dependent on male protection and approval.[9]

---

[8] Women-church is a movement of autonomous groups seeking to actualize "a discipleship of equals." Cf. Mary E. Hunt, "Women-Church: Feminist Concept, Religious Commitment, Women's Movement," *Journal of Feminist Studies in Religion*, 25, no. 1(Spring 2009): 85–98; cf. Rosemary Radford Ruether, *Women—Church: Theology and Practice of Feminist Liturgical Communities* (San Franscisco: Harper & Row, 1985); Elizabeth Schüsler Fiorenza; *Disciples of Equals: A Critical Feminist Ekklēsia-logy of Liberation* (London: SCM Press, 1993). Women-church is a feminist concept that arose in a Catholic context but has since spread well beyond it. From the late 1950s, when Swedish Lutheran women were ordained to the priesthood, to the mid-1970s, when Episcopal women in the United States were ordained, Catholic women named the injustice of being prohibited from ordination and vowed to right it. Their efforts, initiated by Mary B. Lynch in the United States, resulted in a conference in 1975 in Detroit, Michigan, "Women in Future Priesthood Now—A Call for Action." In that conference, Elisabeth Schüsler Fiorenza called for a "New Christian Sisterhood" (fore-shadowing women-church, perhaps) that would unite women, especially those in religious congregations and those who do not belong to such groups (what later became known as the nun-woman/laywoman split). See also, Miriam Therese Winter, "The Women-Church Movement" at https://www.religion-online.org/article/the-women-church-movement/. I am talking about those versions of the Bible for women but that the claim to use feminine gender to refer to God.

[9] "Sisters Tackling Climate Change and Male Destruction of the Environment," presented at the *RADFEM 2013*, accessed September 3, 2018, https://bugbrennan.files.wordpress.com/2013/03/rf2013-programme.pdf.

Radical women vehemently opposed the liberal feminists' demand for equal rights for women and their strategy of incremental change. The liberals were working through the bureaucracy with a hierarchically structured feminist organization, attempting to bring about change through reform and legal amendments. However, radicals did not believe that changing the legal structure or organizational reforms would have shifted the balance of power between men and women.[10]

Even though the concern is not limited to radical feminists, I see a problem in making Feminist theology as an academic discipline in which the system requires memory and not intelligence; a failure to make an impact on the life of the people. It will only be a source for scholarship at a higher level and fail to impress the attitude of the public. Today, while we take feminist concern seriously, we are faced with the difficulty of taking the matter to the grassroots because our knowledge on feminism is too ideological and academic.

While radical feminists are appreciated for their firm stand against the practice that commodify women's body into prostitution and pornography, they have been heavily criticized for their stance on transgender men and women. While not all RadFems today exclude the fight for transgender rights, a select group, often referred to as the TERFs, or Trans-Exclusionary Radical Feminists, have gone so far as to fight for the exclusion of trans-health care and deny recognition of trans-people as deserving of equal rights.[11] In the article "What is a Woman?" in *The New Yorker*, Michelle Goldberg identifies the radical feminist view of gender as "less an identity than a caste position," in which male-to-female trans-people are seen as inherently male, and not entitled to being "female" because they do not embody the essence of the female gender struggle.[12] In addition, a male "seizing" the title of female is seen as an exercise of patriarchy in itself. In the case of trans-female-to-male, the trans-people are seen as traitors to the female sex by abandoning the struggle against patriarchy and, instead, becoming a part of it.[13] The fight to define gender as something biologically determined is surprisingly conservative, and seems to be somewhat counter-productive in ending gender stereotyping.

There are two other minor issues that need to be underlined: First, radical feminism looked at women as one homogeneous group and recognized them to be oppressed by men; this gave the movement a universal

---

[10] Rosemarie Tong, *Feminist Thought: A More Comprehensive Introduction* 3e (Philadelphia, PA: Westview Press, 2009), 191.
[11] "The TERFs," accessed August 17, 2018, http://theterfs.com/.
[12] Michelle Goldberg. "What is a Woman?—The Dispute Between Radical Feminism and Transgenderism," *The New Yorker*, July 28, 2014: 2, accessed August 17, 2018, http://www.newyorker.com/magazine/2014.
[13] Goldberg, "The Dispute," 3.

vision. This is why black women's involvement in the movement was obscured by racism and elitism. Black women have withdrawn from the movement and did not participate just as they did not participate in the liberal feminist movement. They found themselves to be at odds with the radical propositions of putting gender as the primary oppression factor, asserting the universality of sexism oppression, and seeking independence from men since they saw themselves as already having achieved self-sufficiency. They wanted to include the issue of racism with the issue of sexism due to their experience since they have been treated and perceived as something other than women from their experience in the civil rights movement. This perspective made them unwelcome in the radical feminist movement and unable to find their place in these movements.[14] Therefore, Spelman argues that feminism in the West was offensive to black women by putting white, middle class women's issues first and not being inclusive of black women. Therefore, the negative points in radical feminism are class blindness, color-blindness, and heterosexuals. Second, its anti-male stance made it lose out on many women, particularly women of color from poor working classes who were not ready to antagonize men. There are differences in the way women read oppression, and not many women see the primary oppression to be on gender lines. However, we should not misunderstand that today, many women are talking about multicultural feminism in the postmodern and third-wave feminism that includes black women as well. This is especially brought out by the book *Colonize This! Young Women of Color on Today's Feminism* by Daisy Hernandez and Bushra Rehman.

A FEW ISSUES OF DEFINITION

The office and ministry that are considered as soft avenues are being targeted for implementing equal employment opportunities but hard jobs are never sought. Pastoring a church, teaching in Christian school/college, being a church administrator, a parliamentarian, legislator, etc., are often mentioned in arguing for equal gender participation, but women in India have never mentioned that they should form half the size of the Indian defence sector for which one has to undergo arduous training and move around the borders to guard the nation day and night. At the same time, if we talk of equality in terms of numbers, we have about 4.8 million security forces of which men constitute about 89 percent, and so the need is to employ nearly 4.2 million women to ensure gender equality. At the same time, the world today is facing a serious threat from terrorism and there is a need to defend innocent civilians by guarding and patrolling day and night in both plains and hilly terrains. How far are women prepared for

---

[14] Tong, *Feminist Thought*, 213.

such work and why are they not claiming equality in formation of army if there is a need for equal participation to run a society/nation? In the world of production, we have millions of jobs in industries and factories, but who is claiming gender equality in those sectors? As the world realizes the importance of surface connectivity for both market and warfare, there is a lot of road construction work being carried out, and as of today, the workforce is dominantly occupied by men, but why are women silent to claim gender equality in that sector as well?

We all know the issues raised by current feminists that women are paid less than men, and social norms reinforce certain stereotypes like dolls for girls and cars for boys that translate the matter into inequality in life choices, leading to women being under-represented in many high level jobs, especially in certain sectors like finance, technology, etc. Most mainstream feminists propose measures such as quotas or fighting the gender stereotypes prevalent throughout society. But, what if they were not radical enough? One clear area of disappointment is that feminists seldom question what society defines as "high level" or "important" jobs and "worthless" jobs. Why should we have more respect (and more pay) for a CEO than for a nurse?[15]

For instance, a man and woman do different jobs in order to sustain life. Their works are equally important because both of them will not survive if only one job is done. But what happens is, if one could rightfully claim to have more merit than the other, then the task that person has carried out suddenly becomes more attractive since it gives you more "rights" and everyone wants to do that task without realizing that high status and high paying jobs come in short supply. Not all educated persons can become CEOs, and so, even if we decide to educate all our children in the best business/engineering schools, most of them will end up in lower paid jobs. Therefore, what is important for us to understand in relation with gender is that there are jobs that people would want to do, and there are the jobs that are in demand. So, all jobs and status should not be read from the gender perspective. Women deserve to be respected as much as men do. The problem with modern feminism is that it suggests that to be respected, women have to be more like men.[16]

---

[15] Martin Schmalzried, "The Problem with Feminism: It's Not Radical Enough," accessed December 11, 2017, https://medium.com/@marma.developer/the-problem-with-feminism-its-not-radical-enough-dad387a11d24.

[16] Laura Furster, "The Problem with Feminism: It's a Flawed Construct that should be replaced by Gender Equality," *The Hamilton Spectator* (September 13, 2017): 3.

PERSPECTIVE

Previous generations of feminists were willing to die in the trenches for getting women the right to vote, to go to college, to have an equal education, for protection from domestic violence, and workplace discrimination, and equal pay, and fair divorce laws. Because of such challenges, we see today a much different reality as many women have attained a much better position in many places. Present-day women have created a better and more realistic history and a shift in perspective and effort toward total emancipation of women, thus making the dream alive.

For Mark Manson, tribal feminists today are more interested in enforcing thoughts and perceptions about women, rather than actually becoming the women they wish others to see. You want more women in math and science? *Be a woman who pursues math and science.* You want more women as CEOs and winning at business? *Start a business.* You want more women in politics? *Run for office.* These are the real activists. This is where real progress happens.[17]

If we look at the definition of feminism, we find that it refers to a range of political movements, ideologies, and social movements that share a common goal: to define, establish, and achieve political, economic, personal, and social equality of sexes. At this point, what is to be noted is that in the first and second waves, feminism had worked hard toward this goal but modern feminism seems to have narrowed down its goal to some aspects of sexual equality. There are many things that should be done without gender priority. For instance, we say that women's participation in politics is less but when it is election time, no woman comes forward to file nomination papers. Instead, they go around seeking permission from men whether they can file nomination; they have not tried to develop a strategy to organize women for political campaign and when one or two women try to come into the picture, they expect men to campaign for them. If we want to understand women's empowerment, we need to listen to the history and story that the Rwanda women are telling. They have shown the example of success that has not happened with any women group in any part of the world. What Pro-Femmes or Twese Hamwe has done was not just a story of talking and writing, it was not simply organizing programs but they have gone much beyond that and developed a real action plan. The achievement made by women's forum has become very significant in the lives of the people. They have fought and achieved political space in the national parliament; they have been able to pressurize law makers to make laws to protect women; they have trained enough women

---

[17] Mark Manson, "What's the Problem with Feminism?," accessed June 22, 2017, 3–4, http://markmanson.net//whats-the-problem-with-feminism/.

personnel in the legal section to fight against forces of violation. They are proving that they do not simply speak and make claims but have made the nation realize that they are capable of making policies for a nation to bring welfare to all citizens.[18] A time has come for women's movements to get into politics and challenge the existing system because there is a great chance to win the fight. Women have the necessary number of votes to choose their political leaders: Who can stop them if they are able to develop an approach with a combined voice?

Double standards in approach

In the feminist approach, there has always been a double standard element. For instance, what is exclusively for women should be preserved and also claimed from what is traditionally perceived as total humanity. Reservation for women is never questioned. Higher amount in government scholarship to women students is never questioned by them even if they know that it is a gender bias toward women.

Both in secular and religious contexts, women members have been self-centered and exclusive that is portrayed through women's movements,

---

[18] "Rwanda's Path to Gender Equity," See https://bpr.berkeley.edu/2017/10/18/rwandas-path-to-gender-equity/; (Pro-Femmes or Twese Hamwe is a national women's organization in Rwanda founded in 1992, that is recognized internationally for its contributions to rebuilding society after the 1994 Rwandan genocide. These women took on the role of reconstructing what had been damaged. In order to restore Rwanda, the women created projects to improve the economy, establish peace, and offer new opportunities. The 13 women who started this organization were determined to speak out against injustices, especially against women, so they became a voice for change. The genocide incident caused great destruction; however, since 1994 the organization has grown to include 58 member associations. These women work hard to bring about changes and help the minorities grow and develop.

The purpose of the organization is not only about the Rwanda genocide, even though that is when it had its greatest impact, it was created to enhance women activity and provide recognition in favor of women. Due to all of the discrimination women were facing back in the early 1990s, this was an effective way to put up fight. Because of this organization, "Rwanda is amongst the best countries in the world in terms of women representation." Working with women was not enough to help society as a whole, therefore, they ensured all human rights were being met so that there was no social injustice. Their achievements include "peacekeeping, conflict management, mediation, and reconciliation that empower women in leadership roles." In addition, they were involved in helping soldiers, prisoners, and fighting any discrimination within the people. Pro-Femmes received the 1996 UNESCO-Madanjeet Singh Prize for the promotion of tolerance and non-violence "for their outstanding contributions in rehabilitating families and communities devastated by mass violence, through their activities fostering a climate of peace based on tolerance and non-violence." They received the inaugural Gruber Prize for Women's Rights in 2003.

women's society in the church, women's fellowship in the localities, and work places to exclude men in the making of their own space and leadership. If they really want gender equality, they should first think even to forfeit some traditional patterns and privileges that do not promote gender equality. However, one should be clear about the truth that there are possible ways to understand this fact: (1) It could be a method adopted to empower women; (2) if not, it could be a sign of frustration for being denied of leadership and power in the church and society. Thus, the question is: Why are women unable to critique the structure of the Christian church in which women are set aside to run "women's department" so that they do not disturb the main structure that is dominated by men? Why are they happy to participate in fund raising for celebration events or for the purpose of church building construction while they are not given the privilege to utilize the money they raised? Is it not possible for them to read that this model/structure in the church and society has been adopted in order to silence the claim for more women's participation in decision-making? And also, that it does not serve as a means to empower women but turns out to be a quota (in the Christian church) beyond which women should not ask for.

Do we really feel the need of gender implication to the ministry of the church that intends to serve all humanity? We are fully aware that the existing Christian church is dominated by male hegemony but to counter that structure by establishing a "women's church" is a radical theological undertaking that has not provided an answer to the search to serve God.

Perhaps, the initial vision of "total emancipation" was redefined as "equal gender participation" in the ministry of the church and society without defining the term *equality*. The concept of gender equality in terms of number has created further confusion that has threatened the mind-set of the male leaders, that in order to fulfill the claim, they need to appoint women equal to the number of male employees. But, what feminists actually want is not to deny capable persons on the basis of gender but to provide equal opportunity to all.

One of the issues I want the readers to consider is that while talking of equality, we do not need to make claims for a double share. While women are bonafide members of the church that is established for everyone, why should there be claim for a women's department; a semi-church? Doing this simply fragments the church by arranging women's worship beyond and besides general church programs. Thus, we need to properly redefine "gender equality" without referring to the number of representations.

Women's empowerment

Women's empowerment is an important concern until total emancipation is achieved. But my question is: What should we do in order to empower women? For example, because of the painful experiences of victimizing women in the forms of rape, domestic violence, abortion, etc., the government of India has come up with many stringent laws. We have also seen a lot of resources invested in the programs for empowering women. These are the results of the work of women who over the years had constantly pursued the goal, by organizing women groups and articulating on the issues of gender problems. But, the ground reality has not improved in the country. As per the report of Annie Gowen, Bureau Chief in *The Washington Post* on June 27, 2018, India is ranked as the most dangerous place for women.[19] My assessment is that perhaps they have been adopting a wrong approach to the problem. The victims cannot decide the fate of the accused. Therefore, if at all we want to improve the situation of women in our society/country, we should invest more available resources on men. The problem is not with the women but it is with men, therefore we only need to educate and empower them without which improvement in the lives of women cannot be expected. Should we even think of organizing seminars and workshops for those street boys who hold no job but only create problems for women?

Women-ordained ministry

Statistics tells us that there is a good increase in the number of women ordained ministers (at least in the Baptist experience in Nort East India). I expect that more numbers will follow in the near future. However, this fact is a result of a long debate and negotiation with the church administration and we should not take it for granted and think that we have won the war and accomplished our mission. We need to do constant follow-up in order to rectify the patriarchal mentality of the Christians. Even after experiencing this level of reality (ordaining), I still have a lot of doubts about the attitude of the Baptist churches. There is an unexpressed hesitation over this fact. The attitude seems to be "because they keep asking for

---

[19] This report is based on the Thomson Reuters Foundation—the philanthropic arm of Reuters media company—that released a study that ranked India as the most dangerous place because of its high incidences of sexual violence, lack of access to justice in rape cases, child marriage, female feticide, and human trafficking. "India has shown utter disregard and disrespect for women ... rape, marital rapes, sexual assault, and harassment, female infanticide has gone unabated," Manjunath Gangadhara, an official in the southern state of Karnataka, told Thomson Reuters. See https://www.washingtonpost.com/news/worldviews/wp/2018/06/27/india-ranked-worlds-most-dangerous-place-for-women-reigniting-debate-about-womens-safety.

it, we are ordaining them with reservation." Giving ordination to a woman with hesitance (her ordination is only for institutional ministry but her service will not be used in the church) will not bring total emancipation of women in the church and society. This attitude creates negative impact toward the ministry of ordained ministers in general, resulting in their facing more difficulty to make impact on the general populace. For example, even after so many decades, they have not been given enough space to minister; I have not heard and seen any ordained woman solemnizing a wedding in any church. This enables us to read and evaluate the attitude of the Christians as to why their office is not yet accepted. Therefore, my question is: For what are such Christian ministerial permissions given if they are not to be fully accepted and used by the church?

While the demand has become constant, important, and challenging, we should be very careful that failure on the part of the ordained ministers is a serious threat to the future programs. If we fail in ministry, then the door for others will be shut.

With all these, we may now note that starting from the first wave to the third wave of feminism, we can observe two things: (1) It criticizes patriarchy because that is the source of all oppressions and discriminations; and (2) It calls for help and support with the longing to achieve gender equality. To me, this is a grievance narrative that not many people are interested to listen to; a victim mentality does not help anybody. Therefore, we should now call for ideological departure from the present and develop new methodology by adopting a power narrative that is in a way calling for the fourth wave.

Strategizing feminist methodology

The first thing we need to address is the definition of feminism and to redefine feminism not as women doing theology with the support of men but as a human endeavor; a theological outlook of total humanity. A time has come for us to question the implication of the words "help," "support," "cooperation," etc., that are available, provided that man remains as the driver/controller and women as passengers; we may even refer to what Bina Agarwal compares with the "Ladies Compartment" in a long train where women find complete safety, freedom, leadership, etc., but do not know where they are heading to because the driver of the train is a man.

Power narrative

One reality we need to seriously underline is that in our search for women's emancipation, we often experience women calling us "to help" or "to cooperate," and I am confidently writing now that we have not failed to heed their call. Many men have positively responded to women's call to read the Bible together and articulate theology together while many others refuse to be part of the struggle. This is the point I intend to note. If it is a "request," anyone can say no because he owns the decision; the choice to say yes or no is his. So, in order to address this problem, I am proposing the Power Narrative in doing feminist theology because in this approach, we do not talk about "option," but rather "participation." We will have to explain identity, ministry, and achievements, and vision, and invite everyone that their turn has come to fully and positively participate in this endeavor to achieve this vision of humanity. There should be a positive force behind the invitation so that we do not provide the option to say no.

The report of a study in Canada gives us a clear picture of this: for example, 75 percent of men believe their partner's career is as important as or is more important than their own; 87 percent either didn't care or preferred their boss was a woman; 79 percent believed in equal rights for women. While 57 percent were raised to think "being physically tough" is what it meant to be a man, 64 percent now believe "being fair" is more important.[20] We have the capability to bring about a much better picture than this report found. We only need to straighten our approach.

Passivity

If we decide to adopt the Power Narrative approach, then female passivity needs to be seriously and deeply questioned. If our dream is gender equality and our claim is equal recognition, then there should be no room for passivity. Our dream and our mental and practical efforts should not remain in contradiction; because, if they are so, people will not believe what we want to achieve. Women and men are intellectually competitive; they are equal in creativity but often women hesitate to show their capacity or make it available only when pressure is given. My 30 years of teaching in the classroom tell me that things are not right. Generally speaking, while women can do much better in individual or small group discussion/debate, they tend to remain silent in the class discussions. Another related issue is that very often, they are not serious enough. We seldom see women sitting together and seriously deliberating on some important contemporary issues, because they have not had the opportunity to develop the habit of critique or they prefer to have light conversations any time they get a chance to be together. Is this a biological product or mental product? And if it is a mental product, it can be easily changed.

As a part of our attempt to strategize feminist theological thinking, I think that we do not need to teach feminist theology for academic exercise

[20] Gilmore, "Want Men to Support Feminism?," 4.

alone but rather the goal should be to talk/debate and learn to change the attitude of women that would enable them to fully realize their creativity and ability so that they can overcome their own unreasonable passivity. Women have struggled for long and therefore, the time has come for men to listen and hear the cries of the victims of patriarchal system. But, this claim should not be without a question of whether women are psychologically/physically prepared to shoulder social responsibility and face the challenges of the time? We need to consider one of the sharp remarks made on feminism, "Lots of feminist theology is in print but less of it is in action."[21] Feminist issues should not be confined to academic deliberations alone, but they should be taken up as a theological initiative to break the traditional imagination.

CULTURAL EXEGESIS

Exegesis is a term normally applied in biblical studies. Although we know what exegesis is and we are well versed with what the Bible says, human life is not lived exclusively based on the Bible. We need culture in order to define life and identity, and cultural binding has much to do with our personality shaping.

The feminist theological investigation has not done enough to locate the context of cultural formation and explain how every cultural element is formulated by the people at certain periods of time. However, no culture is rigid and every culture evolves with time. Therefore, if there is a need to reformulate and redefine people's culture, it is the people themselves who can do it.

Many people think that their culture and customary laws are golden rules; nothing can be done to them. Their protection goes almost to the extent of admitting that people are created for culture, but not culture for the welfare of the people. I say this because there are instances where people have stood in favor of customary laws even if it causes harm and discriminates half the population of about 49 percent comprised by women.

As a part of the project Jaagore-Push the Pins that initiates debate on the issue of safety of women in India, Manju Mohandas reports that as women constitute 49 percent of India's registered voters, the Power of 49 together needs to demand a tougher India, yet, an India that is sensitive to women. "Women's issues need to be pushed in every lobby until the leaders have no choice but to yield and take a hold on the crisis that looms across every street and every corner of India today... This is the time we own up to ourselves. We stand by each other. Tall and proud. Brave and

---

[21] Hunt, "Women-Church," 88.

unfazed. This is the time we own up to India. No more harassment. We want what we deserve—for us and for our daughters—a safer India for women."²²

In this connection, let me refer to another report that says, "right now, make no mistake about it, we need something that forms the foundation of a safe society: a functioning law-and-order system. No amount of soul searching, cultural self-flagellation, sex education, local activism, and behavioral conditioning will succeed unless our streets are well-policed and our courts function with speed and efficiency." Ravi Pratap continues,

> And this is exactly why I am afraid India will remain an unsafe country for women for the foreseeable future. Now I know this is not the message that many campaigners for women's safety want to hear. Many of them are optimistic that some kind of governmental or non-governmental campaigning will make India safer. But, as long these campaigns are divorced from a substantial overhaul of law and order mechanisms, they will not work.²³

As I have earlier mentioned, doing feminist theology should not be left to women alone; it is an endeavor of the total humanity and when men do the debate, write books, lead the movement, advocate the cause etc., they should not be termed as feminists but "pro-woman" so that they are made more comfortable in their involvement.

Thus, in our undertaking, occupying the office of pastor, teacher, ordained minister, legislature, parliamentarian, etc., is not the first priority. On the part of the women, the attitude to work and ministry should be like that of Sangeeta Talwar, CEO of Nestlé, the woman behind Maggi's 2-minute revolution. She says that she realized much later that she was the first woman executive, as she was so busy understanding what the job was and what she was required to do. She didn't really focus on the fact that she was the only woman executive in Nestlé. She further states, "It may be an unpopular thing to say, but the point is you are there to do a job. Your gender follows. You just happen in that job."²⁴

Work responsibilities are not to be executed on the basis of gender. For instance, the profession of pastor, teacher, or ordained minister, is not to be considered as a soft avenue or an easy job. They are difficult jobs that require 100 percent commitment and effort. Each of them is a job that projects the Fifth Gospel. Therefore, I do not suggest that vacant posts in

---

[22] Manju Mohandas, "Jaagore—Push The Pin," accessed September 4, 2018, https://www.jaagore.com/power-of-49/womens-safety-in-india-a-crumbling-illusion.

[23] An answer by Ravi Pratap of Wynberg Allen School, Mussoorie to the question, "Why is India Unsafe for Girls?" https://www.quora.com/Why-is-India-unsafe-for-girls#.

[24] "Success Story," *Assam Tribune@Campus* (Dibrugarh), August 13, 2018, 1.

these offices should be filled on gender terms. Rather, commitment, accountability, and efficiency should serve as criteria to join the ministry. Selection for leadership based on gender is a wrong practice.

Conclusion

In this chapter, I have critiqued the ideological framework we have so far followed in doing feminist theology. This requires evaluating paradigm shifts in due course of history but instead of a detailed study, I have adopted a random method to put the discussion into perspective. It is important to see the historical factors and basis in the development of the waves until the stage of postmodern thinking. However, I have chosen to focus on methodological issues such as over-dependence on Marxist ideology to deconstruct patriarchy on the principle of destroying the owning class for the sake of the working class; Second, after a long debate feminism seems to remain incapable of changing the passive attitude of both men and women and has made feminist theology an examination/academic oriented undertaking; Third, an attempt has been made to redirect its approach from focusing on women's issues being wrestled by women themselves to making it a male issue because the real cause of women's problems lie in the governance of the men.

Whether we call it the fourth wave in feminism or not, the fact is that we cannot expect success and achievement of the desired goal unless this concern becomes a concern of every one. Our methodology does not need to be feminist but pro-women where active role is taken by men for the total emancipation of women.

9

METHODS AND VALUES OF PEACEBUILDING: A CONTRIBUTION OF TANGKHUL WOMEN

INTRODUCTION

The reason why there has been chaos and restlessness in the tribal areas for a long time is probably because they have not been able to apply traditional methods of peacebuilding and derive the desired values contained in them. The tribal people are never short of methods and means to restore peace, provided they are culturally oriented and respect its directive. Their experiences of military attempt, religious attempt, and that of civil societies have not given them a desired condition of peaceful living except a temporary reduction of violence. It may not be because they do not have tools, but that they fall short of integrating the cultural and traditional mindset of the people. It does not mean that peace efforts have to be carried out by traditional people, but all individuals, civil society, religious groups, and other organizations have to give integrated effort to the cause so as to bring about the desired changes in the region.

Peace is a value that cannot be borrowed or imported from someone and from somewhere. To a certain extent, other methods may be applicable, but the process has to be at the local level by the local people and for the local people. The efforts being made toward creating peace in this region have been either too weak or too little. It is not possible to believe or expect that a state/society would exist without any form of conflict. Conflict itself is a part of human lives and it will continue to exist. But it is also possible for us to maintain lasting peace, provided people are ready to culturally relate with one another. There are different approaches to create peace but relevancy differs according to the context of the people. Culturally oriented people need cultural values to find meaningful results. For instance, approaches to peace include: conquering the weaker nations and colonizing them in order to maintain peace; changing the patriarchal mentality for gender equality; establishing an organizational system that would manifest justice against injustice, provide several economic packages for development of the region, etc. But if these approaches are not culturally relevant, then the outcome will be very different. In this chapter, I will discuss the tribal cultural methods and values by citing the example of the Tangkhuls that may shed some light on developing an appropriate peacebuilding method in the North East Indian tribal people's context.

In most of the traditional tribal societies, peacebuilding was a matter of fair implementation of the available customary laws. The tribal people of the past were genuinely faithful to their laws. We do not hear of any one who tried to twist a law and even criminals were ready to face the consequence of their actions. In their context, law could neither be bought nor could it be easily altered. There was no problem or crisis that was too crucial to be resolved. But, every dispute had to be settled in the best possible way. Today, we are looking for peace in a very different context. Ours is a context where people ask endless questions about the legal system. The system either fails to detect corruption or does not punish and correct the corrupt person. So, there is a clear need to revisit the laws and redefine the customary and modern legal system so that there is no interference in executing a law. This is necessary because the law cannot be pushed aside during the attempts to create peace in any given society.

Perspective

The Tangkhul Nagas have a custom of setting up a village on the hilltops. As such, most of the older villages were situated on the hilltops. According to their stories, this was done for the purpose of defence as waging different kinds of war was constantly taking place. No enemy would be able to attack the village easily; any approach made by enemy toward the villagers would be noticed from the village. Along with this, it is interesting to note that with the founding of each village, a new dialect was formed. Thus, each Tangkhul village maintains a different village dialect besides their common dialect. One can guess that this was done for village security reasons. In a situation when strangers came to a village and if the villagers had to decide or notify any matter to fellow villagers that the strangers should not know, they needed a secret medium of communication. And so, having a distinct dialect was found to be the best method to keep the village safe. Thus, in connection with the concept of village security, the Tangkhuls had serious concerns about the village location and a unique custom of developing village dialect.

The above idea of defence system indicates that the Tangkhuls' history was a violent history in the sense that waging of different forms of war was the order of the day. The waging of war or hunting of human head was not simply a political practice, but it was associated with social, cultural, and religious belief. For instance, a man had to go for headhunting not because he was brave and violent, but because he was required of it by the culture. Until a male adult cuts off a human head, he was not considered as man; he was not qualified for marriage and not permitted to wear a certain traditional shawl (*Haorā*) that exemplifies manhood. In this way, a certain amount of social prestige was attached to the practice of head hunting. For example, it was an honor for a person to have curved symbolic signs on the post of *Lengcheng* (front door post of a traditional house) because the number of the signs indicated the number of heads he had acquired. And again, as very often referred to in the traditional religious discussion, a human skull brought in to the village increased the fertility of the soil and benefited the entire village. Today, when we try to understand the methods and values of peacebuilding, we need to keep in mind that we need to properly deconstruct "the idea of prestige" that was embedded with violence. The proper understanding of tribal theology would emerge only when we are able to make a systematic analysis of the concepts and practices of the tribal people and screen out the destructive elements of their culture and enhance the positive elements of the tribal people's culture.

As violence was the reality, making of peace with a warring group or person was also the immediate concern of the traditional Tangkhul society. The Tangkhuls had adopted different methods of peacemaking and peacebuilding among which the role played by women was considered as the most important one. It was so because their role was what no man was able to do as it involves risk of life. But in the case of the Tangkhul traditional practice, the greatest privilege and respect was given to women to mediate in times of conflict and war.

The idea of peace that was understood and sought for was both positive and negative peace. In the first place, any dispute had to be sorted out within, to make people live in peace, and that was also done in view of external forces that might come any time. At the same time, when outsiders attacked the village, the tribal force was put together. Similarly, though there was practice of headhunting it was done within a strict discipline. For instance, there were four types of war such as: (1) declared war; (2) war of challenge; (3) war of hostage; and (4) secret war. Headhunting was prohibited in the first three wars but done only through the fourth type.

The Tangkhuls' concept of peace was at the same time positive because they knew that community peace did not come only when violence was absent. But, wellbeing of every citizen in the day-to-day living was ensured and the best effort was made to maintain friendship with the neighboring villages who would otherwise become their enemies. To ensure peace within and with neighbors, every possible step for maintaining peace was taken by the law enforcing body. A general understanding of the people was that "No one should be left poor" in the community. And thus, every possible help was extended to the needy. At the same time, peace was understood as a process and not as an event that would have its end. Thus, their administration was carried out with utmost care and also in view of what was to come in the future generations.

It is interesting to note that setting up of *morungs* in Tangkhul villages worked as Peace Education centers, where younger generations learned several things, such as history, folk tales, songs, dance, craftsmanship, etc. To a great extent, *morung* helped the villagers regard (among) themselves as members of a bigger family relationally. At the same time, it promoted dignity of labor and helping one another. A hard-working person who, besides accomplishing his own works, can help others most was regarded as a real hero, and a lazy one as a poverty prone and wanton person.

In our attempt to understand the tribal worldview, we can easily note that the main concept of life and the collective motive of the people were to keep the community in peace. The defence system, the social observances, and customary laws were all directed toward the security and welfare of the people. The taboos and *gennas*[1] were strictly observed. Religion and community festivals were all related to peaceful coexistence of the people in the village that was at the same time extended to the outsiders by inviting them to the cultural festivals.

The Tangkhuls have strict taboos in many matters, some of which are as follows:

1. *Land:* With regard to land ownership, the Tangkhuls had the belief that a person, who knowingly and wrongfully grabs other's lands, is dealt with harshly by the earth-god who tells him in a harsh manner, "since you lust after me, you will be with me soon, and your descendants will follow suit." This means he would die soon.

2. *Land Demarcation Stone*: According to the Tangkhuls' custom, land ownership is marked by distinct boundaries based on hillocks, natural ranges, springs, or three stones, erected to mark the boundary. All boundary materials are *taboo* with serious implications. There was a belief that whoever shifts or removes a demarcation stone will harvest a sorrowful curse, that is, death.

---

[1] A ritual observed by a village or a community during which certain restrictions on the members imposed and visitors from other community or village are not allowed; they believe that breaking a rule of *genna* would invite greater wrath from the deity.

Methods and Values of Peacebuilding

3. *Song and History*: Events and history of the Tangkhuls were passed down through generations in the form of songs and oral narrations. The belief was that those who modify, twist, or wrongfully compose, such songs and narrations would suffer paralysis and die painfully, and even their descendants would also feel the pain.
4. *Trees*: Those who chop down trees or bamboos planted by others will become physically-handicapped—blind, deaf, or mental retardation—early in life.

There were many methods to resolve conflict in the traditional Tangkhul society. Many of them are used to sort out different kinds of dispute. Normally, mediation to the conflict was done by family representatives, clan representatives, villagers, village court, and also by the Long,[2] the apex body of the tribe.[3] Most of the disputes were resolved by imposing fine on the culprit. One of the distinct cultural practices of the Tangkhuls is the role of women in conflict resolution.

PUKREILA: THE POWER OF WOMEN

The term *yorla*[4] in Tangkhul refers to a woman who got married to a man belonging to another clan (exogamy is a strict rule of marriage), who may be of the same village or another village. So, all the married women become *yorla* of their brothers and cousin-brothers. However, even if their citizenship is changed, neither the blood tie is cut off nor attachment to the village is removed. They are always invited to all important events in the family. There is a festival called *Luira* (seed-sowing

---

[2] This term refers to Tangkhul Naga Long of which the birth cannot be ascertained and yet its existence is beyond doubt. The definition has slightly different variants. T. Luikham translates it as "the whole people" or "grouping a nation" (T. Luikham, *Wung (Tangkhul) Naga Okthot Mayonza* (Imphal: G.M. Press, 1961), 53; S. Kanrei uses it to mean Tangkhul government, S. Kanrei, *Tangkhul Ringphatyan* (Imphal: The Gandhi Memorial Press, 1970), 131. When it comes to the question of formation, M.K. Shimray asserted that it had been there from the beginning of their inhabitation with two types of Long, such as *Lam Khangakai Long* (sub-divisional Long) and *Shiyan Khayang Long* (Administrative Long). See M.K. Shimray, *Tangkhul Miyurlung* (Imphal: n.p., 1967), 48; whereas, S. Kanrei traces the date to around 1400 C.E.; whatever the case of definition and formation, the functions of the Long are very clear in its executive, administrative, and judicial roles.

[3] However, there is difficulty in locating the exact time of forming the Long that covers the whole tribe. And yet, it is the fact that the function of the Long is seen from a very early period.

[4] The literal meaning of *yorla* contains a negative connotation as one who is given away. Thus, the Tangkhul women have called for coining a more appropriate word. Mrs. Ningthingla Ruivanao suggests the alternative for the word as *Yola* to mean "most loved and cared person," "most tender and precious," etc.

festival normally celebrated during the month of February) during which the *yorla* becomes the most important person in the sense that this is the special time for the male members to invite the married women (their daughters or sisters), and after the festival they are sent home with many gifts. This is how relations with the married women are maintained. This further indicates that among the Tangkhuls, a female relative is never forgotten as long as she lives.

The *yorla* becomes much more important when there is conflict or war, which was more common in the early days. Her status is changed into *pukreila* in the context of conflict or war; this is another name given with much regard and indicates her dual citizenship in the sense that she owns the recognition of her original villagers and also the favor of her present village. This neutral status of a woman is considered as the best source of mediating during the war. A *pukreila* is called as a peacemaker, the torch bearer of peace and the Red Cross bearer of Naga inter-village war.[5] In the midst of war, at the time of wild, frenzied, and emotional situations when no man's force could control the conflict, *pukreila* could easily enter the battlefield and stop the fight. According to the custom, a *pukreila* cannot be harmed by any side. She is highly respected for her neutrality, for she is related to both the villages. She has a strong bond with her parental home such as with parents, brothers, sisters, and cousins. At the same time, she shares equal bonds with her husband and in-laws. The bond to respect a *pukreila* goes to the extent that if any harm is done to her by any person/party, then the case will be taken to the court of Range Council (Chingsang Long—a council formed by several neighboring villages, mostly those who share a mountain range or/and those who have adjacent paddy fields) and this combined force would wage war against the accused party. Such was the serious penalty that no village would dare to face it. And thus, none would dare to touch or harm a *pukreila*. At the same time, another factor that accords importance to a *pukreila* is that a *pukreila* knows the situation of both the parties and would make the best decision to restore peace. As such, the decision of *pukreila* is always accepted.

One of the historical examples of *pukreila* may be cited here, in the middle part of the nineteenth century (ca. 1850–60) when Kampha Ramhon[6] was attacked and totally devastated within a day by Talui vil-

---

[5] R.R. Shimray, *Origin and Culture of Nagas* (New Delhi: Samsok Publications, 1985), 168.

[6] Kampha was the name of a person from Humbum, who first settled at the village that was named after him. The village was shifted due to water scarcity. Another migrant group came and were let to settle at the place where Kampha first settled, and thus, the name "Kampha Shimphunghon," which, in the course of time, was renamed "Kampha Ramhon." Thus, Kampha and Kampha Ramhon were two

lagers as retaliation for an insult to some individuals who were on their way to Imphal. The attackers were about to attack Kampha also, which was located hardly a kilometer below, when a very old *pukreila* by the name Vakhapla (who had been married from Talui to a Kampha village clan chief) appeared at the village gate and with outstretched arms tried to stop them shouting, "No, brother, I am still alive. As long as I am alive, Talui and Kampha should not wage war among ourselves."[7] Since Talui had vowed to destroy both Kampha Ramhon and Kampha villages, they tried to push her aside. Just at that instant, Vakhapla's brother who happened to be among the group came out crying, "Without heeding my sister's plea if you are to attack Kampha, then spear me to death first, lay my corpse across the gate and by stamping upon my chest, you can enter the gate and attack the village." At this point, the Talui group could not help but break a part of their vow and retreated without attacking Kampha. It is said that, not long after Vakhapla's death, the Kampha villagers stormed Talui village as a vengeance for the attack on Kampha Ramhon.[8]

There are two important occasions when the *yorlas* become very important among the Tangkhuls. They are most important during the time of marriage and death. When marriage takes place in her brother's house, the *yorla* becomes an important person. She would normally take responsibility to monitor the activities during the occasion. She would also contribute as much as she can for her brother's marriage and in return, her brother would also give back as much as he could. The other occasion was during the time of death in her brother's and cousin's family, she would not be forgotten. She would also not come empty handed to pay her last respects to the deceased blood-kin.

The post-war role of the *pukreila* was also very significant. After stopping the fierce fight of the two warring groups, the *pukreila* did not remain silent but continued to act as mediator between the two groups until complete reconciliation was made. In most cases, the mediation took a long time for the *pukreila* to convince the angry men who had not decided the victor of the war. So, the *pukreila* would take the tiresome task of traveling

---

separate villages from different origins and under two separate chieftainships located next to each other. After the Talui attacked few survivors from Kampha Ramhon, they left the village and settled down at Kampha village. Since the arrival of Christianity, they shifted to a new location and the village is named Sirarakhong. Though Kampha and Kampha Ramhon villagers are now living together within Sirarakhong village, each still claims to maintain separate patta and chieftainship. Information obtained by the author during discussion with Mr. Ngakhamsing Woleng, the 18th generation descendant of Kampha in 1971.

[7] Mr. Ngakhamsing Woleng in discussion with the author, 1991.
[8] Mr. Shimrei Woleng of Sirarakhong village in discussion with the author, January 4, 2013.

back and forth between the two villages. And when she had done the task successfully and when the two parties/villages had agreed to reconcile to remain peaceful, then she initiated a feast for them called *Mashit Sashai*, meaning "feast of friendship." This feast was considered very important and thus, normally organized symbolically and with much solemnity. During such a feast, in certain cases, the representatives of the two parties would exchange spears symbolizing that since they hold each other's spears, they should never try to use the spear to kill its owner. This phrase conveyed the idea that from then on, they would never fight again. Such was the contribution of the *pukreila*.

The marriage further leads to closer relationship of two families, clans, and villages. Even when there was no incident where a *yorla* became a *pukreila*, it wove a circle of friendship between the men of the two families, clans, and villages and they are called *āmāk* (brother-in-law). This is a strong concept among the Tangkhuls and people normally do not expect any violence between and among the *āmāk*, but are expected to help and protect one another. Thus, marriage is a source of human relationships and especially more significant in the context of conflict.

Contextualization of *pukreila*

In a world gripped by conflict, division, violence, and destruction, there is no other option than to look for some means to negotiate between warring groups and also any means to control the situation. It is in such a context of need and search that the Tangkhul concept of *pukreila* becomes important, meaningful, and relevant. It is a cultural method of fashioning peace that needs to be rediscovered and activated. Today, we do not need to think of women only in terms of the *pukreila* who can go in between the frenzied menfolk at war. But, we ought to think in terms of endowing such a status and role to women as a whole (both married and unmarried), married within or outside their village. Following this, the respect owned by women and their hearts inclined toward creating a peaceful world would surely become capable of silencing any form of conflict and fight that prevail in the present society. Today, when we search for peace, let us recognize the presence of any woman (of our village or a woman from neighboring village) as a Red Cross bearer who always identifies with reconciliation and peace process so that this redefined concept of women would serve as the greatest means of fashioning peace among different people.

The role of the *pukreila* was not limited to that of the battlefield but also in times of misunderstandings, conflicts, disputes, etc. For instance, when there was any dispute between two villages and when menfolk found it difficult to travel to the rival village, it was the *pukreila* who would take the responsibility to travel and initiate the process of reconciliation.[9] In the recent past, when the political situation in Nagaland was not good because of factional conflict of the National Socialist Council of Nagalim, the *pukreilas* had successfully imparted their role of mediating and creating peace.[10]

Today, when we talk about making our own culture relevant to the people, we cannot speak of a divided culture but rather a united culture. And within that concept of a united, concrete culture, this value and strength of women must be accommodated with priority. Thus, we can affirm our understanding that for the tribal people, the perception of women as peacemakers is not a new idea but an old hidden idea that needs to be uncovered and strengthened. This challenge is not a threat to any patriarchal custom, structure, and form of society, rather it is a call to respect our own cultural values. I think that in our attempt to formulate feminist theology, we have given biased emphasis on exegeting and interpreting Scripture texts but have not given sufficient efforts to exegete cultural texts for interpretation and correction. This has become an important area we must further explore to derive the proper meaning of feminist theology.

This positive tribal value of women, if made practical and realistic, can be opened up to the global academic market. In other words, the tribal people will be able to contribute the most needed method of fashioning peace in the world. Upon full acceptance of this value system by the world, it will become a point of change from the spirit of war to the reality of experiencing peace on earth. And when this happens, the tribal people will be appreciated for recognizing the hidden values of women at an appropriate time.

In our theological deliberations, we very often talk about the empowerment of women. We have also affirmed that theological conceptualization without a good share of feminist concern is incomplete. Such affirmation is, to me, a deconstruction of the mindset that holds, "women's participation in all works of life is very important and they should come forward and take part in leadership role," without seriously considering the factors of why they cannot come forward to the forefront to participate and take a leadership role. This practice of casual talk has been adopted for long enough without realizing that it is not only the duty of women themselves to claim, but the duty of their oppressors to realize their attitude of cultural colonization. Take the example of Naga Mothers Association's efforts

---

[9] There are times when even the *pukreila* acted as a spy. But, that was not common.
[10] *Nagaland Post* (Dimapur), February 5, 2007, 1; *The Telegraph North East* (Guwahati), February 7, 2007, 17.

in peacebuilding: it made tremendous contribution toward achieving a "Dry State" in Nagaland during the mid-1980s; it played a crucial role in the unification process of factions of Naga national movement. However, it failed in its demand of 33.3 percent reservation in politics, especially in municipal elections. The rejection of the demand came from the Naga patriarchal mindset and assumption that it would disturb Naga customary laws that seemed to have caused frustration to women. However, the fight did not end with that rejection but they have gone to the legal court and are expecting a verdict in their favor so that from the next political exercise in the state, they would be able to make their presence felt. This is the reason why I have made repeated calls for cultural textual exegesis to question the norms and reframe/redefine the culture of the people.

The challenge for peacebuilding has become much more crucial as it is no longer limited to peacemaking but is concerned toward keeping society in order. The answer to this does not lie in constant bargaining for reservation and quota within a patriarchal colonial system because it will not take them to any desired destiny. But, we need to make a drastic paradigm shift in approach and enter into the competitive job market. There are many male bureaucrats in the government and politics who have miserably failed and many male Christian ministers have also failed in manifesting the truth. This is one of the best reasons to question patriarchal power and its substitution by an integrated participation of women.

Having realized that we do not need to look for further excuses, we must act upon our convictions to manifest the relevant meaning of women's value and worth. A time has come for us to fully realize that we no longer need to extort the freedom of women but rather endorse greater participation basically for the sake of peacebuilding. However, we need to make it very clear that whether it is done by men or women, violence cannot be retaliated with violence. It is not possible for us to endorse women coming forward to take up weapons to counter violence being done by the rebels.[11]

I would further reiterate that the privilege enjoyed by the women of the traditional Tangkhul society was not simply a right created by themselves and for themselves, but a value that was endowed by the patriarchal society and the status was given by the patriarchal system. But today, we see that male chauvinism has indirectly attempted to weaken women's mediating role. Therefore, to make tribal women important in the process of fashioning peace, it is not a task of women alone, but the society has to reinstate their status and their role so that they will endeavor to use it to

---

[11] A few years ago, the women groups of Kashmir demanded the government to provide guns to them so that they can fight those rebels who brought suffering instead of prosperity, poverty instead of wealth, and death instead of life.

its fullest. We are not advocating for extra privileges but that we should understand tribal society in an inclusive manner where every effort is recognized and respected for the purpose of achieving peace.

Conclusion

Today, we are not to lose time talking about cultural awakening. We have had it for a long time, as substantiated by the kind of theses written during the 1970s and 1980s onward. Since then, theological debate has been continuing, but the impact on the tribal people is weaker than expected. One of the probable factors is that because people continue to think of social or religious transformation within the framework of "individual first" for social change. Such an approach worked until the middle of the twentieth century for evangelization/conversion. But, its capability must be seen in the context where people have become much more educated and there is less personal influence.

Peace cannot be understood apart from the laws of the people. However, I do not mean the laws that can be manipulated to meet vested interests. The need is for laws that would be based on organizational operation. We may further see that the present social crises are not because we do not have individual intellectuals, individually rich and individually religious, but because we do not have a strong organizational framework to execute laws. Therefore, to me, what is important today is not an awakening, but a need for greater intellectual responsibility, that is, an active campaign to put cultural values into action.

On the whole, we must understand and be prepared to make a meaningful critique on the emotional nature of the tribal people; that they are by nature very emotional people and very often act on the basis of emotion. While, emotion has its space in programming, it is not possible for us to allow it to rule over logic/rationale. When it comes to women's issues, very often logic is not applied and decisions are taken on the basis of narrow cultural interpretation. The tribal people need to redefine several phrases referring to women that contain negative connotations like "womanly," "quiet," "disciplined," "silent," etc., because they all carry suppressive ideas. At the same time, patriarchal mindset that is judgmental and biased needs to be brought under question. For instance, the tribal society for long enough has condemned women who are involved in acts of prostitution. A number of wrong factors are given for such acts but the core factor of the people behind such acts, has not been questioned. There is also a need for us to read how customs are formulated and the truth blinded. For example, many of our people do not take very serious note of accumulating public money or giving bribe for a job in the government office, etc. Many of these unjust practices are becoming almost accepted as the norm on the one hand, while there is emphasis on following religious norms such as condemning chewing pan, irregular attending of worship services, travelling on Sunday, etc., as sinful. This is not strictly restricted to gender but the intensity of gender bias against women may not be ignored. This is an attempt to differentiate secular and religious realms in order to derive greater freedom for the secular world and confine religious persons to a limited world.

The above discussed method of conflict resolution was a method traditionally developed and imbibed with the values of respect and fear. It was used so that, by all means disputes were resolved. Perhaps, the people who practiced it had intended that there should be proper mediation for any form of conflict because unless a dispute was resolved, no peace would exist among the people.

The method does not only convey the practical end of conflict but also contains strong morals and ethics of non-violence, to *pukreila*, and strict laws that any harm done to *pukreila* would invite greater penalty from a stronger force.

10

CHRISTIAN INVOLVEMENT IN POLITICS

The involvement of Christians in politics is a widely discussed topic. At the same time, this matter has not received the necessary rigorous and serious attention it needs. The fact is that as long as the Christian church exists on earth, the debate will continue. More importantly, the discussion is being made in a specific Christian context. In this chapter, I will show two stages of participation on how contemporary Christians can look at the issue from different perspectives and also how radical the church can be. We cannot bring politics into the church, but can we take religion into politics?

The church and politics belong to two different institutions that should not be confused. There should not be any interference between the two in any institutional affairs. The church exists in the world but is not of the world. Therefore, Christians cannot remain silent over the negative political manifestation and crime. It is so because, Christians, at the same time, are citizens of the political government.

Church is apolitical by nature and thus it cannot identify with politics that is manifested in party politics. An individual may cast a vote for any party candidate, but the church as an institution cannot belong to a political party. The church is also not the platform for political campaign. No politician has a space in the church as a political representative, but anyone can come to the church as a believer. Thus, the church has no business in political campaign.

After having said this, though the church is apolitical, people cannot remain silent to the reality of human suffering, hunger, and death. They must give a prophetic voice against the misgovernance of people. However, the church cannot speak anything against the government if the members have abstained from casting their votes during elections because they will have no moral right to do so.

Karl Barth, who was considered as the father of modern Christian theology, opined that the church should always be on the left. This means the church should continuously critique the government and also help it carry out its activities for the good of the people. It is the duty of the church in a Christian society to constantly expose the failures of politics.

There are many steps Christians can take to participate in politics without becoming political and while refraining from many other political activities. For instance, a Christian minister commissioning a political candidate and participating in the felicitation of an elected candidate is taking a dangerous step because it indicates identifying with a single political party and rejecting the others who have lost the election. It may have a long-term effect as the minister undermines the sanctity of the office. Christians should not be confused that what is not politically right is not religiously right as well.

The Christian participation in politics can be very active, constant, and also both before and after elections. They need to work hard to motivate Christians on religious principles toward fair governance and to choose the right leader. It is in this context that a "clean election campaign" becomes important. This is an urgent challenge to the tribal communities in North East India to take serious note for the sake of future development and nation building. Campaigning for clean elections is necessary because once the opportunity is not seized during elections, then the elected members will not pay heed to the people's needs and instead work toward recovering their election expenditures. If this happens, the society forfeits development and welfare. This campaign should not be carried out only when elections are near and also should not be limited to urban sectors, but it should be in all possible ways continued as post-election strategy and taken to the grassroots levels that have the greater vote count.

Elections in a Christian society are in the hands of the members of the church and thus, the church can play a major role in endorsing or rejecting candidates. Christian electorates do not need to struggle how to choose one between two or among many selfish persons. A committed person with a clear vision should be allowed to undertake political responsibility to deliver the promises. Anyone who does not have a good standing in the church may not be given another chance to do greater harm and deprive all the entire citizens of the constituency or state of their rightful claims to development. If a candidature of a person is not approved by the church and the person still stands for election, people should exercise their electoral power and vote out such a person. This action should be carefully carried out with strict Christian moral ethics for the sake of the common good.

The post-election role of the church should be to provide a "just principle" to the decision makers. It needs to constantly remind them that the need of the poor is basic and uncompromisable. Social welfare is of much more worth than individual wealth. For this, the political leaders should be made aware that their standing in the church is very essential for the success of their ministries.

For the purpose of successful participation in politics, the church must at the first instance refuse to compromise its principles by accepting monetary donations. Such an act could silence Christian leaders, they will lose their prophetic role and Christian moral ethics, and fail the God-anointed mission. Accountability to the people and to God determines the success of Christian ministry.

Christians who are very concerned for the well-being of the citizens in any given society must know that they have to use their votes diligently in pursuit of social development. They must know that the world in which they live is a corrupt world and any politician they promote should be someone who can face the challenge of corruption and not one who would perpetuate corruption.

Our experiences in the last fifty years clearly show that money shared by politicians with a few individuals at the cost of the common good is not an answer to our search for society's progress. The people who have given their votes should in return get much more than a single package (if at all). Christians must learn that they do not need to be misled again by empty political promises that never come to reality. There is instead the need for sincere and incorruptible representatives in the government. Citizens do not aspire for a government in which lawmakers become rich and the common people have no proper roads, clean drinking water, and electricity for education, health, and development.

The other area of concern is the issue of almost nil participation of women in politics. On this matter, I have a few direct questions: Who is responsible for this? Can the institution of politics belong to men? Is this because of structural problem or social and cultural problem? In addition, there are another two corresponding questions: Why are the indigenous/tribal people not seriously and positively responding to it? Are tribal women prepared to actively participate in politics?

If women are prepared for the task, then, even if there is no reservation, they are very much capable of taking power into their hands and work for the well-being of the people. We have strong women's movements, unions, associations, etc., which if they are able to mobilize and network among themselves, have a strong possibility of entering into politics and making a difference. The reason why I am raising this gender issue in politics is because the time has come for the people to make a paradigm shift in our political thinking. Gender is not necessarily about men and women, but a conflict constructed by the socio-cultural norms of the society between two sexes. Taking the perspective of Christianity and its interpretation of humanhood, it is proper to think that the strong presence of Christian women can be an alternative to the present-day corrupt politics. I do not intend to claim that no woman will be involved in any form of corrupt action, but general reading informs that they can still be more humane when it comes to materialization of programs for social benefits.

For that matter, if committed Christian men and women participate in politics with a clear principle of justice and a genuine vision of the kingdom of God, they would surely do great things for the people. But, this will not happen until the whole Christian community understands the importance of politics. At the same time, in the present culture of politics that is determined by the amount of money one spends, no faithful and committed Christian will be willing to participate because politics operates within the framework of corruption. Thus, the tribal Christian community has the option of either leaving politics to the secular world and allowing corrupt politicians to further manipulate power, thereby causing more human suffering, poverty, backwardness, etc., or the option of taking a new position on politics and electing into office capable, efficient, faithful, trustworthy men and women, to serve the people with all the available national resources.

This debate is not necessarily a borrowed view of *humanism*, but one that keeps in mind that religious belief is highly important and that wrong systems and forces that destroy religious belief and function need to be corrected for the good of religion. The quantum of corruption that exists in our society does too much damage to the total life of the people. Upon reading Subhas Chandra Bose's statement, "tolerating injustice is worse than perpetrating injustice," we ought to examine where we stand on issues of corruption, injustice, etc. The debate on church and politics has been there for a long time since the beginning of those institutions and many people have strongly responded to the issue. For instance, commenting on how Karamchand Gandhi maintained religion and politics, Nirad C. Chaudhuri believed Gandhi did not bring religion into politics to raise it to a higher plane; Gandhi instead took politics into religion to create a new faith of which he was the prophet. After that, Jawaharlal Nehru projected a strong conviction that "politics and religion are obsolete; the time has come for science and spirituality." The point here is that when civil moral value declines, it is the church that should actively involve itself in restoring humanity and religious values that are the focus of Jesus when he said, "the thief comes only to steal and kill and destroy; I have come that they may have life, and have it to the full."

One of the common mistakes Christians continue to make is the confusion between biblical/doctrinal issues and administrative issues. A proper differentiation of whether a person is carrying out the duties of the office of the pastor or working in their individual capacity is necessary to understand an individual's role. Christian ministers should also know how to represent the office they hold. There are several occasions on which they go in their individual capacity and not representing their office. It is only when one can clearly define theological issue and administrative issue that one would be able to distinguish the difference between religion and politics.

What has been said in the above discussion may still be confusing because there is need for clearer understanding to this call. For this, the Christian organizations and Christian-based NGOs may conduct a series of deliberations to generate mass awareness of the real meaning and concern of politics at all levels. These efforts should aim at enabling Christians to rethink their centuries-old interpretation of politics and the church.

Christian intellectuals should become more sensitive to non-performing governments, expose all failures, and file cases seeking explanations from the government. This should be done not with the intention of maligning particular persons, but for the sake of achieving the common good for the people that is a political duty. This has become ever more important because if the people cannot correct the system of the government, then they can never experience the benefits of government that is formed by the people and for the people.

11

HOLISTIC CHILD DEVELOPMENT: ETHICAL AND MORAL VALUES

Perspective

Society is a collective of individuals; without people, there is no society or community. An individual will find no way of existence if one is not part of a society. Society is very crucial in making a person important. At the same time, personal identity is also associated with one's society/community. A person finds it difficult to identify oneself apart from one's society. Having a community name and identity of being Mizo, Naga, Khasi, Assamese, Garo, etc., is important to each individual. Otherwise, when people travel to a city and try to explain themselves, their identity, without referring to their community, the people there will not be able to understand who they are. In a similar way, we cannot understand the meaning of beauty, educated, rich, intelligent, professional, etc., in the world of the self. Thus, while individuals form a society, society in return shapes the personality of individuals.

The thought-forms (psyche) or personality or spirituality of a person is shaped by one's social environment. The socialization of society directs the personality of every individual. This again is the basis of our different worldviews; for instance, compare the different worldviews of a villager and a city/town dweller.

A person is important to the society in relation with others. One cannot own wisdom, and wisdom cannot be important apart from others. Thus, individuals are integral to one another. However, the value of an individual is graded by the perspective of the society. The need/demand of the society is the criterion to judge whether one is important or not. In such a case, knowing the perspective of the society is the way to make a person important in the society. An Information Technology (IT) professional who earns one lakh rupees a month will not find a place in a remote town. The inter-linkage between one's specialty and the society is equally important. Religion also has meaning within the framework of a society. Why we are Christians today has much to do with our historical and contextual experiences. Because the socialization process we have encountered matters very much; it is a sign of our perception of society. Faith/truth cannot be defined beyond and apart from the society. Faith is meaningful from the perspective of the society.

If the society/church is said to be weak/corrupt/wicked and needs restoration and reformation, it should be kept in mind that we who are speaking today are not too old to address the aspects of children. This is so because even if we can restore and preserve all other aspects, if we fail to reshape the lives of children or lose the future of today and tomorrow's children, then we lose everything together.

Critique on general ideology

A traditional mindset among many parents is that in order to train our children, it is okay to inflict physical punishment. This idea is based on "heat when it is hot," "a slap is bitter today but sweet in the future," and "you have to listen and obey what is being told, but you should not speak or react." I want to raise a simple question: What ethical right and moral value do we find in corporal punishment? Why should we continue to define ethics and morals only from adults' perspective? Why should our concept of rearing children go to the extent of owning their lives and forcing them to do what we think is right and not theirs? We are often tempted to think that it is moral enough to punish children because that is for their good.

We fail to reason that children do not think exactly the way we think. Their psychology is disturbed/hampered when they perceive our actions as wrong. They are frustrated. They feel ill-treated. They lose the interest of working hard to learn and give in to duty for duty's sake. They try to fulfill our demands, but in the long run they may not become somebody that we expect them to be. We need to seriously rethink this aspect.

We must understand that today's children are living a fast life according to the context, environment, and avenues. Many children have more computer knowledge than their parents, and are more aware of fashion too. And yet, parents have the tendency to claim greater knowledge more than them. This is ethically wrong.

Education

Education is meant for shaping the worldview of a person through information and knowledge. Education should have a purpose of building a future society. To build a strong nation, we need good education. The present educational system in India is faced with two major problems: (1) It is competitive and profession-oriented, but it has become too commercialized making it difficult for common people to cope with the pressure. On the other hand, there is a government program called basic education for all children. This kind of program becomes very superficial as children are not provided with the kind of education necessary for a highly competitive academic environment. Moreover, at the end, when it comes to employment, their education will not be accepted in the modernized world. For instance, one of the criteria for a gate-keeper's job is having basic computer knowledge. This is so because we now live in a computerized world. (2) We are living in the world of a globalized world. Therefore, people are not talking of national expertise alone now, but of world class education. This is another area where local values and systems get dissolved and become incompatible. We are being challenged to locate the proper perspective to fit in our children, otherwise, their generation will come under threat.

Children in today's world are required to have a wide range of knowledge for professional discipline. In this context, traditional customary modes of teaching have become inferior and insufficient. We know that prospective employers choose the best among the best. And so, if we cannot provide sufficient space for children to attain the best of education, they will not be able to meet the demands of a competitive world. There is a need to prepare for any demands that arise in the future. Otherwise, formal (non-professional) education will not serve the purpose. We need to redefine morality from this perspective. Who is the one who chooses the profession for a son or a daughter? Is it the child or the parents? We must allow the children to live according to their times. We should be ready to participate in the decisions that our children make to achieve their goals. Otherwise, imposing our interests on them may hamper their lives.

Religion

Parents often consider themselves to be more religious than their children. They think they know more about God than their children and attend church worship, and so insist upon their children to follow the same religious rituals. They assume that the children do not know God. There is no question against the parents' desire to let their children know more about God. But, there is a serious problem in their efforts to make children know or follow religion. They insist that they go to Sunday school regularly, and they are very happy to send their children to children camps or Vacation Bible School without critically evaluating what is being taught in all these programs. What kind of memory verses are they made to memorize? Have they been chosen to express children's religiosity meaningfully or chosen because the teachers like them? Why are children being taught many things that are deemed important by the teachers and the children forced to learn what the teachers consider to be right? All these forms of imposition of religious values are ethically not acceptable. This is not an attempt to reject the programs, but the vision and methods need to be reassessed. Children are very intelligent. They must be given the opportunity to exercise their faith without any adult imposition. They should not be made to feel inferior while trying to teach them religion. We need to adopt a method through which their wisdom and freedom can be nurtured. We do not need to produce more nominal Christians, but aim to produce matured Christians. This can happen when we also allow children to make good decisions about their religious calling.

The above issue takes us to another related problem faced by children in the church worship. We can take a simple example in the form of a question: How many sermons have we preached in the church that refer to the needs of the children? Perhaps children's needs do not figure even in the appendix of our sermons and, instead, are completely ignored. This is a serious ethical question that arises in our search for justice for all.

The existence of the problem of neglecting children in the church worship is understandably a by-product of our theological considerations and cultural pattern of decision-making. Christian theology is being done only from adults' perspective. Mission and evangelism are directed only toward adults. This negligence of the needs of children weakens the life of the church. People have the tendency to recognize only those who contribute their intellectual inputs and wealth. The lack of concern in our churches toward children becomes visible through the reports that most of the churches do not have a financial head for children in their annual budget. As such, in the process, the church uses the excuse of "no fund" for any children-oriented program. The church needs to allocate a sufficient amount of money for children because they are the most important group of people who would be responsible for the church.

Economic Issues

There are two classes of parents, the rich and the middle-class parents. Both classes invest their wealth in children's education. The former does not have any problem in meeting the financial demands of their children, whereas, the latter struggles to provide the same demand. I want to refer to two issues involved in our attempt to educate our children. First, both the classes in many cases commit the mistake of providing money without discipline. I have no doubt that many precious lives have been spoiled because of money made easily available to them. All parents love their children but it is dangerous if they do not know how to love them. Giving unaccounted money is not the best way to love children. Parents must cultivate a sense of responsibility and accountability in the minds of the children. Otherwise, children find it very easy to demand money. While it is necessary to meet their needs, it is wrong to meet such demands when they are still young. Second, where does one find the resources to meet the children's demands? It becomes unrealistic for a person who earns a monthly salary of Rs. 40,000 to educate three children in any cosmopolitan city of India while maintaining the so-called "standard/status" at home. But, this is being done by many people today. We must be sensitive enough to realize that an unexplainable source of money may not become the best source to bring up the best kind of children.

Another issue I come across in the management of resources is that most parents give maximum effort to support their children in all their undertakings. They do not worry about spending all that they have for their children, but they do not make investments for each child; parents do not have the practice of a savings system for their children. One can see two perspectives on this: One, parents are ignorant of the future of their children; they tend to rely on what comes to them in future. Two, if this is not the case, it can be an ideological decision to let the children continue to remain under their control even when they grow older, forcing them to depend on the parents so that the parents will continue to have a say in their life affairs.

At this juncture, it is relevant to understand the criteria of adulthood in the West and learn some of the good elements. In the West, when a child reaches the age of 18, the child becomes an independent person. The child's savings are sufficient for them to lead an independent life. This is a sign of attaining adulthood. But in our context, many of the children never become independent. For example, even after getting married, a son continues to depend on his parents. We need to question the system of child-rearing from the perspective of making a total (independent) person. In our attempt to bring up a reasonable child, we cannot rely on a single tool that takes care of one aspect of life, and instead, we need to adopt a holistic approach. Because, investing a huge amount of money or giving religious guidelines alone is not going to help in ensuring a child's holistic development. We are not looking for a child with high education but without responsibility. The goal is to raise responsible citizens and capable leaders. To attain this, we need to take into consideration the entire socio-political and cultural aspects to raise and train a person.

Culture

Very often, tribal people claim to have rich cultural values, good moral codes, communitarian legacy, and right ethical judgment. But, reading tribal culture from a child's perspective, I do not see it as good as it claims to be. We need to critically evaluate the culture in which children are brought up. In the old tribal tradition, children were never considered important in any aspect. They were not given rightful citizenship but were simply attached to the father. Children are entitled or recognized only through their parents. There were very few, if not completely absent, cultural practices that were concerned with children. Children were only taught to obey their parents and elders. They were not trained to become leaders but obedient sons/daughters. Unfortunately, this was how the prime time of learning and shaping of attitude was lost. The fact was that consciously or unconsciously, decision for life was taken before adolescence. From this point of view, I do not endorse the claim that our culture was good or beneficial for children's growth.

In order to make children aware of their own cultural traits and maintain their identity, it is necessary to inform them about their culture. They must be made familiar with their own history and tradition. However, parents or older people should be careful in how they present such values. Any of those practices that have negative values should be avoided and they are to be taught the good cultural values. This is necessary because today, we find many children who do not want to follow any cultural practice or consider their own culture inferior to other modern values.

Conclusion

The question we need to understand today is not limited to who is good or who is not good but we need to consider more important questions in connection with holistic child development, and how we are responding to the needs of children. We must also keep in mind that their future will greatly depend on what we do today. There is no wrong in thinking big, attaining great economic progress, saving the world from ecological crisis, or end of wars. But, one thing we must keep in mind is, it would mean nothing even if we can achieve all these and fail to save our human generation, or if we produce a future generation who would waste all the resources of today. We need to build a society in partnership with our children in order to be realistic and livable. Our attitude toward children as weak, ignorant, incapable, and illiterate beings must be seriously questioned in order to make a difference in our generation and the next generation.

12

CHRISTIAN THEOLOGICAL THINKING ON CHILDREN

If the concern for children is deeply rooted and advocated by the Bible, why has it taken so long to prominently appear in Christian theological thinking? Why is theological thinking so adult oriented? Why is theological thinking so rigid in framed doctrines and less open to the new issues? Why are Christians too Protestant or too Baptist?

I would like to emphasize that while each individual is very important for societal existence, individual effort to bring social change is found lacking in our time. It is so because we do not have any meaningful and relevant contemporary or recent history of social change. The primary concern is what approach our society needs today for the purpose of creating an environment and space for children to grow in a way that leads to "success." Because, as Dave Wiebe explains, they (children) may never be able to point to a date when they "accepted Christ as Saviour."[1] The same can be applied to social development and social history.

All that our children think today is not necessarily an outcome of their independent thinking, but because they have been made to think the way they are. On many occasions and programs, they are made to feel unwanted because we uncritically follow the dictates of our culture, that children should not be present, speak, and participate. Therefore, if at all we are concerned about the well-being of our children, we ought to raise critical questions on our culture. We must be prepared to take the risk for the sake of our children and make them feel accepted in the society and in the church.

I would argue that the adults, in order to place themselves in the center of power, have become unnecessarily legalistic and not loving toward the

---

[1] Dave Wiebe, "Toward a Theology of Children," *Direction—A Mennonite Brethren Forum*, 22 1 (Spring 1993): 41.

children. So, it is the question of vacating the seat of power that decides the functions of the society. I am not thinking in terms of making a young child a pastor of the church, but there are areas in which they need to be considered. Who formulates the culture and customary laws and for whom? Who can reformulate inefficient, destructive laws? Why do people on the basis of customary laws in this modern world continue to refuse women's participation in decision-making? As an example, the rejection of 33.3 percent reservation for women was based on the assumption that it would disturb customary laws, which is a clear projection of patriarchal mentality.

Why is there no provision for children in the church constitutions? No specific reference for children is seen other than the Sunday school program and children camps (this also only in their budget). However, no church has a clear explanation of even these two programs.

Denominational attitude

In the Baptist setup, we do not see enough space for children in the church structure; its democratic decision-making structure is biased against the children.

Mission policy is again highly adult oriented. The Protestant Church does not believe in infant baptism for active church membership. And as such, no proper consideration is given to children's mission and they are expected to tag along with their parents. They are not counted among converts although that is the most important aspect of Christian mission.

However, without referring to whether the system adopted by the Baptist churches is good or not, the one thing we must acknowledge is that Baptist Christians treat children well and with kindness. But, we may further investigate whether the divisive nature of Baptist groups has overshadowed their concern toward children?

Today, our primary concern should not be the size and history of the church/Christians, but the health of the church. Because if she fails in women and children ministry, then she is failing a large and vital section of the church, and if her members offer only lip-service theology without works, then she is not healthy, and; if the church is more interested in maintaining status quo, then her growth and movement are hindered and she fails to meet the needs of the people.

We do not need to point out the factors that discriminate children, but we must start acting against them. I believe we are here to advocate positive concern for the children. And when that is the case, the best thing we can realize is that we need to change our definition of society. In the new definition, children should not be placed in the margins, but they should be made an integral part of society.

We must also see that all the good works and achievements of our world do not end with the present generation, but that progress is sustained and continued when the young take over leadership. The American Indians' saying in relation to the land gives an appropriate sense of this, "we did not inherit the land from our ancestors, but borrowed from our children." The meaning is, if we have inherited something, then it belongs to us and if it is ours, then we have every right to do anything against it; but if we have borrowed it from someone else, then we do not have the right to destroy or damage the land because we will be charged guilty. And so, unless we are able to define new ways of living, the existing adult-centered lifestyle will lead to maintaining the status quo, and the systemic flaws and perspectives of the current generation will be transmitted to the younger generations.

Another aspect we need to understand is that systems are important for evolving society, but we must be aware that systems can also turn out to be wrong. And when a wrong system is brought into being, we cannot speak of equality and the common good because the wrong system will judge us as wrong. Therefore, we need to first of all critically reflect whether the rights and duties laid out by the United Nations serve as the mirror to our policy making and evaluation of societal achievements. We need to make policies based on the concept shown in the Convention and evaluate societal condition using the same yardstick. In so doing, we must be willing to challenge the system if it does not provide sufficient/expected result.

In the debate on religious capabilities of children, theologians like Thomas Aquinas questioned a child's capacity to understand God. He states, "our understanding cannot reach to the divine essence."[2] He is talking of this in terms of fully trained theologians. He further states, "by grace we have a more perfect knowledge of God than we have by natural reason."[3] Taken together, these statements indicate that the distance between the natural reason of any one person and knowledge of God can only be bridged by God's grace. We cannot limit the reach of God's grace to any particular group of people such as theologians or other adults. And so, because knowledge of God depends on grace and not on human achievement, it is possible that children may also be graced with the knowledge of God. However, Aquinas believes that adults have a better chance to understand the essence of God. A similar view is held by Schubert Ogden who describes Christian theology as "the fully reflective

---

[2] Thomas Aquinas, *Summa Theologiae*, vol. 1 (New York: Image Books, 1969), 191.
[3] Aquinas, *Summa Theologiae*, 193.

understanding of the Christian witness of faith as decisive for human existence," and he goes on to explain that "fully reflective understanding" implies that "theology ought to exhibit at least some of the formal marks of any 'science.'"[4] It seems logical to conclude then, that children would be incapable of contributing to theology as scientists using a formal scientific methodology. But to the contrary, Sofia Cavalletti argues that children have the capability to relate themselves to God and inspire the adults to understand the focus of their theology.[5]

The reason why I refer to the above theological position on children is that religion can be made meaningful only in the context of society. An individual can never become religious without referring to other persons. A person's entire personality is shaped by how one is socialized by the society. Therefore, what one thinks about what is right is not necessarily their own choice but the result of socialization of that person and the religious influence. It is so because we cannot define what is right without referring to our religion; our definition of right is determined by our religion. So, children's concerns cannot be looked at in isolation, but they need to be understood in the wholeness of socioreligious situation. This is so because we cannot do anything good for the well-being of the children besides the social norms.

I am aware that there are several analyses on how best we can bring up children; how we need to systematize Child Theology based on cultural values. But, my approach is that we can no longer single out the best culture and use its values as the sole principle; rather, we need to educate children on how best they can interact with three existing cultures. This is because many people in our time, both young and old, are struggling to define what traditional culture is and what is modern, as these are very closely interwoven without a clear line to differentiate between them and each exerts equal pressure on children. The three existing cultures are local culture (for most of us, tribal culture), global culture (values that the media and market provide to the children), and Christian culture (the belief system and its relation with other religious and secular norms). While referring to this principle, Keith J. White asserts that it is of crucial importance that parents and church leaders are aware of this; and that attention is paid to how the cultures interact.[6] They interweave with cultures and history, with geography, gender, economics, religion, and much

---

[4] Peter C. Hodgson and Robert H. King, *Readings in Christian Theology* (Philadelphia: Fortress Press, 1985), 16.

[5] Sofia Cavalletti, *The Religious Potential of the Child* (Chicago: Liturgy Training Publications, 1983), 4.

[6] Keith J. White, *Childhoods in Cultural Contexts* (Penang: Malaysia Baptist Theological Seminary, Compassion International and the Global Alliance for Advancing Holistic Child Development, 2011), 26.

more. Children live at the interface between traditional cultures and these new emerging worlds of meaning.

There are several approaches to deal with the issues of children. All of them may be equally useful but when it comes to special focus, we are practically inclined to think of Christian theological-ethical perspective. It is because we are responsible to the church or the church has a strong influence on us. Following the same pattern, I see that the church needs to be more active toward this concern. It is a fact that the church has been active all through her history. But, we need to ask about the impact she has made on the lives of the children. When we encounter the issues of violence, rape, killing, extortion, etc., can we conclude that all these happen because the Christian church is not able to impart positive values on the children and so when they grow up, they become different? No. This is not a proper assessment. What is important today is what the church is for the children. Is church a new way of living or is it culturally bound, in the eyes of children? Is going to the church their own choice or parents' compulsion? Is taking baptism based on their confession or based on their age? Is the dedication of child(ren) by parents for theological studies or Christian ministries the best method or it is manipulation of their own children? The question of being Christian and going to the church and entering into Christian ministry needs to go beyond cultural binding. Parents should not be satisfied with their children joining their friends in attending church. But, we must work hard to instill deep-rooted faith in the minds of the children so that they willingly abide by the calling of the church rather than blindly following others.

While the role of the church and the commitment of every child are important, we must also consider that the home is equally important for a child's holistic development. There are several habits that the parents should adopt and teach to their children. But, while acknowledging that our environment is different from many rural contexts where strict cultural binding is not available and also the avenues to learn and enjoy are different, we must include a particular principle that is, "What books should be given to children to read?" We may be required to evaluate and re-evaluate the results of different reading habits such as, novel reading, comic reading, story reading, magazine reading, etc. It is necessary because reading also has a great and lasting influence on the mind of a child. If parental guidance is not given to this activity, the child's personality may turn out differently from what we or society expect.

For most of us, our social environment does not permit us to strictly follow the traditional patterns of training children for participation in church ministry. The world we live in is different now and so, we need to adopt different styles of shaping children. For instance, confining children at home is no longer the best method for instilling good morals in a child. The school environment is also not without problems as children pick up habits and lifestyles of their friends. It is not possible to keep them away from friends of different kinds. Teaching children to develop respect for elders and teaching them to learn household chores are two old, relevant cultural values, but which are becoming secondary in today's world.

Children today are doing much more than what they should do at their age. For instance, there is a serious problem of robbing them of their childhood when parents become over-enthusiastic to make their children the best among many. Parents want their child to attain the first rank in the class; they want their child to be the best player in games; they want their child to be the best singer; they want their child to be a musician, the best dance performer, and many more. Will this be possible? Have the parents made sufficient assessment of the capacity, talent, and choice of their child or, are the parents simply pushing their child to excel in all areas. But then, who will be responsible if the child fails in all because of overburden and pressure? The parents must also know that as much as they have the right to educate and train their children according to their wishes, the children also have the right to decide their future, and the right to be free and the right to protest.

There is thus the need for constant reforming of Christian theology in the light of the present reality. We are called to live with a realistic attitude toward children rather than pretend that everything is good and available for them. When reflecting about reforming Christian theology, can we talk about the center of power and ensure that it does not permanently remain in the traditional structure of the family/church? God is not limited to established structural positions/traditions but is also found in the periphery. If such is the case, should there be a way to accept the expression of children's faith for baptism or, we continue to maintain the concept of adulthood to know the truth of God? Can the church move toward the realization of the vision of hope in the Bible by reforming the concepts and structures of the church?[7]

Reforming the church should include taking the status of children as important and dealing with them appropriately for the sake of materializing social and religious justice. They must know the reality of the family and the church to develop their perspective. The responsibility of parents is to ensure that their children do not develop superiority complex and

---

[7] Keith J. White calls Rev 21 and 22 as fragments of the vision of hope; of a new creation; and a new way of living throughout the Bible. Keith J. White, *Introducing Child Theology—Theological Foundations for Holistic Child Development*, rev. ed. (Penang: Malaysia Baptist Theological Seminary, Compassion International and the Global Alliance for Advancing Holistic Child Development, 2012), 211.

undisciplined management of resources, while parents with limited resources should ensure their children do not develop inferiority complex but rather learn good stewardship of their parents' resources.

CHILDREN'S PARTICIPATION (THEOLOGICAL)

The debate in Child Theology (CT)/HCD is a new initiative toward defining what is right and what is wrong in theological thinking. This undertaking does not rely on a biased approach, but rather a realistic approach based on situational resources available to us.

Our approach toward children's participation should be shaped on the basis of our experiences. We should not forget that radicalism in theological approach has led to failure in theology. For example, who attends women's church and who is reading the *Woman's Bible*? Similarly, tribal theology is being criticized as an attempt to take the people back to tradition (This is done most likely by people who do not understand the purpose of tribal theology).

CT is a paradigm of moral discourse that questions traditional definition and, at the same time, attempts to redefine the contemporary concept of the "image of God." How do we include children in our definition of "human?"

It is also a new way of expressing theological anthropology, in which you need God in order to define "human."

I do not have objection to ordain a ten-year boy/girl to full time church ministry, but will that make sufficient impact? We need to find out the areas where children can best participate to make meaning.

Keeping in view the need for a time frame, I prefer to think in terms of a 10 years projection during which all programs may give emphasis not on glorifying children or portraying children's suffering, but on the relationship between children and adults, and also evaluate the mentality of adults toward children for the purpose of getting a new definition of Child Theology and its ministry.

World Environment Day

Can the church collaborate with local schools to observe World Environment Day? We should commit to plant 500 trees every year for thirty years so as to reclaim the normal cycle of rain, and thus make peace with the environment. It is worth noting that certain groups of people have already signed up for this program.

In such collaborations, we need to ensure the selection of the right tree species, as certain trees absorb high quantities of water, and there is also the need to decide if local tree varieties or trees with high carbon removal rates are to be planted. Further, we must design a method to stop unreasonable burning of forests. It may be good to organize program for citizens in order to conscientize them about the impact of wildfires. Can children undertake campaigns on this issue?

Human Rights Day

Is it possible for the church to celebrate Human Rights Day on the 10th December or 2nd September and organize program on peace? Will this be a proper means to create awareness to the masses? Children should take up major roles in such programs based on Covenant on the Right of the Child (CRC).

Children's Day

Our society may identify a day for the children or the present Children's Day may be Christianized during which efforts are made to engage children and church leaders, and also with the policy makers to share their needs. The needs of children are not limited to funds or refreshments) but should include issues such as the regular supply of electricity for study purpose and competition, provision of clean drinking water in the towns and villages, and confidence-building activities, among other things. During the interaction with leaders of the church, society, and government, children should question the leaders about what they want them to inherit. This would make adults to understand that they are living the borrowed land from the children; it would soon return to them.

Mediating role

Taking into account the failures of adults in their attempts to negotiate conflicts, we may now change our approach and ask children to meet leaders of conflicting parties to express the pain and struggles of living in the midst of conflicts and killing.

Children Sunday/World Sunday School Day

Attempt should be made to go beyond the traditional space given to children to sing special numbers, memory verse recitation, skit, etc., by conceptualizing and introducing new kinds of roles and involvement for the children.

Stewardship

Can they serve elements during the Holy Communion? Can you receive these without guilty conscience? If yes, it will show that we are accepting children in the church.

Children workshop

Can we conduct creative workshops for children to orient them on writing their own stories? These stories can become source materials for future programs. Children can be taught to compose songs (if we are not able to get into the shoes of a child to write songs for them). Peace initiatives should be taken up on a war footing.

Participation (social)

Does our approach also involve including children in the decision-making bodies like the board of deacons, village council, Hohos, and development committee? The question is even if this is possible, we will not be able to realize that the vision of CT is materialized. For, it might have the same outcome as the case with women—giving ordination to women and refusing to use them in the church ministry. Why do we only bring about cosmetic changes without seriously considering their call to the ministry? Think about the number of women ordained ministers and compare this number with the utilization of their function. How many of them have got the role of solemnizing weddings? How many times have you received elements (of Holy Communion) from women ordained ministers?

I am not advocating quota for children because they will continue to have no voice in the Council/Board. A quota system will not work unless we call for restructuring or redefining the concepts of "policy making" and "leadership."

In one program on children in Dimapur, Prof. Lanunungsang Ao touched on the importance of mother-tongue. Expressing concern about the increasing trend of Naga households conversing in Nagamese, he said the trend has become a threat to Naga identity. In this regard, he urged that parents should lead by example and discourage the use of Nagamese in the household, while encouraging conversation in one's mother-tongue.[8] His idea is that every Naga tribe has its own mother tongue whereas Nagamese is a corrupted language of Assamese, Hindi, and English that is used for communication between and among different Naga tribes. When their children have become too accustomed to Nagamese at the cost of their own ethnic dialect (mother-tongue), they loss their culture. That trend should be stopped as far as possible.

All these methods and concerns need to be properly oriented to make the children themselves feel the need and they themselves act as agents of change. In doing this, they should not become victims of adults again.

---

[8] *Morung Express*, January 11, 2014.

Adults in the present period must realize that children's involvement can perhaps make one of the biggest impacts on the world.

We need to redefine festivals in order to incorporate children.

While focusing on paradigm shift in thinking, I find it necessary to refer to the modern educational system being adopted in the schools in India. The system and workload are not children-friendly. Children are over-burdened and are unable to cope with the educational demands. The system has provided quality education to only a select few.

The system is too competitive, expensive, individualistic, and foreign. The adverse effect on children is evident in the busy schedule they have to follow daily—daily classes in school are followed by tuition, music/dance class, after which they return home exhausted. And, in between the activities, any short time available is spent in watching television or playing computer games, which adversely impact children's holistic development in different ways.

We need to remodel education, by doing away with education determined by literacy and introducing participatory education. Content knowledge and examination-oriented education is not conducive to meeting the needs of children and society. Either the examination-oriented system has to be drastically reduced, and balanced equally with participatory education, or the examination system can be done away with altogether, like the Japanese system that is based on the principle. In their system, they do not conduct examination up to the fourth standard but they only taught them etiquette. They do not give any pressure on them at this tender age.

In a world where children have multiple avenues to pursue and choose, when knowledge continues to increase at a fast pace, and education becomes extremely competitive, parents need to be more explorative when the rights of children are being advocated. They need to wisely assist their children to locate their culture and its interaction with other new cultures. The parents must be aware of the power of socialization of society that shapes the personality and spirituality of a child. Attempt should be made to properly identify the relationship between ethics and morals of the children so that parents do not overemphasize one over the other. Parents' approach should be both moral and ethical so that their love does not over-ride their children's ethical education.

To do this, traditional disciplines help to a certain extent, but parents need to adopt the modern approach in order to integrate present realities. For instance, if the parents do not know how to deal with consumerism, there are chances of spoiling the ethics of children by fulfilling their unending demands. Similarly, the church should not serve as only a place for learning scriptural memory texts, but should be a place that they are strongly attached to. The church must be a place to which they can go in all situations so that they can grow with the assurance and conviction that they must live not only for themselves but for the people at large.

There is also a need to provide special activities to children for attaining alternative knowledge. The style of building friendships among the children of different context/campus/locality needs to change because what they consider the modern style lacks rationale and its philosophy superficial, and the concept is domineering against other cultural styles. We need a lifestyle that enriches the interest of modern, Christian, and ethnic culture, without which, we will be ill-prepared to effectively tackle the questions and challenges in our future.

13

AGAINST CORRUPTION: A SOCIAL RESPONSE

Corruption is a very general term that does not provide proper meaning unless one adopts a proper perspective to define certain actions. We may take bribe as corruption, and likewise, the ambit of corruption includes unreasonable sanction of grants to undeserving persons or appointment to a government post by taking bribe, siphoning of funds, unfair utilization of administrative power, etc. At the outset, I want to point out that many people who are aware of corruption do not find a forum to speak and act against it. Any form of corruption exists not because a society or nation does not have a law to deal with it, but it is because laws are ignored or there is a weak law-enforcing body. At the same time, corruption takes place only because there is a huge overflow of resource. If there is no money available in the government departments or market/industry, people will have no notion about corruption. Keeping this in mind, we may first see that all religions and national laws speak about truth, fair administration, equal rights, and sharing. Everyone knows the religious implications of corruption, but the act of corruption continues to exist. The church speaks very strongly against this evil. However, very often, the church platform is unable to address the rampant corruption in the society. But, in spite of its seriousness on these issues, it has failed to adopt the right approach.

It has for almost 2,000 years adopted an approach to individual change for social change by teaching people to individually realize the biblical teaching of truth and stewardship. Christian mission has emphasized on individual soul-winning. This is a good thing, but it is difficult to make a sufficient impact on people outside the church. This is practically impossible for Christians in India who form just 2.3 percent of the country's total population. More seriously, there are many Christians who are involved in the so-called corruption. Individual approach becomes a problem because if you listen to the speech of Christians in secular leadership or Christian politicians on the matter of corruption and how to solve it, it is clear that they already know much about it. But, when they return to their workplace, they continue to carry out the same act of corruption. Therefore, one thing that needs to be clear when we try to debate on the issue is that corruption is an individual effort. It is a person who is involved and not the society or the church; though in certain cases, the name of an organization or church might be used but the act is done by an individual. Even if that is the case of pointing out few individuals, it will not bring the expected result of rooting out corruption. I, therefore, think that we need an alternative approach that I call as social approach in order to fight against corruption. At the same time, I do not neglect the existing approach but use the approaches together or as per the demands of the context. My perspective is strictly of a tribal Christian perspective.

It is already several years now since people's movements had sprung up in India to move against corruption. Corruption is not limited to mainland India, but it is very much present in our own land. Whatever society one belongs to, it is a fact that there is no society that is free from this modern disease. And, it is easy to find that all aspects of our society are affected by this reality. It is everyone's knowledge that vote has to be bought, education has to be bought, government job has to be bought, and even a below-poverty-line scheme has to be bought. The list is endless but what is important for us is that if we do not act against this problem very soon, our society will be completely de-stabilized and there would be no more room for us to speak and act against it. Further, we will fail to pass on a livable society to our children and grand-children.

The word *society* comes from the Latin word *socius* that literally means companionship. Later, it came to be defined as a collection of individuals that live together with a distinct or diverse identity. A society and its identity are thus important to each individual. This importance is evident through an individual's dependence on society. No individual will find a way of existence, if left alone. *Dependence on one another is a divine creation and purpose.* This is again the basic element of society. A person definitely finds it difficult to identify oneself apart from one's society. For example, if you go to a city and try to introduce yourself without referring to your society /tribe /ethnicity /race, and the land, people will not be able to understand who you are. The same is true for beauty, truth, wealth, intelligence, profession, etc., because each of these values can be understood only in relation to others and not in the world of oneself. *Thus, individuals form a society and society in return shapes the psyche of individuals.*

A society can be kept in peace and harmony only when there is a strong law-enforcing body and intelligent public awareness. We need an organization that controls the system of the society. It should be able to make a final decision and the verdict should be properly executed so that no individual force is able to challenge the authority of that organization. Any modern society must see to it that individuals do not weaken the organization so that few people can manipulate the organizational authority in order to make their positions comfortable. Such practice weakens the values of society and creates poverty as injustice becomes rampant.

With this brief introduction, we will first look at the reality of our society. Most of us are made to think that in order to become a respectable person in society, we need just two things namely, wealth and education. A simple analysis of our society shows that an individual's values are highly looked upon and sought after. Individual progress happens very well and fast but community/society is not considered. Many of our programs are directed toward individual progress. As a result, we have highly educated individuals, and few extremely rich individuals but majority of the members in society are neither educated nor rich. The so-called common people in the society are forced to live on subsistence mode. They are denied the opportunity to dream of a better life and status one day in their own society. In contrast, the uppermost questions in their minds are: How do we repay our debt? What do we get to eat for the week? How do we support our children's education?

A quick look at the annual expenditure of our states clearly indicates that there is no shortage of finances. We have very high-quality educational institutions. Our educational system is very expensive and competitive. So, for those who can afford to spend on education, accessing high quality education is not a problem. However, we further need to underline two more issues. The first concern is related to the question: Does our educational system produce only administrators and not people with social and cultural values? The second concern is related to the issue that, even though there are high quality educational facilities, the social environment where institutions are located is not good. There are regular reports of killing, corruption, kidnapping, rape, molestation, divorce, looting, etc. Thus, young students are vulnerable to the influence of such reports and may later grow up to either follow the corrupt system or wrongly react to the social realities.

It is difficult to come to terms with the fact that while a huge amount of money is allocated for poverty eradication, the number of poor people continuously increases; when a huge amount of money is allocated for power supply, and the public continues to live under load shedding/power cuts; when so much money is spent for road construction and repair, and the condition of the roads does not improve; when a large chunk of funds are allocated for water resources but the common people have not had the chance to get drinking water; when employment is made not on the basis of merit but on the basis of higher bribe offers, and the list goes on. Where have our state finances gone to? All the misdirecting of state finances is due to a weak state administration and the lack of a people's organization that can strongly raise its voice. To cite an example based on a news report from Imphal, except for a couple of officials, officers of Agriculture Department starting from Director to District Agriculture Officers (DAOs) are unaware of the central sponsored schemes implemented in the state in agriculture and allied sectors as well as the quantum of funds sanctioned for these schemes. The concerned officials denied knowledge of when and how much material has been distributed as the materials were distributed through the MLAs (the elected representatives of the people).[1] In this way, the few officers who have been literally controlling several central sponsored schemes have managed to browbeat the DAOs. In such a scenario, which organization in our society should we rely on? Who is there to stand up for the cause of the people? Are we not all caught up in this together? The situation has become such that the voice of the poor and powerless will never be heard and the leaders are not in a position to speak against any wrongdoing because if one leader speaks up against others, the accused would expose the greater wrong of the one who speaks.

It is heartbreaking to look at the happenings in Manipur. In an article in *The Sangai Express*, it was pointed out that the current government in Manipur has failed the expectations of the people that a stable government will provide peace and well-being to the citizens. The Congress party-led government for three consecutive terms has resulted in the worst form of human rights violation, corruption, and increase in number of private enterprises at the cost of the government sector. The Human Rights groups have termed the preceding decade as a "fake encounter decade." Enjoying a strong majority, the government is following the dictates of politicians without working for the common people. Even after the exposure of a scam amounting to over 200 crores by a number of agencies, the government has not done anything. Even when drug peddlers were caught with drugs worth 25 crores by police commandos and were detained in jail, the accused could get bail on the ground that no charge-sheet is filed against them. Who is responsible and what is the government doing? Or is government inaction due to the fact that the two accused are a sitting MLA's son and an Indian army officer? An equally grave situation is that when any movement/union/organization calls for bandh, the politicians immediately join hands with the entrepreneurs to make fast money. This

---

[1] "Agri Officers in the Dark about Schemes, Funds," *The Sangai Express*, August 10, 2013.

situation is evident when the oil pumps are closed and the roadsides are made free for black marketers who sell petrol at grossly inflated prices.[2]

There are many rich people in the world today, which is a good thing. Some of them have genuinely labored to become rich, but some others have gained wealth by plundering the wealth of the society through unknown sources. Now, we must inquire of them: Did your parents bring you up in such a way that you are trying to bring up your children the same way? If their parents had used honestly-acquired resources, they would not have raised people who steal the money of the poor. The testimonies of many poor parents who had struggled to support their children are beautiful and the reward of their labor and sweat is sweet. But there are many parents who have spent much money from unknown sources and do not have a similar testimony because their children have turned out to be spoiled and unsuccessful. By this, I do not mean that they are not educated, but that they have failed to earn people's recognition and respect.

Have you ever seen or met any person who is educated and wealthy, but is not peaceful and happy? It is said that people who become rich with wealth from unknown sources do not live a happy life, but live a very insecure life. This can however be confirmed only when they admit and testify to it. Not very long ago, I got to hear about the experience of an ordained Christian minister. After many years of working in other places, he came to his village for winter vacation. He met many of his old friends. There was one friend who had became extremely rich. When the minister visited his friend, he was very excited to entertain him. He took him around and showed every corner of his mansion filled with the most expensive furniture. He showed all his properties accumulated from unknown sources. His house was filled with expensive appliances and outside the house, a few cars were lined up. It was not possible for the minister to tell his friend that all this wealth was accumulated from money meant for the poor and also from those who deserved it. As usual, when the Christian minister was about to leave the house, he was asked to offer a prayer. The minister struggled within himself about how to pray. He was very sure that his friend has made himself rich by wrong means and therefore, it was not possible to give thanks for the blessing, nor possible for him to pray for more blessings because the friend may do greater harm to deprive more people. Therefore, the Christian minister refused to sit on the sofa, but he instead asked for a *morah* (cane stool). He sat on it and prayed for his friend, "When he sits on these sofa seats remind him that he is sitting on a stolen sofa, when he lies down on the expensive fluffy

---

[2] "Stability for Whose Sake? Who Stands to Benefit, Political Bandits or the Police?" *The Sangai Express*, July 21, 2013.

bed, let him think that he is lying on a stolen bed and when he travels on those luxury cars, let him think that he is sitting on a stolen car." After the visit, the Christian minister left his village and went back to his place of work. That night, it was a cold winter night but the minister's rich friend could not sleep as he was sweating during that cold night. The minister's prayer continued to disturb him until he realized that there are many people crying because they are deprived of their rightful share of wealth and privileges. The next day, the friend called the Christian minister and asked him what he should do. He was told that there is little he can do except that realization of his wrong deeds would be his best Christmas gift that year. The friend seriously realized the kind of wrong life he had lived and regretted so much that he promised he would not continue his wrong way of living. The point to note here is that, the Christian minister maintains justice as his principle of ministry; he refused to offer a cheap prayer for which he may get a good sum of money; he identifies himself to be a true Christian minister. That is what I call "doing Christian theology."

If we read Jeremiah 32:18, we find that God is a loving God but at the same time, God would judge the children for their parents' sin. No parents will be able to bring up good children from their stolen wealth. They may be able to buy education for them but when they are not careful, their children would do greater sin than them. Remember, when their children realize that their parents' money comes from unknown sources, the children could become frustrated and curse the parents. Is it possible for the parents who accumulate wrongly-acquired wealth to understand that they would surely fall one day because the truth remains as truth and it will surely catch up with those who overrule it.

Wealth is very important for living. There is nothing wrong to own a huge amount of honestly-acquired wealth. Money is required to rescue many lives, and for carrying out many good works. Beautiful kingdoms and cities were all built by money. Money can do many good works and change the lives of many people. But, if money is wrongly accumulated and used, it is very harmful not only to individuals but to the society as well. The lives of many are being destroyed by it; it creates enmity between and among people; it creates selfishness, and people are oppressed.

There is an argument that there will be less human misery on earth if injustice done by a few individuals is stopped, because much of human misery is caused by unjust practices of a few. Now, anyone may honestly start analyzing the cause of human suffering by identifying and understanding what makes people suffer. Is there anyone who has knowingly made the choice to suffer? Or, is suffering imposed on people? For this purpose, one may ask why the relatively few educated people struggle to find any means to survive? Why do people remain in the cycle of poverty

Against Corruption

for decades without access to any national facility? Where is their right to life? There is no reason for people to suffer if they are not denied of their rightful privileges that society offers. There are people suffering only because they are denied opportunities by a few powerful people who are more interested in building their own kingdom by exploiting the poor. In other words, if every citizen is given their equal share of available resources, then there is no opportunity for corrupt people to make themselves rich. This logic is based on the argument that honest government workers cannot acquire disproportionate wealth, based on their salary alone. It is impossible that someone honestly living on government's salary can accumulate huge property estates, live in luxury, and sponsor their children's expensive education. It is thus possible to become rich only when one indulges in unfair means or, only when one takes others' share. This is why it is said that if there is no greed or corruption, human beings would only suffer the misery caused by sickness and natural calamities. Therefore, I would conclude that 85 percent of human suffering is caused through injustice. And the remaining 15 percent of misery only exists in a fair society. I am reminded of a preacher saying that when certain leaders that people look up to (with respect) speak one thing and do another thing, it is shocking to the nation and to the community. It is a loss of personal integrity and for which people would reject their leadership.

This again takes us to another aspect of the problem of corruption—that it is due to the weakness and failure of organizations. Perhaps, our society has forgotten the stewardship of organizational functions and opted to exercise organizational function as a privilege to use its power for serving vested interests. As a result of this, our society is weakened. Do we have any organization that we can fully rely upon? Or, do we think that there is no point to go to the organizational level for the problem we face because the leaders would again demand money and at the end, they will not be able to address the issue since their conscience and decision may be bought by someone who owns enough money? What is societal power and how do we use it? must be properly defined if we decide to serve people through an organization. Each of us should keep in mind that without organization, there cannot be a society that serves the needs of its people. In other words, no individual will be capable of providing well-being to any other individual as this is possible only when a society is administered by the law of justice.

Keeping in mind the issues underlined above, we draw the conclusion that what we are in need of is a method that would usher in peace to the people. There are many people who think that when enmity between the warring parties is sorted out or any conflicting parties are reconciled, and we put wars to an end, everything will be okay. It is not difficult to understand such an idea of peace. This is one form of peace called negative peace. But at the same time, there is another school of thought that the end of violence cannot bring peace. According to this school, violence is necessary in order to bring peace. It maintains that until the powerful state that deprives the weaker nations/sections is destroyed, there will be no peace as it continues to exploit the poor/weak through their powerful strength. Today, most people expect to attain positive peace that can be restored only when every citizen is respected, and justice prevails in the society, and there is equality and love among the members.

And so, in conclusion, I perceive two possibilities. First, there is need for a strong reformation at the organizational level in which common citizens hold the ultimate power, and leadership is given only to those who are willing to serve the people. Anyone who tries to live above society's needs must be immediately withdrawn. No leader should be given a chance to exercise power for selfish ends. If our civil societies become greater and stronger than individuals, things can be changed. The India against Corruption movement has adopted a similar stance. It has also gone to the extent of forming a political party, the Aam Aadmi Party. Similarly, the Krishak Mukti Sangram Samiti (KMSS) in Assam has been raising its voice against corruption for a long time and eventually emerged as a new political party called Gana Mukti Sangram. But, even as I think there should be a movement against corruption, I do not see creating political space as the best strategy.

The other option I see is in line with what had happened in India's national capital New Delhi, when a 23-year-old paramedic student was gang-raped by six accused on the night of December 16, 2012. The incident of gang-rape is not something new in Indian society but unlike other similar events, this incident gave a chance to the citizens of India to pour out their anger against the nation that has a for a long time refused to take appropriate legal actions. After this incident, thousands of protestors from all walks of life, men, women, and people of all religions thronged India Gate, Ram Lila Maidan, and Jantar Mantar. Interestingly, a similar environment was seen in many other cities like Bengaluru, Kolkata, Mumbai, Chennai, Lucknow, Hyderabad, Guwahati, and Jaipur, etc., with citizens demanding a befitting punishment to the rapists, reform of the legal implementation system, and heavier punishment for rapists. Following this, there have been drastic changes as fast track courts were set up to speed up prosecutions. For the Delhi case, the court has given (four accused) a verdict "to send them to gallows till death." Many changes are still expected in order to make India a safer place for women. I would even go to the extent of proposing that judgment against rape and gang rape should be differently and strictly dealt with and a different level of punishment given to the culprits, in view of the high number of rape cases in the country.

The world of the tribal people in North East India is not too far from the menace of corruption. They seriously need to do a critical reflection on their religious system because most of the crises that exist in the society are the outcome of spiritual decay. In order to find a proper socio-religious approach to combat corruption, there is a need for concrete logical understanding of religious directions. Christians in the region need to re-examine their understanding of the Bible and its directives. There are many people in this region who consider the Bible as very important and yet, do not follow biblical teachings. Biblical teachings are in certain cases confused with the biblical principle of revelation and verbal prophecy and this has led to the development of a religion of fear. Christian teaching is not necessarily restricted to arousing human emotion. Every Christian knows confession is an important thing to do, but no one should be threatened to make confessions as they can become psychologically disturbed.

When a person is threatened with religious commands, it leads to fear and prevents enjoyment of religious life. This is illustrated by the incident of a seer in Uttar Pradesh who dreamt that 1,000 tons of gold are buried under the premises of an old fort at Daudiya Kheda in Unnao district. The government of India and the leaders who desperately believed the dream of a religious leader allowed the archaeological department to dig the ground, but they did not find the gold.[3] Is this a civilized and scientific method? Who decides the administrative affairs in a country? My point is that if the tribal people of the region are not careful enough, they may soon face a similar collapse of administration if things like dreams are allowed to dictate the actions of political and religious leaders. Christianity is not a religion that propagates fear, but truth, love, joy, and peace. The tribal people need to urgently reorient their religious thinking.

Adopting a new approach to religious thinking is important because it would provide leaders a way to strengthen their social organizational authority. As long as this world exists, we can never think of being completely free from injustice and corruption. But, we must also know that any corruption/injustice/conflict/crisis is created by human beings, and therefore, human beings are the only beings who can resolve any form of crisis. More specifically, there is no one who will come and solve the tribal people's problems and they themselves have to awake and correct their social vision, and take steps to authenticate their position against corruption. Today, we do not have a strong political entity that governs people

---

[3] See "Unnao: Gold hunt for 1,000 tonne begins at old UP fort," accessed June 6, 2020, https://www.businesstoday.in/current/economy-politics/gold-hunt-unnao-up-fort-shobhan-sarkar/story/199756.html.

with justice. The political system of India is not conducive to bringing about justice and rooting out corruption. The people in NEI must realize that there is no other better option than to revive their own political systems in truth and honesty in order to manifest the principle of justice.

Lastly, my observation is that the tribal people are, by nature, a religious group of people. Religion has served as the backbone of their society. It is further possible to think that even if all other social institutions fail, as long as they have firm religious convictions, their society will survive but if religion fails, then the whole society would collapse. And yet, what is not possible to see in their religious life is that it is not impacting and strengthening the social organizational system. So, the church that is the people's movement should take a proactive role to fight against corruption without any form of compromise. If this happens, other institutions cannot stand against it because people are part of this institution. So, the need is to have a paradigm shift toward conceptualizing justice from a social perspective. In this kind of a framework, individuals are not given space to manipulate social power, but will work to ensure that people equally live under the strong organizational laws. Perhaps, we may even change our attitude of repeatedly telling people to read the Bible and rather let the Bible to read our own lives. For our not knowing the Bible is a lesser issue than living a life not guided by biblical teachings.

We have heard the stories of a few organizations trying to work against corruption. Though their cause is noble we may ask, how realistic is their approach and program? The best possible option I see is that there should be a state Bill that requires transparent governance. Each department should disclose every type of expenditure, either monthly or bi-monthly, and people should be attentive to it. At the same time, every development work taken up should be publicized along with the names of persons responsible to utilize the money, and the community/church/NGOs and other social forums must monitor the work's progress and expenditure. Similarly, the names of contractors who take up road making or construction of government buildings and projects should be published along with the amount of money sanctioned, and other project details.

This information needs to be utilized by the local people in checking the quality and progress of the work. If any person is found guilty of corruption in any work, the local community may take steps to inform the government and demand that such persons are not granted any more projects.

There is a serious need to reorganize the organizational system of the society so that the law becomes powerful to check all the wrongs of individuals. There is no organizational corruption unless there is an individual who is manipulating the organizational system. Thus, no society or government can fail the people if there are no corrupt individuals behind the system. It is better to check individuals than fail the society or government. No individual should be made too powerful to destroy the social system, instead people should be endowed with the necessary power to uphold the laws and follow them successfully.

14

ETHICAL RESPONSE TO THE DANGER OF ENVIRONMENTAL CRISIS

Introduction

This topic is, for some people, an over debated topic that no longer draws mass attention. But this is not the answer to the matter at hand. We must continue to hold debates until full awareness on the issue is created. For the last forty or more years, intellectuals have been discussing and studies have been done on environmental issues although we have not been able to find the solution. The world has invested enough resources for the concern on environmental issues, and yet much more would be further required. However, the answer to this crisis will not and cannot be derived by either scientists or environmentalists alone. It is only when the local people can regenerate their forests to their original state and improve land management system at the local level through local methods, that the crisis may be reduced. The United Nations declared the year 2010 as the Year of Bio-diversity with the theme: *Many Species, One Planet, One Future* that was followed by a series of Earth Summits.[1] The World

---

[1] Among all the declarations and statements of the Earth Summits, the Kyoto Protocol is very significant. *The Kyoto Protocol* treaty was negotiated in December 1997 at the city of Kyoto, Japan, and came into force on February 16, 2005. "The Kyoto Protocol is a legally binding agreement under which industrialized countries will reduce their collective emissions of greenhouse gases by 5.2 percent compared to the year 1990 (but note that, compared to the emissions levels that would be expected by 2010 without the Protocol, this target represents a 29 percent cut). The goal is to lower overall emissions from six greenhouse gases—carbon dioxide, methane, nitrous oxide, sulfur hexafluoride, HFCs, and PFCs—calculated as an average over the five-year period of 2008–12. National targets range from 8 percent reductions for the European Union and some others to 7 percent for the US, 6 percent for Japan, 0 (nil) percent for Russia, and permitted increases of 8 percent for Australia and 10 percent for Iceland." accessed February

Council of Churches (WCC) had begun debating on the issue of environmental crisis as early as 1983 during its Assembly at Vancouver, Canada. But, with the passing of time, it has become more crucial and pressing. Environmental concern is not an economic and technological issue alone, but a serious moral issue that all people of the world need to seriously address. Moreover, our primary concern is limited to the local context and we must seek to find what practical positions people can take to respond to this pertinent reality. Therefore, I will not go into a detailed discussion and explanation of the environmental crisis.

The environmental crisis may be considered as one of the greatest threats human beings have ever experienced. This threat does not make distinctions between races or regions, but places the entire universe under the same risk. It refers to the understanding that environmental and biological balance of the earth's biosphere, home to a multi-million variety of plants and animals both aquatic and dry land, is endangered. Our atmosphere, water, air, and soil are under attack and damaged, leading to natural calamities and erratic climate change.[2] The crisis also refers to the pollution caused by chemical use, greenhouse gases,[3] industrial wastes, and also noise pollution.

A PERSPECTIVAL OVERVIEW

A lesser number of commonly found creatures like butterflies, grasshoppers, and spiders, the drying up of springs and ponds by as early as October or November every year is a reality and not a good sign. I intend to place the issue within the frame of "morals" because our deliberation cannot be limited to studying about nature, but it must center around the very basic source of life. It is not simply an issue that there is less rainfall or degrading fertility of soil, but it is more a question of denying people the right to live a certain quality of life. Water and air pollution and poisoning through the food-chain are causing many people to die. In this kind of a situation, the question then cannot be less than LIFE itself that is the most precious gift of God. Within this framework, we must understand that we are living in a world where many species are heading toward extinction. There is a serious crisis of biodiversity loss.[4]

17, 2015, http://www.kyotoprotocol.com/; Cf. "Disaster Risk Reduction and Resilience Building," www.uncsd2012.org.

[2] T. Swami Raju, *Christian Theological Response: Contemporary Contextual Response* (New Delhi: Christian World Imprint, 2014), 90.

[3] Nick Spencer and Robert White, *Christianity, Climate Change and Sustainable Living* (New Delhi: SPCK, 2012), 13.

[4] It is logical to conclude that when there are no butterflies, bees, and other creatures that help in the process of pollination, then the fruition will be reduced.

In most cases and for a long time, researchers, analysts, and activists have blamed human greediness to meet their wants through destructive development paradigms, which has led to the environmental crisis. This is not a wrong accusation. But, I want to read this context from a slightly different standpoint and place "ignorance" as the main factor for the crisis. In my assessment of forest resources business, particularly timber, during the last 35 years, I do not see many tribal business people who have become rich in proportion to the loss caused to the forests. The hundreds of Shaktiman trucks that ventured into the virgin forests have not made the local people richer, but have instead made many people (outsiders) rich by supplying our resources to them at the cheapest price. Through such timber business, tribal people have made themselves victims; they are making themselves poorer than ever before and living under the threat of losing their livelihood. They may soon become climate refugees in the absence of mother Earth with her rich resources to sustain them.[5] In the following lines, I cite a few research reports of Ukhrul district in Manipur state.

T. Shimrah presents a projected impact of climate change on crops in the 2030s in Ukhrul district and other parts of the North-eastern region. As per the projection on climate change (INCCA, 2010), an overall warming ranging from 1.7°C to 2.0°C by the 2030s for all the regions is projected with the maximum increase in the north-eastern and coastal regions of India. The rise in temperature with respect to the 1970s as base years will range from 1.8°C to 2.1°C. The maximum temperatures are likely to rise from 1°C to 2.5°C and the maximum temperatures may rise from 1°C to 3.5°C. The analysis indicates a crop yield reduction as in the irrigated rice yields by about 10 percent to 5 percent, while the impacts on rain-fed rice are likely to be in the range of 35 percent to 5 percent. Yield of maize crop is projected to reduce by about 40 percent in the north east region.[6]

According to Jubilate Kazingmei, 75 percent of forest in Ukhrul district remains degraded where no flora and fauna grow. Twelve percent of the land remains fallow (soil has not been regenerated after shifting cultivation). The district has just 4 percent of its forests. According to him, the main factors in the eastern and southern areas are shifting cultivation and

---

[5] The terms and concepts of Climate Refugee and Environment Refugee that are attributed to Norman Meyers and Renaud are discussed in Zulunungsang Lemtur, "Climate Change and Climate Refugees," in *Green Theology*, ed. Wati Longchar (Kolkata: SCEPTRE, 2014), 48–49.

[6] T. Shimrah, "Global Environment Change: Perceptions, Challenges and Adaptation Strategies in Tangkhul Indigenous Community," in *Encountering Modernity—Situating the Tangkhul Nagas in Perspective*, eds. R. Vashum et.al. (New Delhi: Chicken Neck, an imprint of Bibliophile South Asia, 2014), 253.

timber business because of which no matured trees are growing while in the western area, ganja (opium) cultivation and excessive use of chemical fertilizers are degrading the fertility of the soil. In the northern area, forest burning and timber business are seen as factors of deforestation.[7]

In the context of climate change and challenges to tea production, Ashok Krishan said, "We are aware that the years ahead are not going to be easy . . . .. We should be prepared to meet the challenges of the environment, and the challenges posed by climate change in relation to tea production."[8] This indicates that climate change in the region is a reality and for which, every group must work hard to face the changing scenario and condition to meet human needs while sustaining the environment.

The environmental crisis is created because of human activities on land, forests, and water. It is not a natural evolution, but a reaction to the activities performed during the last forty to forty-five years. The rationale is that even if all the available trees are felled today, there will be no water scarcity in the near future but that the consequences will be felt much later in about 30-40 years. So, it has much to do with our attitude toward the land and forest that are directly related to water and air. The privatization of land has been one of the major factors for environmental crisis. Many people buy land for their living, but slowly a greater challenge is emerging as land is being used not for livelihood but for business and development. The modern priests argue that they would take the land and make people rich with a lot of facilities (good building, good road, good school, good hospital, etc.). But, the actual consequences of this argument are clear from resistant voices that came out in Nandigram and Singur in West Bengal: *When the mountain disappears, what will be our identity? If you do not want us to cultivate, what will we eat? Do you want our children to die? When all the waters are polluted, what will we drink? When all the air is unsafe to breaths, can we buy air? If we sell our land, money will remain just a few years. If we have land, the land will feed us more than 3,000-5,000 years. We know we will live in peace as long as we have land.*[9] So also a reply of an Australian indigenous leader to a capitalist businessman who wanted to buy a plot of land belonging to the tribal/indigenous people: *How can you buy or sell the sky? The warmth of the land? The idea is strange to us. We do not own the freshness of the air or the sparkle of the*

---

[7] Jubilate Kazingmei, "A Shared Concern for Our Future," a paper presented at Tangkhul's People Consultative Forum—Consultative Meeting, February 27–28, 2015, at Tribal Research Institute, Chingmeirong, Imphal, 2.

[8] "Climate Change and Societal Challenge for Industry," *The Telegraph* (Guwahati), February 15, 2015, 6.

[9] Quoted in Wati Longchar, "Eco-Justice in Primeval Tradition: A Methodological Exploration," in *Tribal Ecology*, eds. Razouselie Lasetso, Marlene Ch. Marak, and Yangkahao Vashum (Jorhat: ETC Program Coordination, 2012), 12–13.

water. How can you buy them from us? Every inch of the earth is holy to our people. Therefore, our land is more valuable than your money. Our land will last forever..... Therefore, we cannot sell the land.[10]

The first paragraph of the Sixth Schedule of the Indian Constitution provides power to form an Autonomous District Council, which is again empowered to make law with respect to the allotment, occupation, use or setting apart of land, any other land that is reserved forest, for the purpose of agriculture or grazing or for residential or other non-agricultural purposes likely to promote the interest of the inhabitants of any village or town.[11] In the context of Assam, the *Assam Wasteland Rules* defines ownership and wasteland in such a way that any land left uncultivated for a season could be called wasteland and taken over without compensation.[12]

One of the main intentions of the modern law tenure system is collection of land revenue. Revenue generation from land tax is an important source of income for the state. While communal ownership of land and forests is protected by the customary laws under the Indian Constitution, the state tries to circumvent it by introducing individual land ownership Bill. When land is individually owned, it is easy for the state to apply the *Land Acquisition Act* (of that particular state) to acquire it. The Garo tribe in Meghalaya has experienced great impact of the new system and has lost much of community land to the government and private companies.[13] The same technique is applied in Manipur and the government is making attempts to convert tribal land into caste non-scheduled land through the state Bills/Land Act.

When it comes to forest conservation, there has been faster degradation after the introduction of forest departments in the hill areas. The state governments through the forest department are incapable of preserving forests in hill areas. This is even realized by the state governments, thus, as per the government circular in June 1990 to all the states and union territories, a guideline was provided for the involvement of village communities and voluntary agencies in the regeneration of degraded forests

---

[10] Quoted in Rongsen, "Continuing Aggression Against Indigenous Peoples and Environment," a paper presented during the Sub-Regional Consultation jointly organized by SCEPTRE, Clark Centre for Peace Research & Action and Eastern Theological College, Jorhat at ETC, Jorhat, November 18–21, 2014, 2.

[11] Sixth Schedule No. 3 (a) of *Indian Constitution,* Article 244 (2) and 275 (1).

[12] H.K. Barbujari, *Assam in the Days of the Company 1826-1856* (Shillong: North Eastern Hill University, 1996), 254–258.

[13] Melvil Pereira, "Impact of Modern Nation-State Land Tenure System on Indigenous Lands," a paper presented during the Sub-Regional Consultation on Doing Theology with Indigenous Spirituality: Asian Contribution to Theology of Creation and Wider Ecumenism at E.T.C. Jorhat, November 18–21, 2014, 4-5.

through the Joint Forest Management (JFM).[14] At one point of time, the Manipur government also introduced the Joint Forest Management system, but it terribly failed because the government did not want people's participation in the decision-making and financial management.[15] In fact, during these few years, many state government departments in the region have, as per the media, planted thousands of trees with a single objective to respond to the global climate change. But, this is not the first time that tree plantation drive is undertaken. Many departments and government agencies have also done this in the past, but there has been little significant positive impact as trees were planted without care and nurture or these were done for publicity.

In many places, the indigenous people had bitter experiences when they were thrown out of their land in the name of development and the ecosystem is destroyed. Looking at such a reality, Wati Longchar makes a strong argument when he writes, "the indigenous people who live and work closer to the land are the worst affected communities because of rampant ecological destruction and exploitation . . . . They have been uprooted from traditional earth-centered life and cultures which eventually lead to an identity and spiritual crisis."[16]

The traditional Tangkhul society had a great respect for nature and lived in harmony with nature. Tangkhul people would take permission to clear the forest for the purpose of jhum or farming and the same was done when they wanted to cut down any big tree. It may not be wrong to argue that maintaining continuity would be worthwhile for which we must adopt a similar attitude of the past. We do not need to think in terms of appeasing malevolent spirits, but rather in terms of acknowledging the value of land and forest. This principle is echoed in one of the strong appeals sent out after one of the Earth Summits, that the only option to sustain the earth is going back to 1980 levels. This was said in reference to the consumption level of energy.

THEOLOGICAL-ETHICAL REFLECTION

We need development to restore the environment, but not to destroy it. We must understand that today we are made to believe "values" in the name of modernity (a scientific explanation). In most cases, modernity tends to

[14] Franky Varah, "Indigenous Forest Management: Trends in Tangkhul Naga Community," in *Encountering Modernity*, eds. R. Vashum et.al., 283.

[15] One of the factors for the failure of that system was that there was no proper direction about the terms of collaboration between the government and the people.

[16] Wati Longchar, *Returning to Mother Earth; Theology, Christian Witness and Theological Education: An Indigenous Perspective* (Kolkata: PTCA/SCEPTRE, 2012), 14.

dismiss people's values as unscientific, superstitious, and backward. For instance, the Western world had lost several mysteries just because they were termed as traditional.[17] Considering the long-drawn debate on the crisis, it may be possible for us to perceive the ecological crisis from the perspective of Christian ethics as a justice issue that demands a substantial discussion. In the present modern world, the value of life is almost always determined by the wealth one possesses and not the intrinsic value that defines life. Unfortunately, our socialization process accepts such an attitude and makes the younger generation think the same way too. The natural resources are seen as commodity for generating wealth. Taking the indigenous people's perspective, Wati Longchar sums up like this: "the earth, the environment, natural resources, and eco-system has (have) been misunderstood as a machine that humans could maneuver (them) as we like. The mindless destruction of the earth's resources, and marginalization and subjugation of the marginalized people, like tribals through war, cultural genocide, alienation, denial, and suppression are deeply rooted in such (a) view of life. This wrong notion must be challenged and corrected."[18] Andrew Hamilton argues that in order to respond to climate change, we need to develop a moral framework because the issue is about how humans are to live humanly in this world.[19] Our approach may be developed by addressing the attitude of the people that has given rise to in the present reality. For instance, we need to consider for what reason people burned the forest? For some, it is done so as to watch the fire while others claim it to be a means for hunting birds and animals. But what is difficult to understand is, even if people are able to hunt five deer a day, it is not worth the amount of destruction they made to nature. Poisoning of water for the purpose of fishing is another illogical practice because a long stretch of river is being poisoned in the name of catching some fish. Another destructive practice is disrespecting the mating season of animals that the Tangkhul people strictly observed in the past.

The dualistic concept that was developed through the influence of Greek metaphysics has resulted in maintaining dichotomy of sacred

---

[17] Today, traditional knowledge (TK) system is eroding fast throughout the world before its value is realized. With the coming of Christianity and modern formal education, younger generations no longer give importance to the traditional knowledge system. Sometimes, they have a wrong notion that believing or practicing TK system is a primitive way of life. Thus, in pursuit of higher education as a result of enhanced inspiration and aspiration and to have a better way of life, much of the TK system has been neglected. This resulted in moving further away from land-based activities and ultimately detachment from nature. Cf. Shimrah, "Global Environment Change," 255.

[18] Wati Longchar, "Eco-Justice in Primeval Tradition," 24.

[19] Andrew Hamilton, "The Ethics of Climate Change Solutions," *Eureka Street*, 18/15 (August 1, 2008): 5.

and secular, soul and body. This dichotomy that is being upheld by the Christians to maintain the hierarchical structure that justifies human dominion over nature[20] remains at the center of the problem. The assumption is that only creatures with conscience and reason can be aware of their rights. The non-human world exists for humans and has no innate rights.[21]

Sallie McFague in her book, *A New Climate for Theology: God, the World, and Global Warming*, writes that "theology must deal with global warming because one of the basic marks of the church is its ecological catholicity, which must be lived out in a political context. In other words, Christian faith is concerned with a just and sustainable existence for all of God's creation."[22] It is so because according to her, the problem lies in our theology and our humanity. "The environmental crisis is a theological problem, a problem coming from (a) view of God and ourselves that encourages or permits our destructive, unjust action."[23] Christian theology that teaches that humanity is the crown of creation, i.e., they are superior over the rest of creation and other forms of life seemed to be one of the main reasons for our disrespect for other life forms. So, such a theology needs to be rectified if we are to save the earth from ecological imbalance. This is the reason why McFague suggested that "who God is and who we are must be central questions if we hope to change our actions in the direction of just, sustainable planetary living."[24] To her, we need a God who understands our present problems, not only about the life in eternity. We should understand God as one who is fully involved in the present life of the people.

We cannot argue against the growth of manufacturing and production. We must produce as per the demand of the people but what is important is that it should not be done at the cost of the environment. After many years of debate on alternative to jhum cultivation, we have not been able to adopt an acceptable method. Jhum cultivation is a suitable means of production in the hill areas and it may not be right to advocate banning it. But, we should be able to maintain the system by keeping in mind the importance of protecting the environment. For instance, the duration of fallow may be extended to 10 years in order to give the land sufficient time to regenerate the soil. Meanwhile, we may introduce fast growing

---

[20] George Mathew Nalunnakkal, *Green Liberation: Towards an Integrated Ecotheology* (Delhi: ISPCK, 2004), 148.
[21] K.C. Abraham, *Transforming Vision: Theological Methodological Paradigm Shift* (Tiruvalla: CSS, 2006), 192.
[22] Sallie McFague, *A New Climate for Theology: God, the World, and Global Warming* (Minneapolis, MN: Augsburg Fortress Press, 2008), 3.
[23] McFague, *New Climate for Theology*, 31.
[24] McFague, *New Climate for Theology*, 31.

native shrubs and carbon-absorbing trees during and after the cultivation to help regenerate soil fertility. At the same time, there should be attempts to learn from past practices that were beneficial both to humans and the environment. For example, in the Tangkhul traditional practice, when trees are felled, oak and alder are never cut and uprooted completely. They are cut just at or above the chest level and also just above tree node and the trunks are usually left so that more coppices grow fast and in four to five years' time, the trunk is ready for pollarding again.[25]

Going back to the Tangkhul/tribal worldview, it may be said that indigenous spirituality is derived from their relationship with nature but the underlying principle of that relationship was not simply living harmoniously with nature, but a deep consciousness of caring and protecting nature. Keeping in peace had a rich meaning for the Tangkhuls. The present Christians must revisit the tribal worldview in order to derive true meaning of life with nature. It is for this reason that Huang Po Ho asserts, "The recovery of a proper relationship between humans and the rest of God's creation is thus key to preserving a full and harmonious universe."[26]

My simple line of argument is that if we are not able to keep creation that sustains the physical aspect of human life, then we are not ethical. The tribal people/Tangkhuls have such a strong claim of communitarian life, but if our definition of communitarian life does not include nature, then we are talking of skin-deep relationship. For the tribal people, justice cannot be limited to human social system, but extended to the rest of creation as well.

ALTERNATIVE RESPONSIBILITY

There is a need to develop an ideology that calls for contextual eco-friendliness. In this alternative, contrary to the earlier experience of the government trying to use people as its instruments, it should rather participate in the people's program through technical and financial assistance. This means that people make the policy and program in which the government participates through financial assistance in order to accomplish the program and benefit the people.

For this cause, we do not need to differentiate between secular and religious organizations but join hands to be active campaigners for environmental protection. On the part of religion, there are people in different parts of the world who have practically materialized environment-friendly Christianity by adopting the Green Church

---

[25] Shimrah, "Global Environment Change," 272.
[26] Huang Po Ho, *Embracing the Household of God: A Paradigm Shift from Anthropocentric Tradition to Creation Responsibility in Doing Theology* (Kolkata: PTCA, 2014), 24.

concept. They build the church using green materials and concepts, decorate the church with green, and preach about the green; their green mission is successful.

We are called to change the pattern of fuel consumption by shifting from firewood to gas and biogas system. This would enable us to think in terms of sustaining our forests. The people, organizations, and unions, have to make a strong demand to increase the supply of LPG gas to all areas so as to meet the cooking fuel demands and needs of the population.

If the Christian churches (no matter which denomination) fail to actively involve as a peoples' movement for environmental protection, then I do not see any positive reality coming out within our lifetime. This is where the Christian churches can actively involve in campaigning against wrong methods, practices, and attitude to help people understand the concern that we cannot boldly look to the future due to ongoing environmental degradation.

As I have mentioned earlier, we need to plant trees but our attitude must first change toward this program. For instance, if we talk in terms of planting trees, then thousands of trees have already been planted by the government, individuals, NGOs, etc. But, they are not to be seen anywhere. We do not have a rejuvenated forest. Some of the trees planted by the forest department are found to be destructive because they are meant for another soil and region. For instance, eucalyptus trees absorb a huge amount of water and so, there is water shortage in the areas where many such trees are planted. Thus, what is important is to identify local plants that are most suitable to the soil in our region.

In addition, care and nurture of the trees are as important as planting them. If we are not able to care for the trees and let them grow to maturity, then our labor is wasted. We should be discerning enough to ensure that our activities help the land and forest so that water and air are preserved and maintained. And in return, they would sustain us for long. In the end, I would like to refer to what K.M. Bujabaruah, the vice chancellor of Assam Agriculture University, in his address to the gathering at the 60th technical session of Assam Science Society on March 21, 2015 said, "it is time to do something to restore the original form of the environment which man [sic] had destroyed."[27]

In conclusion, it is necessary for the people of the region to take note that there are reactionary voices, crying, groaning, and inviting people to be involved in reclaiming the environment, especially for the coming generations. We must listen to all those voices. There are many other parts of the world where the soil has completely lost its fertility and cannot be

---

[27] "Save Planet Call at Meet," *The Telegraph*, March 22, 2015, 6.

revived anymore. The topsoil of forest areas is wasted and it would be extremely difficult for the people to think of planting trees there because even if they do it, the trees will not attain the normal height. This is so because while topsoil is an important factor, groundwater is polluted and unhealthy, thus rendering tree planting projects a failure. The soil and water in North East India have not degraded beyond restoration, and people of the region should take advantage of it and double up their efforts in order to make their goal of restoring forests possible.

15

UNDERSTANDING CONFLICT SITUATIONS IN NORTH EAST INDIA

People in other parts of India understand the people of the North East region as one homogenous group with a common political problem or social system and custom. But, the region is more complicated than that. There is a danger in considering the North East people as one as far as ethnic composition and cultural differences are concerned. The region has an extraordinary diversity in terms of ethnicity, language, religion, and culture. The region is marked by diversity in religious persuasion with the presence of all major world religions—Hinduism, Buddhism, Islam, and Christianity—and a small number of people still hold to their traditional beliefs. There is a multiplicity of languages and dialects used in the region. According to L.P. Singh, they number 420 out of a total of 1,652 languages in India. All these diversities, however, do not nullify the commonness shared by the people in the nature of struggles and difficulties.

We need to first of all understand that the struggles in the region are not for the same cause. There are different people with different aspirations who again struggle through different means. In the process, there have been conflicts between and among the ethnic groups of the region. Unfortunately, the people of the region are again faced with the so-called inter-state disputes. In addition, the North East India is one of the most severely affected regions of the Armed Forces Special Powers Act (1958) that endows the Indian *jawans* with extra constitutional powers. This Act has inflicted scars and countless deaths in the region. Thus, the history of the region is scripted with the stories of conflicts, divisions, pains, and sufferings. The North East region has had a troubled past.[1]

---

[1] L. Jeyaseelam, "Conflict Situation in North East India: The Church's Response," in *No More Gun! People's Struggle for Justice*, Tribal Study Series No. 7, ed. A. Wati Longchar, 2nd ed. (Jorhat: Tribal Study Centre, 2006), 18.

To lend clarity to our understanding, I want to treat the region as a whole and view the problem from a regional perspective. This is necessary because it is the region as a whole that suffers first and the outcome is seen in segmented forms. It is relevant at this point to present a brief political background of the region. The North East in the past had a very different look from the present North East. Each of these seven sister states and Sikkim has a long-standing political history. To put this in the simplest manner, all these states were part of Assam but they slowly disintegrated into independent or full-fledged states. Nagaland was created as the sixteenth state of the Indian Republic by a Special Act in 1963. The state of Meghalaya and the Union Territories of Arunachal Pradesh[2] and Mizoram[3] came into being in 1972 and they ceased to be a part of Assam. The Union Territories of Manipur and Tripura were also raised to the status of state in 1972.

In Assam, precisely until 1920, the Assamese Association that was then the only political organization of the Assamese was playing its moderate role as a royal supporter of the British government. But in December 1920, they closed that chapter and adopted the Congress Program of Non-co-operation to achieve India's freedom and along with it, Assam's freedom within India.[4]

But, six decades of hard experiences taught them the lesson of what India was to them. They lost their confidence in Indian leadership and launched protests against continued Indian colonial exploitation in 1979. During the next six years, the Assamese had undergone a wild agitation led by All Assam Student's Union (AASU) until the Asom Gana Parishad (AGP), their own regional political party, was brought to power under the chief ministership of Prafulla Kumar Mahanta in December 1985.

After the annexation of Assam in 1826,[5] the British consolidated the state administration and thereafter, began to think of territorial defence

---

[2] Arunachal Pradesh was earlier known as North East Frontier Agency (NEFA) under the administration of the President of India through the Governor of Assam under the provision of the Sixth Schedule (Part B) of the Constitution.

[3] Mizoram became a full-fledged state in February 1987.

[4] Udayon Misra, *Northeast India: Quest for Identity* (New Delhi: Cosmo Publications, 1988), vii.

[5] Around the middle of the eighteenth century, the Maomarias, a religious sect rebelled against the Ahom King and drove him away. So, the Ahom King sought British assistance. The British rulers, on the request of the Ahom King came to Assam to suppress the Maomarias' rebellion in 1792. The British troops left Assam to settle at Calcutta in 1794. The Burmese invaded and conquered Assam in 1822. The British came back to Assam and fought the Anglo-Burmese war in 1824. The Burmese were defeated and driven out from Assam. Finally, the Treaty of Yandabo was signed between the British and the Burmese King on February 24, 1826.

and expansion. Meanwhile, their extension of land for plantation to the foothills of the surrounding Hill District inhabited by the hill people caused friction between them and the hill tribes. Moreover, the frequent raids on the British subjects by the Naga and Mizo or other hill tribes continued and became bolder and more destructive. Thus, the British had to adopt a kind of law in order to protect the plain people from the frontier tribes and vice versa. Hence, the Bengal Eastern Frontier Regulations 1873, that is also known as Inner Line Regulation, came into existence. This "Inner Line" was not concretely defined to indicate the territorial frontiers. Yet, the said Regulations empowered the Lieutenant Governor of Bengal to determine the boundaries of the hills and plains. Or, this Line only distinguished the administered area from the un-administered area of Assam.[6] Till today, the "Excluded Area" Act of 1935 continues to be enforced in Arunachal Pradesh, Mizoram, and Nagaland. However, its rationality in the present-day world is constantly debated.

For many reasons, we are excluded from the rest of India and from the world. No Indian can visit us without permission and a foreigner finds it even more difficult to reach us. We are called "excluded people" living in an "excluded area." We are made to think that we live "beyond boundaries." This is one of the main reasons why the people/students of this region face endless suffering in mainland India. The class and caste factor work very strongly in the minds of the Indians toward the people of North East India. Regrettably, such isolationist policies persisted in the post-Independence period under the mistaken motives of "protecting" the tribal population against exploitation by "outsiders." The cumulative impact of these policies was a deepening of fissures between tribal and non-tribal populations, as well as a contrived and unsustainable exclusion of these regions from the processes of modernization and democratization.[7]

Economically, the central government continues to maintain the fear that this region may one day become disintegrated and therefore, it might be a loss to implement all the national development policies on a permanent basis. If one compares the flow of national money, it becomes very discouraging to see that there is an unequal flow of money. The existence of hidden agenda is felt when we see that the money that comes to the region is not much in terms of budget, but in the form of development packages and non-lapsable loans. One must be aware that any money that comes in the form of package is utilized with less transparency and often

---

[6] See the political changes on the *Inner line Regulations* under the government of India Act, 1919, 1935, in Misra, *Northeast India*, 77.

[7] Ajai Sahni, "Survey of Conflicts & Resolution in India's Northeast," accessed November 17, 2010, http://www.satp.org/satgtp/publication/faultlines/volume12/Article3htm#@/.

becomes easier to corrupt such kind of money. It is discouraging to note the slow phase of development in the region. With the present level of development program, it is extremely difficult to calculate the number of years it would take to make all the remote villages connected by proper jeepable roads, making them fully electrified and providing them with regular water supply.

There are different forms of conflict in the regions. It will be difficult to put all of them together. But, some of the prominent ones are the ethnic/tribal conflict with the Centre, ethnic or tribal conflict between or among groups, political conflict between the hills and the plains like that in Manipur.

The following are the few common factors that should help us understand the rationale for the above identified conflicts in the region.

1. We may consider the role of invisible force. The force of ethnicity/tribalism/clan is so strong that no policy is able to control that force. At a certain level, we find that each ethnic group finds it difficult to go beyond the ethnic line. This feeling has led to -ism. Even the truth is not respected if it hurts the sentiment of community members. People often fail to see that people would take advantage of us if we do not establish wider friendship in the region. The people of the region have been too sensitive to ethnic identity and have failed to see beyond their own community concerns.

2. It is also possible for us to understand that most of the conflicts we experience in the region centers on the land. Land is an important source from which people draw their identity. When people become aware of the limited size of their land and exhaustion of their resources, they begin to feel seriously threatened. This results in consciousness of the importance of land, leading to claims of ownership or attempts to expand the boundaries, etc. Further, there is a serious problem in the concept of owning the land. Often, we come across the claims and counter-claims that not an inch of our ancestral land will be sacrificed to the cause of other people. Though the mass media have used the terms like ethnic clash, ethnic conflict, ethnic cleansing, etc., the problem is not because I do not want to live with another ethnic group, but because of an attempt to own and control the land. If such mentality was not behind the conflict, we would not have experienced many land-related conflicts in the recent past. Internal conflicts in India's North East are overwhelmingly conceptualized within the framework of unique ethnic identities that are threatened by, and in confrontation with, the nationalist state, which is often seen as a representative of an inchoate cultural "mainstream." While some of

the conflicts in the region certainly fit into this general framework of interpretation, few, if any, are completely explained by it; others, moreover, are entirely unrelated to this reductionist scheme of "freedom struggles" by ethnic minorities against the "homogenizing state." Indeed, even where militant groups direct their rhetoric and their violence against the symbols of the state, the underlying motives and ideologies are more correctly interpreted in terms of conflicting tribal identities and histories of internecine warfare based entirely on tribal, sub-tribal, or tribal-outsider rivalries, and corresponding competition over limited resources, especially land.[8]

3. The central government of India has, in many instances, played a role in intensifying conflicts by maintaining a double-standard attitude. It may not be wrong to claim that in several instances the government takes side with one group simply to create unrest in the region. It has always had an attitude to maintain different systems to control the North East region. One of the clear-cut examples may that, the government is willing to dilute the Armed Forces Special Powers Act, 1958, in Jammu and Kashmir, but the government's position for the North East is that the military forces should adopt stricter strategy to tackle the separatists in the region, as stated by P. Chidambaram, then Home Minister, in Guwahati on November 12, 2010. "In the backdrop of the massacre of 24 people, many of them Hindi-speaking, by Bodo (anti-talks) militants, Union Home Minister P Chidambaram today asked security forces to launch an "all-out" operation against the ultras and tackle them with an "iron hand."[9] The North East Indians are not only mis-identified but also face imposition of Indian traditions like wearing sari on those who work in the Indian cities. This gives a clear mis-reading of unity in diversity in the Indian context.

L. Jeyseelam identifies cultural differences among the people in the region as one of the factors for conflict. He writes that many regional tensions can be traced to cultural differences. Cultural majorities sometimes try to keep out influences, and minorities defend tooth and nail their separate existence and identities.[10] While this is the case at the regional level, he further claims that there is no cultural affinity between the rest of the Indian states and the North East. Several ethnic groups and the cultural majority and minorities were brought together under one umbrella of administration. The eighteenth-century British occupation can be considered as partially responsible for this.

---

[8] Sahni, "Survey of Conflicts.".
[9] *The Assam Tribune* (Guwahati), November 13, 2010.
[10] Jeyaseelam, "Conflict Situation," 20.

The conflict dynamics are different from state to state and also the official conflict management has been different as initiatives are not uniform for all states and groups. There are national movements fighting to be free from Indian political rule, there are others who demand autonomous status within the existing state, and some others are fighting for separate statehood. It should also be noted that there are movements that are not within this frame of demands. They operate with a purpose of cleansing evil practices in the society. But, the problem is that while they use the card of eradicating social evils, they are heavily involved in extortion of money/collection of taxes. When it comes to official conflict management adopted by various states, the surrender policy is one that is being upheld by all state governments. But, the result of such a strategy is seen as less than what is expected.

The prospects for peace in India's North East remain mixed. There has been a steady erosion of the popular base of all insurgent movements in the region, and there is growing public pressure for a peaceful resolution of grievances. Significant declining trends in violence are also visible in most states. Continuous demographic destabilization as a result of migration, both within the country, and illegal population flows from Bangladesh, have created some of the most significant threats to present and future peace in several states in the region.

The most significant obstacle to peace in the region is the crisis of governance. Levels of corruption in governments in the states of the North East are higher even than the extremely high averages in the rest of India, and the quality of governance is abysmal. Consequently, despite substantial investment of public resources in a wide range of developmental programs, the "trickle down" to the intended beneficiaries has been negligible. The problem is compounded by the collusive arrangements between political parties and "legitimate" businesses, on the one hand, and the lucrative criminal economy of terrorism that has now become entrenched in the region, on the other. With the passage of time, this underground economy of terrorism has grown stronger, and its linkages with the overground sector, immensely complex and intractable.

To make the situation better in this region, it will not be possible for one to think of a single strategy to be adopted and restore peace to the people. We need to consider varied aspects: (1) The first thing we need to consider is that peace cannot be expected from outside the region. People of the region have to realize the need. It is necessary to acknowledge the works of the civil societies who have been making tireless efforts to restore peace. Besides that, we need to make people a part of the movement. They must learn what to reject and whom to support. There is no question that all insurgent groups are able to exist only because of the common people's support; though civilians are often made victims in the process. Therefore, if the common people take a strong stand against evil practices, no other forces would be able to shake them and trample upon them.

The central government also needs to adopt a more people-friendly attitude toward the people of North East India. There is an urgent need to develop political will on the part of the central government so that many of the social and political problems can be addressed. Based on a lot of experiences, General Roy Choudhury, then Army Chief, and several other Army top brasses have gone on record on more than one occasion to state that the insurgency problem cannot be solved militarily. The Army can contain insurgency only to a certain extent. The solution has to be found politically.[11] This should relate to equal laws for all people so that the rights provided by the Constitution will not be overshadowed by other Special Acts or Bills.

On the part of the ethnic groups who are in conflict situation, they need to seriously consider whether the violent means they had adopted to protest and counter-protest have had the desired results or not. Considering the need of building peace in the region, all conflicting parties should develop a Dual Positive Approach toward each other. It is necessary because reconciliation cannot be initiated by one party. Even if one is willing to negotiate peace, as long as a positive response does not come from the other end, peace cannot be restored.

In the context of the insurgency movements in the region, it is further necessary to address the involvement of external forces that provide logistic support, training, and shelter to the insurgent groups. For instance, the role of Pakistan's ISI becomes very obvious as many of the groups receive support from it. Further, as Sahni observes, the problem is aggravated by the fact that most such terrorist groups operate out of safe havens in neighboring countries such as Bangladesh, Bhutan, and Myanmar, and the weak regimes in these countries find it impossible to check such activities on their soil.[12]

As the motives of different insurgent groups are different, we should think of a separate strategy for each of them. Even if many of their demands can be settled through negotiations, it is not possible for the government to initiate talk for those groups whose aim is to reform the social systems. The law must take its own course and allow people to operate within the framework of the law of the nation.

It is also necessary to mention that the above strategies are long-term in nature to counter conflicts but, for practical purposes, we may also

---

[11] *The Eastern Panorama*, September 1997, 9.
[12] Sahni, "Survey of Conflicts."

refer to short-term strategies. This is necessary because before the long-term strategy is implemented, we need a situation where the process should take off. Referring to the initiative taken by the church bodies and organizations, it is necessary to take care of the victims of conflicts. In the tribal context, love feast is also said to be helpful to re-establish friendship between conflicting parties. Such feast is based on a cultural method of peace-making. A more Christianized form is seen in pulpit exchange of the pastors between the conflicting village or tribe. Civil societies also have their own part to play in this process.

Peacemaking is the process of forging a settlement between the disputing parties. While this can be done in direct negotiations with just the two disputants, it is often also done with a third-party mediator, who assists with process and communication problems, and helps the parties work effectively together to draft a workable peace accord. Usually, the negotiators are official diplomats, although citizens are getting more involved in the peacemaking process. While they do not negotiate final accords, citizen diplomacy is becoming an increasingly common way to start the peacemaking process, which is then finalized with official diplomatic efforts.

However, peacemaking is not the final step in the peace process. As the situation of signing peace accords so well demonstrate, it takes more than a peace accord to bring peace to a region. The peace accord is just a beginning, which must be followed by long-term peacebuilding—the process of normalizing relations and reconciling differences between all the citizens of the warring factions. It is therefore necessary to note that reconciliation is not to be taken as an event. Shaking of hands by the disputing parties, putting signatures on the paper, and witnessing of event by the public is not itself peace. It has to be made a continuous process. Because the moment reconciliation process is broken, the same enmity is revived and violence follows. Therefore, peacebuilding should not be understood from the perspective of events but, it is rather the change in attitude of the people to make it a reality.

16

HUMANISM AND CONTEMPORARY CHRISTIANITY

We are living in one of the most difficult times in human history not because we are threatened by possible wars or ecological crises, but because our religion is being challenged from different corners. One of the most difficult threats we face is the challenge of humanism. Many of us are forced to believe and accept so many things that are not biblically, doctrinally, and theologically true. The terms "modern" and "standard" are interpreted in such a way that one is not accepted if one does not fulfill the criteria for modern and standard. These interpretations are harmful as many young Christians are being misled and have compromised their Christian ethics.

The term *humanism* conveys a positive meaning, but it has given space to overemphasize human values over divine values. According to the Webster dictionary, humanism means:

1. devotion to the humanities: literary culture;
2. devotion to human welfare: humanitarianism;
3. a doctrine, attitude, or way of life, centered on human interests or values *especially*: a philosophy that usually rejects supernaturalism and stresses an individual's dignity and worth and capacity for self-realization through reason.

Humanism is a philosophical and ethical stance that emphasizes the value and agency of human beings, individually and collectively, and generally prefers critical thinking and evidence (rationalism and empiricism) over acceptance of dogma or superstition. The meaning of the term *humanism* has fluctuated according to the successive intellectual movements that have identified with it.[1] The term was coined by

---

[1] Nicolas Walter, *Humanism—What's in the Word* (London: Rationalist Press Association, 1997). Walter gives an account of the evolution of the meaning of

theologian Friedrich Niethammer at the beginning of the nineteenth century to refer to a system of education based on the study of classical literature ("classical humanism") he planned to offer in German secondary schools. Generally, however, humanism refers to a perspective that affirms some notion of human freedom and progress. It views humans as solely responsible for the promotion and development of individuals and emphasizes a concern for man(sic) in relation to the world.[2]

In modern times, humanist movements are typically non-religious movements aligned with secularism, and today, humanism typically refers to a nontheistic life stance centered on human agency and looking to science rather than revelation from a supernatural source to understand the world.[3] At present, prominent humanists have gone so far as to declare that a humanist must be an agnostic or an atheist. Human science begins with physics while religion believes the supernatural force beyond science; the divine.

At this point, I would like to refer to R. J. Rushdoony who has observed that in the present day, humanism has brought all things, including most churches, under the sway of man (sic) the lord. The purpose of state schools, as laid down by Horace Mann, James G. Carter, and others, was twofold: first, to establish centralism, the priority of the state over every area of life; and second, to eliminate biblical faith. The founders of statist education in the United States were Unitarians. They rightly believed that control over the child through the schools is the key to controlling society. Control over the schools will determine control over state and church ultimately.

Christianity and humanism are diametrically opposed religions; one is the worship of the sovereign and Triune God, the other is the worship of man (sic). Some of the key points of difference between Christianity and humanism as they affect education are as follows:

Christianity

The sovereignty of the Triune God is the starting point, and this God speaks through his infallible word.

We must accept God as God. He alone is before Lord.

---

the word *humanism* from the point of view of a modern secular humanist. A similar but somewhat less polemical perspective appears in Richard Norman, *On Humanism: Thinking in Action* (London: Routledge: 2004).

[2] Domenic Marbaniang, "Developing the Spirit of Patriotism and Humanism in Children for Peace and Harmony," in *Children At Risk: Issues and Challenges*, ed. Jesudason Jeyaraj, (Bangalore: CFCD/ISPCK, 2009), 474.

[3] See for example, "The 2002 Amsterdam Declaration," http://iheu.org/humanism/the-amsterdam-declaration/, issued by the International Humanist and Ethical Union.

God's word and Person is the Truth.

Education is into God's truth in every realm.

Education is discipline under a body of truth. This body of truth grows with research and study, but truth is objective and God-given. We begin by presupposing God and his Word.

Godly standards grade us. We must measure up to them. The teacher grades the pupil.

Man's will and the child's will must be broken to God's purpose. Man must be remade, reborn by God's grace.

Man's problem is sin. Man must be recreated by God.

The family is God's basic institution.

Humanism

The sovereignty of man and the state is the starting point, and it is the word of scientific, elite man that we must heed.

Man is his own god, choosing or determining for himself what constitutes good and evil (Gen 3:5).

Truth is pragmatic and existential: it is what we find works and is helpful to us.

Education is the self-realization and self-development of the child.

Education is freedom from restraint and from any idea of truth outside of us. We are the standard, not something outside of man.

The school and the world must measure up to the pupil's needs. The pupil grades the teacher.

Society must be broken and remade to man's will and the child's will is sacred.

Man's problem is society. Society must be recreated by man.

The family is obsolete. The individual or the state is basic.

TRUE CHRISTIAN EDUCATION

The Christian school must, therefore, teach every subject from a God-centered perspective, or else, it will be teaching humanism. Mathematic, for example, has no validity in a universe of change: it rests on the presupposition of a sovereign and predestinating God.[4] Unlike Christian humanism, religious humanism does not appeal to God's relationship to

---

[4] John Shook, "Christian Humanism, Religious Humanism, and Secular Humanism," *CFI-Centre for Inquiry* (*Transforming Vision: Theological Methodological Paradigm Shift* (December 8, 2009), 1; cf. https://centerforinquiry.org/blog/christian_humanism_religious_humanism_and_secular_humanism/.

humans to justify our inherent dignity and liberty. Religious humanism puts humanism first and religion second.[5]

The humanistic history book not only eliminates biblical history and the great and central role of our Christian faith, it also sees history as chance rather than purpose. History for the humanist is at its best simply man's determination, whereas for the Christian, it is God's determination. Standing apart from Christian humanism and religious humanism is secular humanism. Secular humanism leaves all divinity and religion out of humanism entirely. Judging that religions are unworthy, and uninterested in spiritual enlightenment, this secular humanism grounds the humanist life and its ethical principles on reason alone. Whether secular humanism will succeed in this effort remains an open question, as it has only just begun to formulate its stances on the great questions of life and living.[6]

In the sciences, we must again deny the "rule" of chance. Materialistic determinism is no better. The Newtonian view of causality has collapsed because its single and purely naturalistic view is inadequate. There is no single cause in nature. Moreover, the multiplicity of causes does not suffice to account for the fact of order, design, and meaning. Only the presupposition of the God of Scripture can properly undergird science.

Let me refer here to Robert L. Waggoner's strong assertion on humanism and Christianity especially in the West. He states that the entire Western civilization, which was built on Christian principles, has been in moral decline. In our lifetime, the social fabric of American society appears to have been unraveling. Christian homes have not been immune to this process of social and moral deterioration. While Christianity may have appeared to be strong superficially, it has nonetheless been undermined by insidious philosophical, social, cultural, and political forces. Many have commented upon the moral deterioration of our civilization. "Western civilization has entered a period of breakdown from which it may never recover." "Civilization is collapsing before our eyes." "American society is an impasse similar to that of the Hellenic world at the time of Christ."[7]

We are living in times comparable to the decline and fall of the ancient kingdoms of Israel and Judah. While all may appear prosperous on the surface, as it did in the days of Jeroboam II in the northern kingdom of Israel, there is real danger of national collapse. Jeroboam II's reign was a time in which Israel extended her borders further than at any period

---

[5] Shook, "Christian Humanism," 2.
[6] Shook, "Christian Humanism," 2.
[7] Robert L. Waggoner, "Humanism vs. Christianity: The Greatest Battle of Our Times," accessed October 23, 2019. See http://www.thebible.net/biblicaltheism/humanchrist.htm.

following the days of Solomon. It was a time of ease and prosperity, but at the same time on the horizon was Assyria that would eventually swallow up Israel. When a nation sows immorality, as ours now does, with its excessive fornications, abortions, and other indecencies, it must eventually reap the consequences.[8] The way human beings define "morality" on the basis of human "freedom" and "conscience" is disturbing. For example, legalization of homosexuality, lesbianism, same-sex marriage, and transgender is based on personal rights and clarity of conscience. This is the influence of the humanist view because humanists derive their standards of sexual conduct from human experiences, and since personal pleasure is the primary standard by which most humanists determine their sexual conduct, then it follows that, for humanists, there should be no restraints upon sexual freedoms except as each person prefers. If any particular person, in any given situation, determines that fornication (i.e., adultery, incest, bestiality, homosexuality, lesbianism, or whatever) is right, then in that situation, for the humanists, it is considered all right![9]

A reading of *A Secular Humanist Declaration* and the Bible together clearly indicates the differences between a humanist and a Christian. Three basic differences about the nature of humanity separate humanists from Christians. First, humanists believe that humanity is only physical. Humanists "find that the traditional dualism of mind and body must be rejected." Humanism declares "there is no credible evidence that life survives the death of the body." Humanists conclude therefore "that the ethical life can be lived without the illusions of immortality or reincarnation." On the other hand, Christians believe that humanity is both physical and spiritual, having been made both from "the dust of the ground" and also "in the image of God."

Second, humanists "can discover no divine purpose or providence for the human species." Humanists declare that "man is at last becoming aware that he alone is responsible for the realization of the world of his dreams, that he has within himself the power for its achievement." "Secular humanism places trust in human intelligence rather than in divine guidance." On the other hand, Christians believe that humans are unable to direct themselves and that humanity is dependent upon God for purpose and guidance in life.

Third, humanists' declarations indicate their conviction that goodness is as basic to human nature as is humanity's physical existence. They declare that "promises of immortal salvation or fear of eternal damnation are both illusory and harmful." They say that "salvationism, based on mere

---

[8] Waggoner, "Humanism vs. Christianity," 7.
[9] *Humanist Manifesto II*, Sixth. Cf. https://americanhumanist.org/what-is-humanism/manifesto2/, accessed April 15, 2020.

affirmation, still appears as harmful, diverting people with false hopes of heaven hereafter." On the other hand, Christians believe that sin entered into the world through Adam, that everyone is a sinner, and that, therefore, everyone is in need of salvation.[10]

Christian religion is not a mere ritual; it is doctrinal and eternal. If there is no mission commitment, we may not call it a Church and her ministry may be limited to a few aspects of life. If the teaching of Christianity about the eternal salvation through Jesus Christ is not real, then we would not have the history and testimony of Christians we have today. Thus, what is important for us is to understand the truth of the religion and follow its teachings faithfully.

To do this, the task at hand is not simply to worship inside the church buildings, but to understand the trends, waves, achievements, and threats so that we may be able to keep the Christian faith intact. One simple example is the way in which the Bible is being circulated in "soft copy" in order to reduce the number of printed copies. There are people who do not like the fact that the Bible holds the rank of being the most printed book in the world. To undermine this status, the Bible is freely distributed in "soft copy" so that Christians download it in their handsets and carry it to church instead of the print version. Such practice is propagated as indicating a high "standard" that everyone must adopt, while holding a "printed copy" of the Bible is considered as outdated standard. Two implications may be noted: (1) By doing this, the popularity of the Bible would be lost; and (2) If one properly evaluates the moral standard of the people who measure the Bible with human standard, it becomes clear that they are the ones who fail the church.

In a similar manner, Christian celebrations like Christmas, Good Friday, Easter, etc., that have been very popular and meaningful to believers for centuries are being challenged by introducing many secular-oriented celebrations and observations. The more serious issue with this trend is the way young Christians and the churches have adopted these events and celebrations, such as valentine's day, friendship day, environment day, national day, tree day, water day, organ day, boy's day, girls' day, pensioner's day, workers' day, elders' day, blood day, cancer day, etc.; most of these have no religious rooting, but are being observed with religious fervor. It is important to know the rationale behind the celebrations and discard those that are not designed for religious celebrations. Consciously and unconsciously, secularization is being accepted as standard and fashionable. We should know the harm they do to the Christian values so that we will be able to prevent the intrusion of humanism into the Christian church to a certain extent.

---

[10] Waggoner, ""Humanism vs. Christianity." 7.

Conclusion

After having discussed the principles of humanism and Christianity, I would like us to reconsider some of the framework under which Christianity is being exercised or nurtured to be able to see better the trend toward which we are moving. Why do people give tithes and offerings to the church? Is this for the purpose of sustaining church employees or for the purpose of developing church infrastructure? Are people investing their money with God who would in return give greater money? It needs to be clearly stated here that believers do not give to the church for these reasons. People acknowledge the blessings they have received from God through their various occupations, and they want to be involved in the ministry of the Church. And thus, they entrust the church with the task of utilizing the tithes and offerings to reach out to the neediest persons in their society and beyond. Therefore, their tithes and offerings should not be diverted toward endless expansion and renovation of church buildings while neglecting the needs of the poorest members. The priority of the church should be ministry and not physical/material development.

The church leaders should be sensitive to the influence of humanism in various forms. For example, people very often take the name of God and religion to fit their interests. Using Christian language such as "prayer fellowship" to invite people so that they can talk ill about others is a very harmful trend in the society. There are people who have the motive of showcasing their wealth and property and they use the term *prayer fellowship* to bring in people to their home. Christians need to check the motives behind their actions.

On the whole, we need to examine whether Christian ministry is focused on the needs of spiritual growth of the members or is diverted to human interests? We need to constantly check the spirit of humanism that destroys Christian morals/ethics. When the church is not able to safeguard Christian values and principles and does not cater to the spiritual needs of the members, then the blow of humanism will become too strong and the church will face the danger of being turned into a club, movement, or non-governmental organization, that do similar works like the church and yet, is not a church.

BIBLIOGRAPHY

Abraham, K.C. "EATWOT TRENDS." In *Doing Christian Ethics*, edited by Hunter P. Mabry. Bangalore: BTESSC, 1996.

Abraham, K.C. *Transforming Vision: Theological Methodological Paradigm Shift*. Thiruvalla: CSS, 2006.

Abraham, K.C. *Global Warming*. Bangalore: SATHRI, 1994.

Achtemeier, E. R. "Righteousness in the Old Testament." In *The Interpreter's Dictionary of the Bible, Vol. 4,* edited by George Arthur Buttrick, 79–86. New York: Abingdon Press, 1962.

Aquinas, Thomas. *Summa Theologiae*. Vol. 1. New York: Image Books, 1969.

Arthur, G.L. Jr. "Covenant." In *Baker's Dictionary of Theology*, edited by Everett F. Harrison. Grand Rapids, MI: Baker Book House, 1979.

Augustine, Mithra G. "Introduction." *Theology of Our Times*, no. 4, (January, 1997): 8–15.

Balasundaram, Franklin. *EATWOT IN ASIA: Towards Relevant Theology*. Bangalore: ATC, 1993.

Barbujari, H.K. *Assam in the Days of the Company 1826–1856*. Shillong: North Eastern Hill University, 1996.

Basu, Rumki. *The United Nations: Structure of Functions of an International Organisation*. New Delhi: Sterling Publishers, 1993.

Blackman, Rachel. *Peace-building Within Our Communities*. Teddington: Tear Fund, 2003.

Blenkinsopp. "The Book of Deuteronomy." In *The New Biblical Jerome Commentary*. Bangalore: Theological Publication of India, 1991.

Borowitz, Eugene B. "The Torah, Written and Oral, and Human Rights: Foundations and Deficiencies." In *The Ethics of World Religions and Human Rights,* edited by Hans Küng and Jürgen Moltman. London: SCM Press, 1990.

Brackney, William H., and Ruby J. Burke, eds. *Faith, Life, and Witness: The Papers of the Study and Research Division of the Baptist World Alliance, 1986-1990.* Birmingham: Samford University Press, 1990.

Brandon, S.G.F. *Jesus and the Zealot.* New York: Scribes, 1968.

Caird, G.B. *Saint Luke The Pelican NT Commentaries.* Middlesex: Penguin Books, 1974.

Carmichael, Calum M. *The Laws of Deuteronomy.* London: Cornell University Press, 1974.

Charles, R. H. *The Apocrypha and Pseudepigrapha of the Old Testament with Introduction and Critical Explanation Note of the Several Books,* vol. II. Oxford: Clarendon Press, 1913.

Christiansen, Ellen J. *The Covenant in Judaism and Paul—A Study of Ritual Boundaries as Identity Markers.* New York: E. J. Brill, 1995.

Cohn-Sherbok, Dan. "Covenant and Law." In *Creating Old Testament,* edited by Stephen Bigger. Oxford: Basil Blackwell, 1989.

Dauer, Sheila. "Indivisible or Invisible: Women's Human Rights in Public and Private Sphere." In *Women, Gender, and Human Rights: A Global Perspective,* edited by Marjorie Agosin. NP: Rutgers University Press, 2001.

De, J. D. "Rights, Human." in *New Dictionary of Theology*: The Master's Reference Collection. 594–595. Downers Grove, Illinois: InterVarsity Press, 1988.

Delotavo, Allan. "Towards A Christ-Centered Way of Doing Theology." *Asia Journal of Theology* 3, no. 1 (April 1989): 328–337.

Desrochers, John. *Toward A New India.* Bangalore: CSA, 1995.

Dewitt, Calvin B., ed. *The Environment and the Christian.* Michigan: Baker Book House, 1991.

Dodd, C.H. *The Founder of Christianity.* Fontana, London: Collins, 1973.

Dorff, Elliot N. "A Jewish Theology of Jewish Relations to Other Peoples." In *People of God, Peoples of God.* edited by Hans Ucko. Geneva: WCC Publications, 1996.

Driver, S. R. *Deuteronomy.* Edinburgh, 1902.

Ellul, Jacques. *The Theological Foundation of Law.* London: SCM Press, 1961.

Evans, Robert A., and Alice Frazer Evans. *Human Rights: A Dialogue Between the First and Third Worlds.* Maryknoll, NY: Orbis Books, 1983.

Ferguson, Sinclair B. "Image of God." In *New Dictionary of Theology*, edited by Sinclair B. Ferguson and David F. Wright. 328–329. Leicester: InterVarsity Press, 1994.

Feuillet, A. "The Reign of God and the Person of Jesus According to the Synoptic Gospels." In *Interpreters Bible*, 785–786. New York: Abingdon, 1951.

Foster, R.S. *Restoration of Israel*. London: Darton Longman & Todd, 1970.

Freire, Paulo. *Pedagogy of the Oppressed*. New York: Herder and Herder, 1970.

Gabris, Karol. "The Issues of Human Rights." In *Human Rights is More than Human Rights*, edited by Eric and Marilyn. Rome: IDOC International, 1977.

Gaspard, Francoise. "Unfinished Battles: Political and Public Life." In *The Circle of Empowerment: Twenty-five Years of the UN Committee on the Elimination of Discrimination Against Women*, edited by Hanna Beate Schöpp-Schilling and Cees Flinterman. New York: Feminist Press, 2007.

Gillingham, Susan. "The Ethics of Love Doing the Right Thing in the Christian Tradition." *The Expository Times* 106, no. 8 (May 1995): 230–237.

Gnanadason, Aruna. "Women, Economy and Ecology." In *Eco-Theology: Voices from South and North*, edited by *David G. Hallman*. Geneva: WCC, 1994.

Gottwald, Norman K., ed. *The Bible and Liberation*. New York: Orbis Books, 1983.

Gutierrez, Gustavo. *Theology of Liberation*. New York: Orbis Books, 1973.

Gutierrez, Gustavo. *Truth Shall Set You Free*. New York: Orbis Books, 1990.

Hallman, David G., ed. *Eco-Theology Voices From South and North*. New York: Orbis Books, 1994.

Harrelson, Walter. *Ten Commandments and Human Rights*. Philadelphia: Fortress Press, 1980.

Harries, Richard. *Questioning Belief*. London: SPCK, 1995.

Harrison, R. K. *Introduction to the Old Testament*. Grand Rapids, MI: William B. Eerdmans, 1969.

Harry, Kuitert. *Signals from the Bible*. Grand Rapids, MI: William Eerdmans, 1972.

Hauerwas, S. *The Peaceable Kingdom*. Notre Dame: Notre Dame Press, 1983.

Hengel, Martin. *Was Jesus a Revolutionist?* Philadelphia: Fortress Press, 1971.

Herzog, Frederick. *Liberation Theology.* New York: Seabury Press, 1972.

Ho, Huang Po. *Embracing the Household of God: A Paradigm Shift from Anthropocentric Tradition to Creation Responsibility in Doing Theology.* Kolkata: PTCA, 2014.

Hodgson Peter C., and Robert H. King. *Readings in Christian Theology.* Philadelphia: Fortress Press, 1985.

Holland, Joe., and S.T. Peter Henriot. *Social Analysis Linking Faith and Justice.* Indore: Satprakashan Sanchar Kendra, 1984.

Hollenbach, David. *Claims in Conflict: Retrieving and Renewing the Catholic Human Rights Tradition.* New York: Paulist, 1979.

Hunt, Mary E. "Women-Church: Feminist Concept, Religious Commitment, Women's Movement." *Journal of Feminist Studies in Religion*, 25, no. 1 (Spring 2009): 85–98.

Irene, Nowel. "Covenant." In *The New Dictionary of Theology*, edited by Komonchak Joseph, Mary Collins, and Dermot A. Lane, 243–246. Dublin: Gill and Macmillan, 1987.

James, Emmanuel E. *Ethics: A Biblical Perspective.* Bangalore: Sevadasan Training Institute, 1992.

Jenkin, David. "Human Rights in Christian Perspective." *Study Encounter* 10, no.2 (1994): 2–7.

Jeremias, Joachim. *Jerusalem in the Time of Jesus.* Philadelphia: Fortress Press, 1969.

Jeremias, Joachim. *New Testament Theology,* Vol. I. London: SCM Press, 1971.

Kashyap, S.C. *Human Rights and Parliament.* New Delhi: Metropolitan, 1978.

Koslowski, Jutta, ed. *Prospects and Challenges for the Ecumenical Movement in the 21st Century.* Geneva: Globethics.net Global, 2016.

Krusche, Günter. "Human Rights in a Theological Perspective: A Contribution from the German Democratic Republic," *Lutheran Word 1* (1977): 59–65.

Küng, Hans and Jürgen Moltmann, eds. *The Ethics of World Religions and Human Rights.* London: SCM Press, 1990.

Lalfakzuala. *Human Rights in Deuteronomy—A Sociological Approach.* Delhi: ISPCK, 2004.

Larue, Gerald, A. "Biblical Ethics and Continuing Interpretation." In *Biblical Vs Secular Ethics—The Conflict*, edited by R. Joseph Hoffman and Gerald A Larue. New York: Prometheus Books, 1988.

Lasetso, Razouselie, Marlene Ch. Marak, and Yangkahao Vashum, eds. *Tribal Ecology*. Jorhat: ETC Programme Coordination, 2012.

Lemmon, Gayle, Tzemach. "The Hillary Doctrine." *Newsweek*, June 3, 2011.

Levenson, Jon D. "The Universal Horizon of Biblical Particularism." In *Ethnicity and the Bible*, edited by M. G. Brett. New York: Brill, 1996.

Lobo, George. *Human Rights in Indian Situation*. New Delhi: The Commission for Justice and Development Catholic Bishops' Conference of India, 1991.

Longchar, Wati. *Returning to Mother Earth; Theology, Christian Witness and Theological Education: An Indigenous Perspective*. Kolkata: PTCA/SCEPTRE, 2012.

Lorenzen, Thorwald. "Christian Perspective on Human Rights" (Unpublished paper, Canberra, 1993).

Luf, Gerhard. "Peace and Human Rights as Seen by the Churches." In *Peace for Humanity*, edited by Andreas Bsteh. New Delhi: Vikas Publishing House, 1996.

Marbaniang, Domenic. "Developing the Spirit of Patriotism and Humanism in Children for Peace and Harmony." In *Children At Risk: Issues and Challenges*, edited by Jesudason Jeyaraj. Bangalore: CFCD/ISPCK, 2009.

Mabry, Hunter P., ed. *Doing Christian Ethics*. Bangalore: BTESSC, 1996.

May, Melanie A. "The Unity We Share, the Unity We Seek." In *A History of the Ecumenical Movement: Volume 3, 1968-2000*, edited by, John Briggs, Mercy Amba Oduyoye, and Georges Tsetsis. Geneva: WCC Publications, 2004.

McAfee, Robert. *Theology in a New Key*. Philadelphia: The Westminster Press, 1978.

McCarthy, D.J. *Old Testament Covenant: A Survey of Current Opinions*. Oxford: Basil Blackwell, 1973.

McConville, J.G. *Law and Theology in Deuteronomy*. Sheffield: JSOT Press, 1984.

McFague, Sallie. *A New Climate for Theology: God, the World, and Global Warming*. Minneapolis, MN: Augsburg Fortress Press, 2008.

McGrath, Alister E., ed. *The Christian Theology Reader.* Cambridge: Blackwell, 1995.

McKim, D.K. "Creation, Doctrine of." In *Encyclical Dictionary of Theology,* edited by Walter A. Elwell. Grand Rapids, MN: Baker Book House, 1985.

Meeks, Michael Douglas. *God the Economist.* Minneapolis, MN: Fortress, 1989.

Mendengall, G.E. "Covenant." In *Interpreter's Bible Dictionary,* edited by George A. Buttrick, Thomas Samuel Kepler, John Knox, Herbert Gordon May, Samuel Terrien, and Emory Stevens Bucke. New York: Abingdon Press, 1962.

Mendenhall, George. *Law and Covenant in Israel and the Ancient Near East.* Pittsburgh: Biblical Colloquium, 1955.

Miller, Allen O., ed. *Christian Declaration on Human Rights.* Grand Rapids, MI: William B. Eerdmans, 1977.

Mingthing, Y.L. "Keynote Address." In *Tribal Theology On The Move,* edited by Shimreingam Shimray and Limatula Longkumer. Jorhat: Tribal/Women Study Centre, 2006.

Moltmann, Jürgen. "Christian Faith and Human Rights." In *Adventurous Faith & Transforming Vision,* edited by Arvind P. Nirmal. Madras: GLTC & Research Institute, 1989.

Moltmann, Jürgen. *Theological Basis of Human Rights.* Fernery: WARC, 1976.

Mott, Stephen Charles. *Biblical Ethics and Social Change.* Oxford: Oxford University Press, 1982.

Mott, Stephen Charles. "The Contribution of the Bible to Human Rights." In *Human Rights and the Global Mission of the Church,* edited by Arthur J. Dyck. Massachusetts: Boston Theological Institute, 1985.

Nalunnakkal, George Mathew. *Green Liberation: Towards an Integrated Ecotheology.* Delhi: ISPCK, 2004.

Nineham, D.E. *Saint Mark—The Pelican New Testament Commentaries.* Middlesex: Penguin Books, 1975.

Norman, Richard. *On Humanism—Thinking in Action.* London: Routledge, 2004.

North, Robert. *Sociology of Biblical Jubilee.* Rome: 1954.

O'Grady, R. *Bread and Freedom: Understanding and Acting Human Rights.* Geneva: WCC, 1979.

Panikkar, K.M. *In Defence of Liberalism*. Bombay: Asia Publishing House, 1962.

Paton, David M., ed. *Breaking Barriers, Nairobi 1975: The Official Report of the Fifth Assembly of the WCC, Nairobi, 23 November-10 December 1975*. London: SPCK, 1976.

Petersen and Helmick, eds. *Religion, Public Policy and Conflict Transformation*. Radnor, Philadelphia: Templeton Foundation Press, 2001.

Pratt, Douglas. "The Imago Dei in the Thought of John Macquarrie." *Asia Journal of Theology* 3, no. 1 (April 1989): 78-85.

Richardson, Alan. *The Political Christ*. London: SCM Press, 1973.

Ringe, Sharon H. *Jesus, Liberation and the Biblical Jubilee*. Philadelphia: Fortress Press, 1985.

Ringgren, Helmer. "Miswa." In *Theological Dictionary of the Old Testament*, edited by G. Johannes Botterweck, Helmer Ringgren, and Heinz-Josef Fabry. Grand Rapids, MI: William B. Eerdmans, 1997.

Robinson, Gnana. "A New Economic Order: The Challenge of the Biblical Jubilee." In *A Vision for Man*, edited by Samuel Amirtham. Madras: CLS, 1978.

Robinson, John. "Honest to God." In *The Honest to God Debate*, edited by David L. Edwards. London: SCM Press, 1955.

Ruether, Rosemary Radford. *Women-Church: Theology and Practice of Feminist Liturgical Communities*. San Francisco: Harper & Row, 1985.

Schilling, Katharina. *Peacebuilding & Conflict Transformation: A Resource Book*. Berlin: Brot für die Welt, 2012.

Schneiders, Sandra. *Beyond Patching: Faith and Feminism in the Catholic Church*. New York: Paulist, 1991.

Schrage, Wolfgang. *The Ethics of New Testament*. Philadelphia: Fortress Press, 1988.

Schwelb, Egon. "Human Rights," in *Encyclopaedia Britannica*. 15th edition, 1975.

Scott, E.F. *The Ethical Teaching of Jesus*. New York: The Macmillan Company, 1957.

Segundo, Juan Luis. *Liberation of Theology*. Maryknoll, NY: Orbis Books, 1976.

Sherlock, Charles. *The Doctrine of Humanity: Contours of Christian Theology*. Illinois: Inter Varsity Press, 1996.

Shimrah, T. "Global Environment Change: Perceptions, Challenges and Adaptation Strategies in Tangkhul Indigenous Community." In *Encountering Modernity—Situating the Tangkhul Nagas in Perspective*, edited by R. Vashum, A.S. Yaruingam, A.S. Shimreiwung, and Yuimirin Kapai. New Delhi: Chicken Neck, an imprint of Bibliophile South Asia, 2014.

Shimray, Shimreingam. "Towards Paradigm Shift of Human Rights," *Asia Journal of Theology* 27, no. 1 (April 2013): 70–79.

Shimray, Shimreingam L. *Theology of Human Rights: A Critique on Politics*. Jorhat, Assam: Ruth Shimray, 2002.

Shiva, Vandana. "Let Us Survive: Women, Ecology and Development." In *Women Healing Earth: Third World Women on Ecology, Feminism and Religion*, edited by Rosemary Radford Ruether, 65–73. Maryknoll, NY: Orbis Books, 1996.

Shiva, Vandana. *Staying Alive*. Delhi: Kali for Women, 1989.

Shook, John. "Christian Humanism, Religious Humanism, and Secular Humanism." *CFI-Centre for Inquiry* (December 8, 2009):1–6.

Spencer, Nick and Robert White. *Christianity, Climate Change and Sustainable Living*. New Delhi: SPCK, 2012.

Spriggs, D.G. *Two Old Testament Theologies*. London: SCM Press, 1974.

Stackhouse, Max. *Creed, Society and Human Rights*. Grand Rapids, MI: William B. Eerdmans, 1984.

Stuhlmueller, Carroll. "The Foundation for Mission in the Old Testament." In *Biblical Foundations for Mission*, edited by Donald Senior and Carroll Stuhlmueller. Maryknoll, NY: Orbis Books, 1983.

Swidler, Arlene, ed. *Human Rights and Religious Traditions*. New York: Pilgrim Press, 1982.

Syiemlieh, Brightstar J. "The Future of Tribal Christian Theology in Northeast India: Possible Directions." In *Tribal Theology on the Move*, edited by Shimreingam Shimray and Limatula Longkumer. Jorhat: Tribal/Women Study Centre, 2006.

Talbert, Charles H. *Reading Luke*. New York: Crossroad Publishing Company, 1986.

Thampu, Valson. "The Church and the Nation." *Evangelical Review of Theology* 22, no. 2 (April 1998): 116–119.

Thielicke, Helmut. *Theological Ethics: Foundation*, vol. 2. Philadelphia: Fortress Press, 1969.

Thompson, J. Arthur. "Covenant." In *The International Standard Bible Encyclopedia, vol. I*, edited by Geoffrey W. Bromiley, 790–792. Grand Rapids, MI: William B. Eerdmans, 1979.

Torres, Sergio and John Eagleson, eds. *Theology in America*. Maryknoll, NY: Orbis Books, 1976.

Trocmé, André. *Jesus and the Nonviolent Revolution*. New York: The Plough Publishing House, 2011.

Villa-Vicencio, Charles. *The Art of Reconciliation*. Östervåla: Life & Peace Institute, 2002.

Volf, Miroslav. *Exclusion and Embrace: A Theological Exploration of Identity, Otherness, and Reconciliation*. Nashville: Abingdon Press, 1996.

Von Rad, G. *Old Testament Theology*. Vol. I. Edinburgh: Oliver and Boyd, 1962.

Von Rad, G. *Deuteronomy*. London: SCM Press, 1966.

Walker, D. M., ed. *The Oxford Companion to Law*. Oxford: Oxford University Press, 1980.

Walter, Nicolas. *Humanism—What's in the Word*. London: Rationalist Press Association, 1997.

Weston, Burns H. "Human Rights." *Human Rights Quarterly*, 257 (1984).

White, Keith J. *Childhoods in Cultural Contexts*. Penang: Malaysia Baptist Theological Seminary, Compassion International and the Global Alliance for Advancing Holistic Child Development, 2011.

Wickeri, Philip L. "Toward a Kenosis of Mission: Emptying and Empowerment for the Church and for the World." In *Scripture, Community, and Mission—Essays in Honour of D. Preman Niles*, edited by Philip L. Wickeri. Hong Kong: CCA/WCC, 2002.

Wielenga, Bastian. "Market Friendly Society and Its Implications." *Theology for Our Times*, no. 4 (January 1997): 28–35.

Wielenga, Bastian. *It's a Long Road to Freedom—Perspective of Biblical Theology*. Revised Edition. Madurai: TTS, 1988.

Witcover, Jules. *85 Days: The Last Campaign of Robert Kennedy*. New York: William Marrow, 1988.

Yoder, J. H. *The Politics of Jesus*. Grand Rapids, MI: William B. Eerdmans, 1972.

Reports

Baptist World Alliance, *Celebrating Christ's Presence Through the Spirit: Official Report of the Fourteenth Congress, Toronto, Canada, July 8–13, 1980* (Nashville: Broadman Press, 1981).

Religious Freedom Main Statement by the WCC, Report of Section V of the Fifth Assembly, Nairobi, 1975, on "Structure of Injustice and Struggles for Liberation Human Rights."

Evanston to New Delhi 1954–1961. The Report of the Central Committee to the Third Assembly of the World Council of Churches (Geneva: WCC, 1961).

Report on the Church and the Disorder of Society, WCC First Assembly (Amsterdam, 1948).

A Declaration on Religious Liberty, WCC First Assembly (Amsterdam, 1948).

The New Delhi Report. The Third Assembly of the World Council of Churches, 1961 (London: SCM Press, 1962).

WORK BOOKS for the Fifth Assembly of the WCC, Nairobi, Kenya, 23 November–10 December 1975 (Geneva: WCC, 1975).

Vienna Declaration and Programme of Action, United Nations. *Women's Rights are Human Rights* (Geneva: United Nations Publications, 2014).

UN Women, *Beijing Declaration and Platform for Action: Beijing+5 Political Declaration and Outcome* (Geneva: United Nations Publications, 1995, reprinted in 2014), point no. 134.

UN Women, *Summary Report: The Beijing Declaration and Platform for Action Turns 20* (March 2015, New York).

Websites

Women Rights in India: Constitutional Rights and Legal Rights, http://edugeneral.org/blog/polity/women-rights-in-india/, accessed September 28, 2016.

The Human Rights of Women, http://www.unfpa.org/resources/human-rights-women#sthash.2HrW9XK1.dpuf//, accessed September 27, 2016.

World Conferences on Women, https://www.unwomen.org/en/how-we-work/intergovernmental-support/world-conferences-on-women, accessed October 5, 2016.

Step It Up for Gender Equality, http://www.unwomen.org/stepitup, accessed October 5, 2016.

The 2002 Amsterdam Declaration issued by the International Humanist and Ethical Union, https://centerforinquiry.org/blog/christian_humanism_religious_humanism_and_secular_humanism/, accessed July 22, 2019.

Robert L. Waggoner, *Humanism vs. Christianity: The Greatest Battle of Our Times,* http://www.thebible.net/biblicaltheism/humanchrist.htm, accessed October 23, 2019.

Unnao: Gold hunt for 1,000 tonne begins at old UP fort, https://www.businesstoday.in/current/economy-politics/gold-hunt-unnao-up-fort-shobhan-sarkar/story/199756.html, accessed August 23, 2019.

www.ingramcontent.com/pod-product-compliance
Lightning Source LLC
Chambersburg PA
CBHW020409080526
44584CB00014B/1241